Risk Management in Organisations

T0292959

Risk management is vital to organisational success, from government down to small businesses, and the discipline has developed rapidly over the last decade. Learning lessons from the good and bad practice of others is a key feature of this book, which includes multiple illustrative examples of risk management practice, in addition to detailed case studies.

Combining both theory and practice, the early chapters compare the ISO 31000 and COSO Enterprise Risk Management frameworks and the relevant regulatory regimes in both Europe and the United States. The core of the book is three highly detailed case studies of risk management in the manufacturing (Akzo Nobel), retail (Tesco), and public sectors (Birmingham City Council). Using the lessons learned from the case studies, together with material from elsewhere, the author then outlines four lessons for risk managers that can be used in any organisation seeking to develop a truly enterprise-wide risk management system.

This completely revised edition contains updates on regulations and practice, together with new chapters covering technology risk and COVID-19, which are major risks faced by all organisations today. As such the book is essential reading for risk management professionals and postgraduate and executive learners.

Margaret Woods is Emeritus Professor of Accounting and Risk at Aston Business School, Aston University, UK. A founder of the EU-funded European Risk Research Forum, her work on bank risk management during the global financial crisis stimulated national and international media interest.

"The case studies set out in this book, based on sound research and set firmly within the context of the most up-to-date governance and standards frameworks, make a real contribution to the understanding of managing risk within organisations. The book will be an excellent resource for students and practitioners of risk management."

Stephen Sidebottom, *Chair, The Institute of Risk Management*

"Providing analysis of the evolution of various risk types via detailed case studies and snapshots of risk events across large and small organisations, this unique and valuable book delivers profound insights for risk management scholars and practitioners."

Marco Maffei, *University of Naples Federico II, Italy*

"*Risk Management in Organisations* remains an invaluable resource and this new edition will be of interest to risk management practitioners, students and academics internationally."

Chris Peace, *Te Wāhanga Tātai Hauora Victoria University of Wellington, New Zealand*

"Combining theory and regulation, this new edition is an indispensable guide to risk management. With new insights around technological development and COVID-19, the book is required reading for risk practitioners globally."

Marie Gemma Dequae, *Risk Management Practitioner*

Risk Management in Organisations

An Integrated Case Study Approach

Second Edition

Margaret Woods

Routledge
Taylor & Francis Group

LONDON AND NEW YORK

Cover image: Andy Roberts/Getty Images

Second edition published 2022
by Routledge
4 Park Square, Milton Park, Abingdon, Oxon, OX14 4RN

and by Routledge
605 Third Avenue, New York, NY 10158

Routledge is an imprint of the Taylor & Francis Group, an informa business

© 2022 Margaret Woods

First edition published by Routledge 2011

British Library Cataloguing-in-Publication Data
A catalogue record for this book is available from the British Library

Library of Congress Cataloging-in-Publication Data
Names: Woods, Margaret, 1954– author.
Title: Risk management in organisations : an integrated case study
    approach / Margaret Woods.
Description: 2nd edition. | Abingdon, Oxon ; New York, NY :
    Routledge, 2022. | Includes bibliographical references and index.
Subjects: LCSH: Risk management. | Management—Research.
Classification: LCC HD61 .W66 2022 (print) | LCC HD61 (ebook) |
    DDC 658.15/5—dc23/eng/20211228
LC record available at https://lccn.loc.gov/2021059888
LC ebook record available at https://lccn.loc.gov/2021059889

ISBN: 978-1-138-63233-2 (hbk)
ISBN: 978-1-138-63231-8 (pbk)
ISBN: 978-1-315-20833-6 (ebk)

DOI: 10.4324/9781315208336

Typeset in Bembo
by Apex CoVantage, LLC

Contents

Illustrations

Tables

Foreword

Bismarck (German chancellor in the late 1800s) is reputed to have said, "Only a fool learns from his own mistakes. The wise man learns from the mistakes of others." Understanding the correct decisions of others is similarly beneficial, and this book uses examples of good and poor risk management practice to provide lessons that are applicable to many different types of organisations.

In doing so, it fills an important gap in the market, as many textbooks arguably still focus on the theoretical aspects of risk management. What has been needed for some time is a more practically focused book for use by employees studying risk management professional examinations that better fits the modern assessment process and provides students with knowledge that can be usefully applied to their own organisation.

This book is a good mix of theory and its practical application, and one of the biggest attributes is that it is well structured and very easy to read and digest. The first five chapters, full of real-life examples, focus on the theoretical and regulatory aspects of risk management, providing an historical context that explains present-day risk management practices. There is interesting evidence that the cost of implementing Sarbanes-Oxley (SOX) far outweighs the losses, a discussion of how companies are selective in response to varying regulations about where they are listed, and on how geopolitical and cyber risks are becoming increasingly important. Chapter 5, new to this edition, introduces "technology risk," which is seen by many as the biggest emerging risk outside of climate change.

Three detailed case studies (Tesco, Akzo Nobel, and Birmingham City Council) are semi-longitudinal and describe the risk management of these organisations over a period of fifteen years. In so doing they reveal, as Toft and Reynolds[1] clearly affirm, that learning from other organisations can be of great benefit. The case studies introduce the practical element that organisations are looking for, and Chapter 9 summarises the lessons learned from across all three case studies, providing a pro forma for those seeking to introduce enterprise-wide risk management to their organisation.

The concluding chapter focuses on the COVID-19 pandemic (still rife at the time of publication) from a risk management perspective and delivers six key lessons that should be learned from a pandemic.

Finally, there is no doubt that this book plugs an important gap in the market and clearly adds value to the risk management body of knowledge.

Douglas Smith MSc,
Fellow of the Institute of Risk Management (FIRM)
and Chief Examiner of IRM

Note

1 Toft, B., & Reynolds, S. (1997) *Learning from Disasters: A Management Approach.* 2nd edition. Leicester: Perpetuity Press.

Preface

How do organisations manage risk? The COVID-19 pandemic has massively raised the profile of risk management and raised important questions about the consequences of risk failures. Learning about current practice is challenging, however, as risk management case studies are scarce, and case studies that trace how systems develop over a long-time frame are non-existent. This updated and accessible book fills this gap via a highly detailed set of risk management cases straddling fifteen to twenty years, covering the retail (Tesco), manufacturing (Akzo Nobel), and public sectors (Birmingham City Council). How such huge organisations identify, manage, and respond to risk is of interest to the wider public, as well as students of the discipline.

The author sets the world of risk management in the context of an evolving global regulatory framework and a fast-growing interest in the concept of enterprise-wide risk management, particularly in the United States. The case studies, as well as multiple shorter examples of practice, are used to illustrate how organisations manage risk in accordance with the varying regulations across different industrial sectors. They illustrate very clearly how the concept of enterprise risk management remains an ideal rather than a reality for most organisations, but they also reveal the key drivers of risk management success.

This completely revised edition of the book contains updates on regulations and practice, together with new chapters covering technology risk and COVID-19, which are of huge importance to organisations today. Both new and revised case studies covering the last twenty years provide the core of the revised edition.

Margaret Woods is emeritus professor of accounting and risk at Aston Business School, Aston University, Birmingham. She was a founder of the EU-funded European Risk Research Forum and is co-editor (with Philip Linsley) of *The Routledge Companion to Accounting and Risk*. She has published numerous articles in both academic and practitioner journals, and her work on bank risk management during the global financial crisis stimulated national and international media interest.

Acknowledgements

This book could not have been written without help from a wide range of people and organisations. I am grateful to the Chartered Institute of Management Accountants (CIMA) who provided financial support for the initial research which generated the first edition of this book. Additionally, I would like to thank the Institute of Risk Management (IRM) for their endorsement in the foreword to both this and the previous edition. It is great that they believe the cases will be helpful to their students and members.

I would also like to thank my editor, Terry Clague, for his endless patience in waiting for me to complete this second edition. I retired from Aston University in the middle of the process and realised that writing longitudinal case studies of this magnitude is a very time-consuming process!

Lastly, I owe huge thanks to my husband for his IT skills, which I harnessed to draft most of the more complex figures and diagrams in the book. He also made a very diligent and demanding editor. I suspect he is hoping that the book's completion will draw a line under my endless conversations about risk.

1 Introduction to This Book

Why This Book Is Important

Sometimes it's the things you don't see that have the biggest impact.

(Enron advertisement, 2001 Media Guide for the Houston
Astros baseball team)

Enron's Chief Executive and its Chairman were both jailed for accounting fraud following the company's collapse in 2001, and the company's auditors. Arthur Anderson , lost their license to undertake public accounting. Clearly things not seen in the organisation had a catastrophic impact. Furthermore, the lesson from the quote is one that has been hard learned by the many businesses that have failed as a result of the COVID-19 pandemic. The World Economic Forum (2021) has commented on the way in which "most countries," let alone businesses, have struggled with aspects of crisis management during the pandemic. The forum suggests that the pandemic has provided great opportunities to improve the governance of risk by encouraging more holistic approaches to the understanding of risk impacts and a greater demand for better risk information leading to increased organisational resilience.

The post-COVID world thus offers huge potential for risk management to develop further as a profession. This book is intended as a learning tool for both current and future risk managers who seek to enable their organisations to be better prepared and resilient in the face of a crisis. Whilst recognising that it is impossible to eliminate uncertainty, the chapters in this book demonstrate how having plans about how to respond to surprises – from a ransom attack by hackers to a global pandemic – can significantly reduce their impact. The text combines detailed information on international governance and risk regulations, together with unique longitudinal case studies of risk management practice in major organisations. Learning from both the successes and failures of others across a range of sectors can help to nurture best practice in the profession.

Contents and Use

This book is aimed at risk practitioners studying for ERM (or similar) qualifications. University students, particularly those taking MBA or executive

DOI: 10.4324/9781315208336-1

development courses, will also find it useful. The book is intended for use by a wide range of readers, who may be looking for anything from a complete introductory course in risk management to simply filling specific "knowledge gaps" and gaining greater insights into risk management practice. More broadly, the book can be used within organisations as a training tool, with staff being asked to read particular chapters/sections as preparation for a training session or discussion group.

Chapters 2 and 3 detail the regulatory requirements on governance and risk management that provide the framework around which most organisations construct their risk management systems. They outline the ground rules for how to draft an internal governance and risk management framework (as described in Chapter 4), as well as providing a point of reference to ensure compliance. Chapters 2 through 4 all include "Key Learning Points," which highlight particularly important features that are critical for readers to understand. Chapter 4 marks the transition into a discussion of risk management practice rather than theory, and so also includes brief snapshots of risk events and their impact across a wide range of large and small organisations.

This is the second edition of the book, and the types of risks faced by organisations have evolved and will continue to do so. In recognition of this, Chapter 5 reviews the concept of technology risk and makes clear the important distinction between the broader technology risk and the more specific term cyber risk. An end-of-chapter glossary is provided to help readers struggling to understand the specialist terminology commonly used when discussing technology risks. The chapter includes a useful case study of the time frame and impact of a data breach at British Airways and a template that can be used to construct a governance and risk management structure for technology. Both of these features can be used for in-house training to increase general staff awareness of technology-related risks. Whilst writing the book, the world was hit by the COVID-19 pandemic, and so additional content, Chapter 10, was added to address this new risk and how it was or was not managed at the organisational level.

The book's title describes "an integrated case study approach," and the three case studies (Chapters 6 to 8) are a key attribute of the text and great learning tools. Their value derives, in part, from the extended time frame covered in each case and the fact that whilst the systems are all developing over a similar time frame (2000–2020), they illustrate how organisationally specific risk management systems can be. Learning from the differences between the approaches of Tesco, Akzo Nobel, and Birmingham City Council, rather than their similarities, is particularly informative. Each case raises specific risk management issues that may be open to debate and interpretation, and these form the basis of end-of-chapter discussion topics, which can be used in universities or elsewhere as examination questions. Chapter 9 integrates the lessons learned from all three case studies and translates these into a list of factors influencing the effectiveness of risk management systems in practice. In so doing it highlights the massive challenge of introducing a system that straddles an entire organisation and embeds risk awareness into organisational culture. Chapter 9 concludes that the ideal scenario of an organisation where everybody, enterprise wide, is continuously aware of and talks about risk and the risk of surprise is minimised is extraordinarily difficult to achieve.

Warren Buffet's view is that risk comes from not knowing what you are doing, and this book confirms that risk management is about preventing this problem arising in practice. I would suggest that this book demonstrates that whilst the profession has developed massively over the last twenty years, there is still a lot of work to be done.

Reference

World Economic Forum (2021) *The Global Risks Report 2021: 16th Edition.* World Economic Forum, Geneva, Switzerland.

2 Risk and Governance

Aim

The aim of this chapter is to briefly review the recent history of risk management and governance regulation in order to illustrate:

- The link between risk management and corporate governance
- The history of governance regulations and alternative forms of regulation
- The need to recognise that regulatory compliance can create an illusion that risks are under control

The conclusion that compliance with governance regulations does not necessarily translate into good risk management provides a backdrop for the case studies which follow. The cases illustrate that risk management practices within companies are widely variable in both style and effectiveness, reflecting different organisational cultures and management styles. Such variations offer huge opportunities for the rapidly growing risk management profession.

What Is Corporate Governance?

The UK Corporate Governance Code (FRC, 2010, p. 1) describes the purpose of corporate governance as being "to facilitate effective, entrepreneurial and prudent management that can deliver the long-term success of the company." The code takes the view that a company's board of directors is "collectively responsible for the long-term success of the company" (FRC, 2010, p. 6) and includes responsibility for determining the nature and extent of the significant risks it is willing to take in achieving its strategic objectives and overseeing the maintenance of "sound risk management and internal control systems."

Regulators therefore see risk management as a core component of corporate governance, and this is also widely recognised within the academic literature. Spira and Page (2003) suggest that risk management is central to corporate governance, as risks are managed through a framework of accountability which encompasses financial reporting, internal control, and audit. The emphasis on accountability is important because as we see in the next section of this chapter,

DOI: 10.4324/9781315208336-2

demands for increased accountability have been the stimulus for the development of worldwide governance and risk management regulations, codes, and standards. We will also see that over the last twenty years, the term internal control has gradually been redefined as "risk management" and a new profession of risk managers has appeared. This issue is discussed in more depth in Chapter 3.

History of Corporate Governance Regulations

Phase One: 1990–2010

The late 1980s and early 1990s saw the emergence of regulatory concerns over corporate scandals, such as the savings and loans crises in the United States and BCCI and Polly Peck in the UK, and a resulting decline in confidence in the quality of financial reporting in both countries. Concerns were expressed about the consequences of poor controls over the behaviour of company staff and members of the board of directors, and clearer specification of the responsibilities of companies and their boards were seen as essential. This consciousness marked the start of the first decade of governance initiatives across the world.

UK History

In 1991, a research report by Coopers and Lybrand Deloitte in the UK highlighted a lack of legislation that would help ensure companies were being managed "honestly and competently." The report claimed there was an urgent need to codify the responsibilities of those involved in corporate governance and identify best practice in the field (Coopers and Lybrand, 1991, p. 1). The following year "The Financial Aspects of Corporate Governance" (more usually known as the Cadbury Report) defined corporate governance as "the systems by which a company is directed and controlled" and laid the foundations for the current UK code of corporate governance and principles of best practice. In retrospect, what is commonly referred to as the Cadbury Code can be viewed as a landmark development in changing the governance landscape. The report placed directors centre stage by recognising that "all directors, whether or not they have executive responsibilities, have a monitoring role and are responsible for ensuring that the necessary controls over the activities of their companies are in place – and working" (Cadbury Report, p. 11, 1992).

Its key recommendations included:

- An implicit requirement on directors to ensure that a proper system of internal control is in place
- Publication in the report and accounts of a statement by directors on whether they comply with the code and identifying and giving reasons for any non-compliance

- The encouragement of directors to make a statement in the annual report on the effectiveness of their system of internal control, with such statements subject to review by the auditors before publication
- Separation of the role of the chief executive officer (CEO) and chairman
- The appointment of sufficient non-executive directors to ensure they can exercise influence in decision making
- The establishment of an audit committee made up of non-executive directors
- A committee made up of a majority of non-executive directors should be responsible for setting the remuneration of executive directors

On paper Cadbury was a "voluntary" code, but its credibility was immediately confirmed because compliance became a condition of listing on the London Stock Exchange. Not surprisingly, the rate at which it was adopted was rapid. Demonstrating compliance with best practice to shareholders was seen by many as providing easier and more extensive access to capital. Furthermore, any companies opting not to comply with sections of the code were required to explain their reasons for so doing, which further increased management transparency.

Box 2.1   Pros and Cons of Comply or Explain

The primary benefit of the comply or explain approach is that it facilitates the monitoring of compliance whilst offering a degree of flexibility to the reporting entity. This perhaps explains why the comply or explain component of the Cadbury Code has since been incorporated into governance codes all around the world.

For shareholders, however, questions about usefulness of the explanations for non-compliance remain. The reasons given need to be both understandable and justifiable if they are to be useful to stakeholders.

The code's primary recommendation was that the directors were responsible for establishing and maintaining a system of internal controls over financial management. It encouraged, but did not require the board to express an opinion on the *effectiveness* of the system. This proved controversial, however, as in these early years of governance regulation, few companies had well-established and tightly documented formal procedures for risk management, and there was a lack of clarity about how assurance on effectiveness might be achieved. As a result, neither management nor auditors were willing to comment on control effectiveness (Page and Spira, 2004), and it was not until the publication of the Turnbull Report in 2009 that the issue was finally resolved.

The Greenbury Report (1995), Hampel (1998), and the so-called Combined Code, issued in 1999, built on the Cadbury Code to consolidate the governance guidance issued in the UK. The Turnbull Guidance for Directors on the Combined Code (ICAEW, 1999) focused on the specific issue of directors' responsibilities in relation to internal controls and included guidance on how internal control effectiveness might be assessed by management.

Key Learning Point

The requirement to comply with the Cadbury Code as a condition of stock exchange listing significantly increased the importance of this "voluntary" code.

Regular review of risks (both past and future) and ongoing monitoring and internal reporting were seen as integral to evaluating effectiveness. Accountability to shareholders was embedded in the report's requirement for the board to report on risks and the fact that they had made an annual review of control effectiveness. There was, however, no requirement to report on the findings of that review.

By the start of the new millennium, therefore, the UK had in place a well-established governance code, the credibility of which was reinforced via the capital markets. The basic principles of the Cadbury Code were subsequently copied or adapted by every member state in the European Union (EU), together with more than sixty countries elsewhere. Examples of regulations that built on the Cadbury Code include the Criteria of Control Board Guidance on Control (CoCo) issued in Canada in 1995, the OECD Principles of Corporate Governance (1999 & 2004), the Dutch corporate governance code (2009), and the King Code in South Africa (2009).

The period 2000–2010 was largely one of refinement of governance regulations in the UK, with no wholesale changes being made to the framework laid down in the Combined Code (1999). For example, an update to Turnbull in 2006 required boards to report and confirm that they had taken corrective action in respect of failings or weaknesses identified in their annual review of internal controls. The Combined Code was updated in 2006 and 2008, and a revised code was then published in 2010. The most important change in 2010 was the introduction of a requirement for the internal control review to include **all material controls**, including financial, operational, and compliance controls. It also laid out very clearly the responsibilities of the board of directors vis-a-vis risk management:

- "The board's role is to provide entrepreneurial leadership of the company within a framework of prudent and effective controls which enables risk to be assessed and managed" (Principle A.1)

and

- "The board is responsible for determining the nature and extent of the significant risks it is willing to take in achieving its strategic objectives. The board should maintain sound risk management and internal control systems" (Principle C2)

By 2010, therefore, regulators had affirmed that the identification, understanding, and management of risk was a key item on the board agenda.

US History

In the United States, the Committee on Sponsoring Organizations (COSO) was established in 1985 with the remit of looking at the causes underlying fraudulent financial reporting. The world's first major internal control framework was published by COSO in 1992, and it defined internal control as:

"a process, effected by an entity's board of directors, management and other personnel, designed to provide reasonable assurance regarding the achievement of objectives" in relation to:

- Effectiveness and efficiency of operations.
- Reliability of financial reporting.
- Compliance with applicable laws and regulations."

Source: COSO 1992

The COSO report defined internal control as being made up of five inter-related components:

- Control environment
- Risk assessment
- Control activities
- Information and communication
- Monitoring

These five components are inter-connected and combine to provide assurance about three core objectives: the effectiveness and efficiency of operations, the reliability of financial reporting, and compliance with laws and regulations.

Key Learning Point

COSO refers to operational and compliance controls in addition to financial controls.

Cadbury only references financial controls. It was not until the Combined Code of 2010 that the UK extended its definition of internal control.

COSO requires that for each objective, a control environment must be designed, risks assessed, controls put in place and monitored, and the outcomes reported to management. This is most effectively achieved when the controls are built into the organisational infrastructure and not seen as a separate consideration, but instead a part of the "essence" of the business. The complexity of achieving such integration is a recurring theme in this book.

The establishment of guidelines on internal controls and codes of behaviour does not, however, guarantee their widespread adoption. A US survey of 300 senior executives and 200 non-management employees conducted by Coopers and Lybrand in 1996 (Krane and Sever, 1996) found very limited take-up of the COSO model in the United States, with only 10% of executives saying they were even aware of its existence. The implication was that "COSO 1992 was more of a philosophical treatise written by a group of accountants to draw the attention of C suite executives to the concept of internal control as a fundamentally sound business practice" (Gupta, 2006, p. 59). The key reason for the limited take-up of the COSO model of internal control was that in contrast to the UK's Cadbury Code, there was no requirement for listed companies to comply with its guidelines.

Key Learning Point

The wording used in the COSO definition of internal control was echoed in governance codes subsequently issued elsewhere, including COCO (Canada, 1995) and the Turnbull Report (UK, 1999).

The common theme that links COSO, COCO, and Turnbull is that internal controls are a mechanism through which management can provide assurance regarding the pursuit and achievement of corporate objectives.

Some years later, the new millennium in the United States was marked by a spate of corporate scandals and malfeasance. The Bermuda-based telecommunications company Global Crossing filed for Chapter 11 bankruptcy in January 2001 amidst accusations of artificially inflated profits, and the energy trading company Enron collapsed in late 2001 amidst an accounting scandal that engendered comments that it was a "virtual company earning virtual profits." Its bankruptcy triggered a number of accounting and governance reforms in the United States, at the centre of which was the Sarbanes-Oxley Act of 2002 (SOX), which came a full decade after COSO. Ironically, the same month that SOX became law, Worldcom filed for Chapter 11 bankruptcy in what at the time was the largest such filing in US corporate history.

Box 2.5   Key Elements in the Sarbanes-Oxley Act 2002

- Section 302 requires company executives to certify that they have undertaken an evaluation of the effectiveness of their internal controls over financial reporting and where the controls are classified as not effective, disclose any material weaknesses that have been identified.
- Section 404 requires that a company's annual report for the Securities and Exchange Commission (SEC) includes:

  - A statement of management's responsibility for establishing and maintaining adequate internal control over financial reporting
  - A statement identifying the framework used by management to evaluate the effectiveness of internal control
  - Management's assessment of the effectiveness of internal control as of the end of the company's most recent accounting year end
  - A statement that the company's external auditor has issued an attestation report on the management's assessment

- The Public Company Accounting Oversight Board (PCAOB) was established to oversee the activities of the auditing profession
- All audit committee members must be independent (i.e. non-executive directors)

SOX directly linked the reliability of financial statements to the maintenance of effective internal control systems, and in so doing it transformed the COSO (1992) internal framework from a useful philosophical treatise into a core requirement for compliance with US legislation.

Following some delays in implementing Section 404, the New York Stock Exchange and NASDAQ incorporated the SOX requirements into their listing regulations, and in so doing forced a spectacular shift in awareness of the interface between governance, internal control, and financial reporting in the

United States. In addition, SOX posed major challenges to the audit profession in its requirement for them to attest to the views of directors regarding the effectiveness of financial reporting controls. Not surprisingly, the legislation drew huge protestation from companies and the accounting profession, wary of the costs of compliance and the potential for litigation.[1]

Control effectiveness can be demonstrated (under SEC rules) through provision of evidence that a suitable internal control framework is in place. The COSO 1992 guidelines are one example of a "suitable framework" (SEC, 2006, p. 5), with the Canadian "CoCo" guidance and the UK's Turnbull Guidance serving as suitable alternatives. Not surprisingly, therefore, one consequence of SOX was that COSO 1992 rapidly became the dominant model for internal control design amongst US companies, and a redrafted, re-titled version issued in 2004 "Enterprise Risk Management – Integrated Framework" (COSO, 2004), soon became the most commonly used governance framework to assess compliance with SOX.

Box 2.6   Key Differences Between UK and US Governance Regulations Post-SOX

1. Compliance with SOX and the linked internal control guidance (e.g. COSO) was legally binding in the United States for all companies filing accounts with the SEC. The Combined Code in the UK was not legally binding, but indirectly enforced by the listing regulations.
2. UK firms could opt out of compliance with specific aspects of the code if they explained the reasons for so doing.

SOX is an example of management of governance via statute, but such an approach can be problematic. Criticisms of SOX rapidly emerged and focused largely around the costs incurred by companies in ensuring compliance (see, for example, the Wall Street Journal article by Solomon and Peecher, 2004). The arguments suggested that the regulations in SOX are:

*   A form of hidden taxation.
*   Economically inefficient. Estimates suggest that the total cost to the US economy of implementing SOX was US $1.4 trillion, compared with total losses of US $427 billion from the major scandals of Enron, WorldCom, Tyco, and Global Crossing.
*   Damaging to the attractiveness of the US markets to foreign listings. In a speech in 2006 Alan Greenspan said he was "acutely aware and disturbed" by the shift in initial public offerings away from the United States and towards London as a result of SOX.

The United States had little time to familiarise itself with the implementation and enforcement of SOX, however, before attention was refocused on a new crisis.

The Global Financial Crisis

In spite of almost twenty years of efforts to regulate behaviour and reduce the risk of corporate scandals, the world was suddenly hit by a banking crisis which originated in the United States and was caused largely by "failure and weaknesses in corporate governance" (OECD, 2009). Extended debate on the causes of the financial crisis are beyond the scope of this book, but it is clear that the **existence** of internal control and risk management systems offers no guarantee of their **effectiveness**, either at national or institutional levels. Reporting that you have complied with a particular governance code and saying you have reviewed the control system does not mean that it is actually working effectively. Furthermore, if the boundaries of the control system (for regulatory purposes) are tightly defined, as in SOX, then the controls outside of that boundary may also be potentially ineffective. Good financial controls may mean little if operational risks are not managed well.

Box 2.7   Narrow Versus Broad Definitions of Internal Control

SOX only talks about internal control in terms of the controls relating to financial reporting. In other words, it seeks only to provide assurance about the reliability of financial reporting. In practice, firms are open to a much broader range of risks and require a much broader set of internal controls which encompass the full range of company activities and extend well beyond financial issues.

The King Code (2009, p. 8) is critical of the approach taken in SOX and notes that "SOX – with all of its statutory requirements for rigorous internal controls – has not prevented the collapse of many of the leading names in US banking and finance."

The scope for contradiction between perception and reality in terms of risk management and internal control can be usefully illustrated by reference to the failed US bank Lehman Brothers. In September 2008 Lehman Brothers filed for bankruptcy despite the fact that in its annual report for 2007 Lehman described their approach to risk management as follows:

> While risk cannot be eliminated, it can be mitigated to the greatest extent possible through a strong internal control environment. Essential in our approach to risk management is a strong internal control environment with multiple overlapping and reinforcing elements.

The annual report goes on to state that management used the COSO framework to review the internal control system over financial reporting and found it to be effective. This statement of effectiveness is further confirmed in the auditor's report.

The subsequent bankruptcy clearly showed that controls over financial reporting are only one part of good governance, and there is a need for the management of broader, enterprise-wide business risks. For example, within Lehman Brothers, a risk committee was in place, but it only met every six months, despite the fast-moving pace of financial markets. Similarly, seven out of the ten directors were retired CEOs of non-banking companies, and a former theatrical producer was a member of the audit committee. Structures can look good on paper but only have merit if they are managed by knowledgeable staff who are empowered to make them effective. As noted in a 2008 report by the Institute of Chartered Secretaries and Administrators, many companies treat governance as "a compilation of rules and regulations which add little value" (Skypala, 2008).

Whilst the financial crisis originated in the banking sector, its impact was far wider, and in a report analysing the corporate governance lessons to be learned from the crisis, the Organisation for Economic Co-operation and Development (OECD) (OECD, 2009) concluded that accounting standards and regulatory requirements had failed to safeguard against excessive risk taking and:

- Risk management was a silo-based activity rather than enterprise wide
- Disclosures about foreseeable risks and the systems used to manage them left a lot to be desired
- Board competence and composition were potentially weak
- Incentive systems encouraged and rewarded substantial risk taking

The Walker Review (2009) in the UK, which also investigated the causes of the crisis, similarly referenced board composition and qualifications as issues requiring review, together with remuneration and the way in which performance is evaluated in organisations. Walker also recommended that banks and insurance companies listed in the FTSE 100 should appoint a risk committee, separate from the audit committee, responsible for oversight of risk strategy and risk exposures. In a similar vein, the Turner Review (FSA, 2009) also highlighted the need to raise the risk management skills of board members and particularly the role played by non-executive directors in advising on risk taking.

By 2010, therefore, in both the UK and the United States there was a much heightened awareness of the importance of good risk management to corporate governance and a growing recognition that compliance with regulation did not necessarily equate to good risk management.

Phase Two: 2010–2019

This period is characterised by increasing convergence of regulatory thinking in the United States and the UK in relation to internal controls and governance.

The key difference between the legislative approach as used in SOX versus the more flexible non-legislative Combined Code in the UK[2] remains in place, but in other ways the principles adopted in both countries have moved closer. This is perhaps because the decade has been one of refinement, rather than whole-sale redrafting, of existing rules, and this has provided opportunities for different regimes to learn from one another. Notable examples of such convergence are discussed in the following sections.

Separation of the Role of Chairman and Chief Executive

The UK's Combined Code (2010 and revised 2012, 2014, and 2018) requires separation of the role of the CEO and chairman, as originally recommended in the Cadbury Report. In the United States, the Dodd-Frank Wall Street Reform Act of 2010 introduced a requirement for companies to comply with rules laid down by the SEC, demanding that they explain their reasons for either having a single person taking on the role of both chairman and CEO or opting to separate the roles. In so doing it introduced the idea of separate roles, which was previously not part of the US governance debate.

"Say on Pay"

In 2010 the Dodd-Frank Act proposed that shareholders should be given non-binding advisory votes on directors' compensation. Although non-binding, companies that receive low levels of shareholder approval on pay have found themselves subsequent to strong pressure to revise the pay packages. Subsequently, the Enterprise and Regulatory Reform Act (2013) in the UK introduced a requirement for listed companies to grant shareholders a vote on executive pay packages.

Risk Committees

As noted earlier, the 2009 Walker Review in the UK recommended that banks and financial companies should appoint a risk committee that is independent of the audit committee. The Combined Code does not specify the remit of the risk committee, but, in common with guidance on remuneration and audit committees, the implication is that the risk committee will be made up of a majority of non-executive (independent) directors, one of whom will be the chair. These rules were echoed in the United States the following year under Section 165 of the Dodd-Frank Act, which specified a requirement for certain bank holding companies and publicly traded non-banking financial institutions to appoint a similarly independent risk committee. The risk committee is held responsible for oversight of enterprise-wide risk management within the company.

Chief Risk Officer

Section 165 of the Dodd–Frank Act also required specified classes of major bank holding companies and other financial institutions operating in the United States to appoint a chief risk officer (CRO) to implement and maintain appropriate enterprise-wide risk management practices for the company. The CRO reports directly to the risk committee and chief executive. This legislation, like that relating to risk committees, largely mirrored the recommendations contained within the Walker Review in the UK, which called for the financial regulatory authorities to review and strengthen the role of the CRO[3] in banks and major financial institutions.

A survey by Deloitte in 2011 noted that the trend in favour of appointing CROs has now extended well beyond the financial sector, although the role is still primarily confined to organisations that could face ruin if certain financial, operational, or reputational risks were crystallised. The case of the Canadian Utility Company, Hydro One, as discussed in Aabo et al. (2005) provides a useful example of such an appointment outside the financial sector. In addition, the precise job title may vary, as well as the level of appointment – executive or below. These issues are discussed in more depth in Chapter 3.

Other debates on risk-related issues are running in parallel across both sides of the Atlantic and the wider world – see, for example, the revised governance principles outlined in OECD (2015). The stewardship role to be played by institutional investors in the oversight of risk taking and broader aspects of governance is one example of this. The Stewardship Code in the UK encourages institutional investors to be proactive in influencing managerial behaviour, whereas in the United States the board of directors retains much more power, although the scope for institutional shareholder intervention is now being discussed.

One key area of difference remains, however. Whilst the role of the board of directors in actively overseeing risk management is well recognised by regulators worldwide, its precise role in respect of internal controls is still open to debate. In the United States SOX and COSO regulations specify responsibility for evaluating and reporting on the effectiveness of internal controls on financial reporting, *but not elsewhere*. In contrast, the UK's 2014 revisions to the Combined Code reaffirmed that the board of directors has ultimate responsibility (across the piece) for risk management and internal control, which "should be incorporated within the company's normal management and governance processes, not treated as a separate compliance exercise" (FRC, 2014, p. 2). Moreover, it established a requirement for the board of directors to publish a viability statement attesting that they are reasonably certain that the company can continue to operate and meet its liabilities as they fall due over the period of assessment, taking into account its current position and principal risks. The assessment period is not specified but is expected to be "significantly" longer than twelve months. Thus the viability statement complements and extends

the going concern principle that has traditionally underpinned annual accounting statements, and in so doing it has substantially raised the profile of risk
management.

As of 2019, the regulatory pressures across the globe serve as a powerful
force to encourage strong corporate governance even if some divisions remain
between the legislative versus "comply or explain" approaches to regulation.
The net result of all of this is a rise in the profile of risk management and a growing professionalisation of the associated roles, as explained in the next section.

Governance Regulation and the Rise of Risk Management

Prior to 2002 both COSO (1992) in the United States and the Combined
Code in the UK regarded risk assessment and monitoring as one element
within a broader internal control framework which served to support good
corporate governance. Risk management was subsidiary to internal control.
The requirement under SOX (2002) for directors to attest that internal controls
were effective (albeit only financial controls) served to catapult risk management up the corporate agenda. When the COSO framework was redrafted in
2004, it was retitled "Enterprise Risk Management – Integrated Framework,"
thereby reversing the relative importance of risk management and internal control. Enterprise risk management became a term "that incorporates the internal
control framework within it" (COSO, 2004, foreword, p. v). This change has
impacted heavily on both the risk and internal audit professions.

Despite the growing importance of risk management in the new millennium, however, the banking crisis revealed that the risk profession in the financial services sector was often silo based and divorced from operational practice.
Furthermore, risk managers were often dealing with issues poorly understood
by the board and hence lacking in board oversight. Post-crisis there has been
substantial growth in the number of organisations choosing to appoint a risk
committee and also a rapid rise in the number of CRO appointments. Other
risk management roles, such as that of chief compliance officer, have also been
growing in both number and stature. At a humbler level, the Global Association of Risk Professionals, which is US based but whose membership spans
almost 200 countries, boasted in excess of 150,000 members and associates in
2014. Similarly, the UK-based Institute of Risk Management draws over half
of its fast-growing membership from outside the UK and offers many different
certificate courses in the field of risk management.

Importantly, the growth of training opportunities and career prospects in
the field is not limited to financial institutions and financial risk management.
Companies of all sizes and levels of complexity are realising that risk and governance are strongly inter-linked, and consideration should be given to the
upside of risk taking as well as the downside. As a result, there is currently
much debate about the role of risk managers in influencing corporate strategy
and the need for all staff in an organisation to be risk aware. Importantly, also,

there are some, such as Power (2009), who are strong critics of the high profile given to risk managers.

Key Learning Point

The financial crisis drove changes in governance regulation within the financial services sector that have since begun to spread across into non-financial sectors.

In Turnbull, the view was clearly expressed that internal control should be embedded within the normal processes of a business rather than being seen as a separate exercise undertaken to ensure regulatory compliance. Similarly, CoCo (Canada) confirmed the idea that "internal control is integral to the activities of the company, and not something practiced in remote corners" (IFAC, 2006). From an empirical perspective, however, this embedding has proved extraordinarily difficult to achieve. Organisations find it easier to "tick a box" to indicate that they have complied with rules and that a control is in place, but in such situations the monitoring focuses on the existence of controls and not their effectiveness. The risk management function can become wrapped up in dealing with issues of compliance and be isolated in silos, which mean that it has little direct contact with day-to-day operations and holds little meaning for front-line staff.

One of the recurring themes in this book is the extent to which internal controls – and specifically risk management – can become divorced from the operational realities of a business. The case studies reveal very different corporate mindsets in relation to this important issue and show that embedding risk management into operations is an extremely challenging and long-term process.

The case studies also illustrate that governance regulations and risk management standards and rules merely provide a skeleton on which the flesh of a control system can be overlaid and used in practice. The underlying skeletal structure may be identical across different organisations, but the resulting internal control system will reflect individual organisational traits, linked to the business model, corporate culture, and management style. Consequently, it can be argued that on a standalone basis, the value added by standards and regulations is minimal – the real value is added by the way that they are used in practice to ensure the achievement of organisational objectives. The case studies in this book provide an ideal way of discovering and analysing the differences between the theory and the reality.

Conclusion

In this chapter we have looked at the way in which the regulations and codes relating to corporate governance, internal control, and risk management have developed concurrently, but concluded that regulations are just the starting point for good governance. Ultimately, the quality of governance and risk management is a matter for the individual organisation. No amount of legislation can force good governance if there is a lack of corporate willingness to engage with the underlying principles. As a result, risk management and governance approaches will vary from organisation to organisation, even in the context of common sets of regulations.

Notes

1 It is very important to note that the report and attestation relate solely to the internal controls on financial reporting and *not* all forms of internal control.
2 The UK does have legislation on governance, most notably the Companies Act 2006 and disclosure rules published by the Financial Conduct Authority, but a "comply or explain" approach continues to dominate.
3 A survey of global financial institutions by Deloitte Touche Tohmatsu Limited (Wall Street Journal, 2013) found that in 2002 just 65% of financial institutions had a CRO, but this rose to 86% by 2010 and 89% by 2013.

References

Aabo, T., Fraser, J., & Simkins, B. (2005) "The Rise and Evolution of the Chief Risk Officer: Enterprise Risk Management at Hydro One." *Journal of Applied Corporate Finance*, Vol. 17, No. 3, pp. 62–75.

Committee of Sponsoring Organizations (COSO) (1992) *Internal Control – Integrated Framework (1992).* Committee of Sponsoring Organizations of the Treadway Commission, NJ.

Committee of Sponsoring Organisations of the Treadway Commission (COSO) (2004) *Enterprise Risk Management – Integrated Framework.* AICPA, New York.

Confederation of British Industry (1995) *Greenbury Report-Final Report of the Study Group on Directors' Remuneration.* July, London.

Coopers and Lybrand (1991) *Corporate Governance and Accountability.* January, London. https://cadbury.cjbs.archios.info/_media/files/CAD-01003.pdf

Financial Standards Authority (FSA) (2009) *The Turner Review. A Regulatory Response to the Global Banking Crisis.* FSA, London.

FRC (2014, September) *UK Corporate Governance Code.* Financial Reporting Council, London.

Gupta, P. (2006) Internal Control. COSO 1992 Control Framework *and Management Reporting on Internal Control: Survey and Analysis of Implementation Practices.* IMA, Montvale, NJ.

Hampel (1998) *Final Report of the Hampel Committee on Corporate Governance.* Gee Publishing, London.

ICAEW (1999) *Internal Control Guidance for Directors on the Combined Code.* Institute of Chartered Accountants in England and Wales, London.

IFAC (2006) *Internal Controls – A Review of Current Developments.* International Federation of Accountants, New York.

King Code of Governance for South Africa (2009) *Institute of Directors in Southern Africa*. Downloadable from: www.iodsa.co.za/downloads/documents/King_Code_ 2009.pdf.

Krane, D., & Sever, J. (1996) *The Coopers & Lybrand Survey of Internal Control in Corporate America: A Report on What Corporations Are and Are Not Doing to Manage Risks*. Louis Harris & Associates, New York.

OECD (2009) "The Corporate Governance Lessons from the Financial Crisis." In Kirkpatrick, G. (eds.), *OECD Financial Trends* Vol. 1. OECD Publishing, Paris. https://www.oecd.org/finance/financial-markets/42229620.pdf

OECD (2015) *G20/OECD Principles of Corporate Governance*. OECD Publishing, Paris. http://dx.doi.org/10.1787/9789264236882-en.

OECD Principles of Corporate Governance (2004) Downloadable from: www.oecd.org/dataoecd/32/18/31557724.pdf/.

Page, M., & Spira, L. (2004) *The Turnbull Report, Internal Control and Risk Management: The Developing Role of Internal Audit*. Institute of Chartered Accountants of Scotland, Edinburgh.

Power, M. (1997) *The Audit Society Rituals of Verification*. Oxford Economic Press.

Power, M. (2009) "The Risk Management of Nothing." *Accounting, Organizations and Society*, Vol. 34, pp. 849–855.

SEC (2006) *Management's Report on Internal Control over Financial Reporting*. [RELEASE NOS. 33-8762; 34-54976; File No. S7-24-06]. Washington.

Skypala, P. (2008) "Time to Reward Good Corporate Governance." *ft.com.*, November 18. Downloadable from: www.ft.com/cms/s/0/a308a71e-b275-11dd-bbc9-0000779fd18c.html.

Solomon, I., & Peecher, M. (2004) "SOS 404- A Billion Here, a Billion There." *Wall Street Journal, Managers' Journal*, November 9.

SOX (2002) *Sarbanes-Oxley Act*. US House of Congress.

Spira, L., & Page, M. (2003) "Risk Management: The Re-Invention of Internal Control and the Changing Role of Internal Audit." *Accounting, Auditing and Accountability Journal*, Vol. 16, No. 4, pp. 640–661.

UK Corporate Governance Code, Financial Reporting Council (2010) Downloadable from: www.frc.org.uk/documents/pagemanager/Corporate_Governance/UK%20Corp%20Gov%20Code%20June%202010.pdf.

Walker Review (2009) *A Review of Corporate Governance in UK Banks and Other Financial Industry Entities*. H.M. Treasury, London.

Wall Street Journal (2013) "CROs in Financial Services Sector Rise in Numbers and Stature." New York, November 13.

Useful Web Links

1. www.sarbanes-oxley-forum.com/
    This forum includes many links to discussion threads and comment about the act, as well as providing access to a downloadable PDF version of the Sarbanes-Oxley Act 2002.
2. https://www.ferma.eu/about-ferma/
    This is the home page of the Federation of European Risk Management Associations, spanning 21 countries, and is a useful site to gain more information about European initiatives and practice in risk management. The site

also offers free access to many useful publications such as a sustainability risk guide for European risk managers.

Discussion Questions

1. Suggest examples of situations in (a) your daily living and (b) your work life where strong emphasis is placed on compliance with rules. Use these examples to discuss the extent to which the rules are being used either to help achieve sensible and clearly articulated objectives or as a cushion to protect against accusations of failure.
2. In preparation for this, it may help to review the ideas of Michael Power on how modern society seems to be characterised by people checking up on each other, demanding accountability and monitoring risk. Look at Chapter 6 in his book *The Audit Society Rituals of Verification* (1997) Oxford Economic Press.
3. Analyse the governance structure of your own organisation (or one of your choice) and look at the extent to which it tries to link controls back to the organisational objectives. Are any elements missing? Could the governance structure be improved at all and, if so, how?
4. Does the payment/incentive system in your organisation encourage risk taking? If so, how and what controls exist to restrict the risk taking to a level that matches the organisational appetite for risk?
5. Discuss the relative merits of allowing poorly governed companies to collapse versus the merits of tighter governance regulations for all companies.

3 International Standards for Risk and Enterprise Management

Aim

The aim of this chapter is to outline the two main frameworks – ISO 31000 (2018) and COSO's Enterprise Risk Management (2017) – which are used globally as guides on risk management systems. Neither guide is industry specific, and both can be used within private- or public-sector settings. Standardised frameworks for risk management are a vital complement to the governance regulations described in Chapter 2, because they provide a frame of reference for compliance with the regulations. As already stated, control or risk management effectiveness can be demonstrated by the provision of evidence that a "suitable" internal framework is in place – for example, COSO 2017. Standards are also valuable in adding detail to the role played by senior management in relation to risk and internal control, emphasising the importance of the risk culture that is engendered by management and setting out the core definitions, principles, and processes for use by all levels of management in designing and implementing a risk management system.

The chapter concludes that risk management frameworks in every organisation have common features based around the standards, but the detail and complexity of systems will vary to reflect the organisational context. We also conclude that the core concepts of good risk management, as expressed both by the Committee on Sponsoring Organizations (COSO) and within ISO 31000, are similar. Compliance with either serves as evidence of compliance with the governance regulations described in Chapter 2. Nonetheless, the calls for risk management to be "fully integrated" across all levels and segments of an organisation remain ambitious. There has been significant progress in the understanding of enterprise risk management over the last decade, and many more organisations now claim to have implemented such a system. Establishing a structured and well-documented system which appears to comply with COSO or ISO 31000, however, does not automatically imply that risks are well managed. As we see in the case studies, evidence suggests that fully integrating risk management into all areas of operations remains extraordinarily challenging in practice. Theory and practice do not yet match up.

DOI: 10.4324/9781315208336-3

The chapter is broken into the following sections:

- Risk Management Standards: Background
- COSO 2017
- ISO 31000
- Conclusion

Risk Management Standards: Background

A core requirement for any standard on risk management is a definition of risk. ISO 31000:2018 defines risk as "the effect of uncertainty on objectives." This simple definition incorporates both opportunities (upside risk) and threats (downside risk), and risk management is thus concerned with providing mechanisms through which to control both aspects of risk.

Why Do Standards Exist?

Risk affects every decision made within an organisation, and as demonstrated in Chapter 2, risk and governance are closely interlinked. Risk management practice needs to evolve to keep pace with both changes in business practice and changes in the types of risks that companies face.

Standards help to ensure that there is agreement on:

- The objective of risk management
- Terminology
- Risk management processes
- Organisational frameworks and structures for risk management

Standards provide tools that are helpful for both private- and public-sector organisations in establishing and maintaining their own risk management systems. Their intention is not to be prescriptive, but simply to provide a mechanism through which organisations of any size can better understand and manage the risks that may impact upon the achievement of their objectives. Whether or not such a laudable aim feeds through to risk management systems in practice is an issue which will be explored in the case studies that can be found in the next section of this book. For now, we focus on the standards which establish the core principles that should underpin a risk management system.

Historical Development

The world's first risk management standard, AS/NSZ 4360, was issued jointly by Standards Australia and New Zealand in 1995 and subsequently revised in 1999 and 2004. It not only provided a basis used by other countries to develop their own standards but also established a framework for the implementation of risk management approaches in a wide range of organisations. The increased globalisation of businesses over the next few years led to increased pressures for an international standard, and the result was ISO 31000, published in November 2009. Simultaneously, Standards Australia adopted the international standard in place of its own by releasing Australian/New Zealand Standard Risk Management Principle and Guidelines AS/NZS ISO 31000:2009. Similarly, in Canada ISO: 31000 was adopted as a national standard, and in March 2010, the British Standards Institute also integrated the international standard into its own portfolio, as BS ISO 31000. By 2015, the standard had been adopted as a national standard in fifty countries, as well as being used by several United Nations bodies and national governments as a basis for establishing their risk management systems. In 2018 a more concise revised version of ISO 31000 was issued, which was hailed as easier to understand and described as supporting risk management and decision making across all activities and all levels of an organisation.

Running in parallel with the development of ISO 31000 was the evolution of the COSO Enterprise Risk Management (ERM) framework in the United States. As we saw in Chapter 2, one consequence of the Sarbanes-Oxley (SOX) legislation was to transform the COSO ERM framework into the most commonly used governance system used to assess SOX compliance. But this was in the United States, whilst the rest of the world was referencing ISO 31000 to build their risk management systems. The key message of COSO is that risk management is enterprise wide, and this idea can be seen to have significantly influenced the development of risk management thinking and practice post-2004.

Box 3.1   COSO 2004 Definition of ERM

A process, effected by an entity's board of directors, management, and other personnel, applied in strategy setting and across the enterprise designed to identify potential events that may affect the entity and manage risk to be within its risk appetite to provide reasonable assurance regarding the achievement of entity objectives.

Over the course of the last decade, the starkness of choice between ERM and ISO 31000 has become more muted, and whilst both standards still exist, it has become more common for ISO 31000 to be used in parallel with COSO in a single organisation. Both public- and private-sector organisations have adopted this approach – for more detail see, for example, these web links on Statoil, the Norwegian state oil company, and the Federal Highway Administration in the United States.

1. Federal Highways Agency "Getting Started in Agency Risk Management"
   https://international.fhwa.dot.gov/scan/agencybroc/
2. Axiom Group Presentation on Risk Management in Statoil
   https://axiomgroupe.com/images/strategic_presentations/Enter-prise_Risk_management_may_2013/Statoil_-_Mr._Eyvind_Aven.pdf

The 2018 version of ISO 31000 mirrors COSO's ERM framework in its emphasis on the need to integrate risk management across an organisation, starting at the governance level. In a similar vein, the Institute of Risk Management (IRM) describes enterprise risk management as a "fundamentally important component of good governance" (IRM, 2018, p. 3). Implicit in this comment is the idea that COSO (2017) and ISO 31000 (2018) are mutually compatible.

COSO 2017: Enterprise Risk Management: Integrating With Strategy and Performance

The 2004 version of COSO defined enterprise risk management as the overarching framework for internal control, implying that "risk is embodied within the corporate strategy of an enterprise" (Dickinson, 2001, p. 364). Consequently, when corporate objectives are aligned with those of shareholders, then ERM also provides a mechanism for managing and enhancing shareholder value. The link between risk management and shareholder value was one of the core philosophies underpinning COSO 2004, which argued that "value is maximised when management sets strategy and objectives to strike an optimal balance between growth and return goals and related risks." This idea is well supported in the practitioner literature, particularly in the area of financial services, and some companies make the link very explicit in their annual reports.

Box 3.3   Zurich Insurance Company: Annual Report (2019)

One of the objectives of risk management is to "enhance value creation by embedding disciplined risk-taking in the company culture." In managing risks "the Group's risk appetite and tolerance reflects Zurich's willingness and capacity to take risks in pursuit of value" (pp. 129–130).

The concepts of risk appetite and risk tolerance, as mentioned by Zurich, underpin the link between strategy and risk management, but can be difficult to elucidate in practice. Examples of the associated problems can be found in the case studies found in later chapters.

The 2017 COSO ERM framework sought to be clearer about how ERM can be linked to stakeholder expectations, and it explicitly connects ERM with performance, arguing that "risk influences and aligns strategy and performance across all departments and functions." Perhaps the biggest change between COSO 2004 and COSO 2017 is the transition from a backward-looking to a forward-looking focus. The rather complex 2004 COSO cube viewed ERM as concerned with value *preservation*. COSO 2017 uses a helix to portray ERM as a set of tools for value creation. By emphasising the role of risk management in respect of strategic decision making, COSO emphasises the forward-looking dimension of risk management. What are the risks to existing strategies being fulfilled? Are the strategies correct in view of the risks we anticipate?

Figure 3.1 shows how the ERM framework is made up of five core principles. Adherence to the principles will indicate to management that their organisation understands its risks and is managing them in accordance with its business objectives. Enterprise management sits above and straddles all aspects of organisational activity, working from left to right across Figure 3.1, from defining its mission, through the implementation of strategies, to the end result of enhanced value. The five principles of ERM shown below the diagram are woven into the fabric of the organisation in the form of a helix, which goes left to right and back again in a continuous loop, indicating that the ERM process is constantly evolving. As new information arises, corporate strategies and objectives evolve accordingly, and risk management systems and techniques need to simultaneously evolve. The framework very clearly highlights the dynamic nature of ERM when it is working effectively, but therein lies the challenge.

Figure 3.1 Components of ERM: The ERM helix

Table 3.1 Twenty Components of ERM 2017

Twenty Components of ERM 2017				
Governance and Culture	*Strategy and Objective Setting*	*Performance*	*Review and Revision*	*Information, Communication, Reporting*
Exercises board risk oversight 1. Establishes operating structures 2. Defines desired culture 3. Demonstrates commitment to core values 4. Attracts, develops, and retains core individuals	5. Analyses business context 6. Defines risk appetite 7. Evaluates alternative strategies 8. Formulates business objectives	9. Identifies risk 10. Assesses severity of risk 11. Prioritises risks 12. Implements risk responses 13. Develops portfolio view	14. Assesses substantial change 15. Reviews risk and performance 16. Pursues improvement in ERM	Leverages information and technology Communicates risk information Reports on risk, culture and performance

The five principles that interweave in the helix are:

- **Governance and culture** – Setting the tone, ethical values, and understanding of risk.
- **Strategy and objective setting** – ERM is integral to strategic planning and establishing a risk appetite.
- **Performance** – Risks that may impact on objectives are identified and assessed, risk responses are selected, and risks are aggregated in a portfolio view. Results are reported to key stakeholders.
- **Review and revision** – By reviewing performance against objectives, ERM practice can be evaluated and amended as necessary.
- **Information, communication, and reporting** – ERM requires ongoing collection and sharing of information across the entire organisation.
  Adding detail to the ERM framework are the twenty components that are contained within the principles. These define the risk management components integral to each principle (Table 3.1).

Although the term "components" is used differently in the two standards, the principles and components within the COSO ERM framework can also be found within ISO 31000 (2009) and its predecessors.

ISO 31000 (2018)

The update to ISO 3100 that was published in 2018 defined risk management as the set of coordinated activities used to direct and control an organisation in respect of risk, with risk seen as "the effect of uncertainty on objectives." The purpose of risk management is regarded as being the creation and protection of value through improved performance, encouragement of innovation, and support for the achievement of objectives.

In common with the 2009 version, the standard is made up of three linked components: risk management principles, process, and framework. ISO 2018 revised the principles and highlighted the importance of governance and leadership, together with the case for integration of risk management across the organisation and an iterative approach to risk management systems. The net result is a standard which strongly echoes the thinking that underpins ERM.

The interaction between the three components is shown in the diagram in Figure 3.2.

Figure 3.2 shows that the principles are used as an input to the creation of a risk management framework, which in turn is used to establish the risk management process. The diagram clearly illustrates that neither the framework nor process are static, as monitoring and continual review result in changes which refine the overall risk management system. The idea is that the structures and mechanisms used to manage risks are continually evolving.

The individual components that make up each of the principles, framework, and process are vitally important, so we will now look at each in some detail.

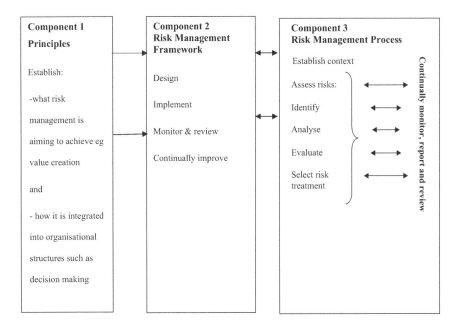

Figure 3.2 Linking the three components of ISO 31000

Principles

Central (see Figure 3.3.) to the principles is the purpose of risk management – value creation and protection. The principles form the foundation stones upon which an integrated risk management system is built, but they are not formulaic. Instead, they take account of the organisational context, including the human and cultural factors, meaning that investment in risk management systems should be proportional to organisational needs. In this way the standard can be adapted to suit different types and scales of organisation. The principles have very strong overlaps with the underlying intentions contained within the COSO definition of ERM and again illustrate the overlap between the ISO 31000 and COSO systems.

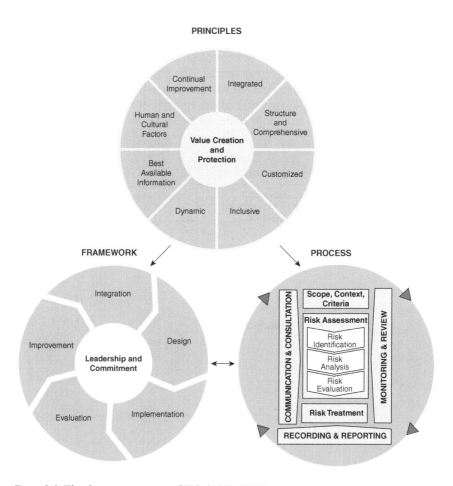

Figure 3.3 The three components of ISO 31000 (2018)

Framework

Leadership and commitment lie at the core of this component of ISO 31000, reflecting the need for senior management to demonstrate their commitment to risk management. This requires the formulation of clear risk management policies linked to organisational objectives; the allocation of resources, lines of responsibility, and accountability; and the establishment of lines of communication that ensure the effective identification, assessment, and management of risks. The initial design of the framework is framed around the principles already laid down, so that it reflects the organisational context, what they want to achieve from risk management, and how it is to be embedded within the organisation, as indicated in Figure 3.2. Implementation of the framework is rapidly followed by implementation of the process (Component 3), and both are the subject of continual internal reporting and monitoring so that both processes and the framework can be continually improved and refined.

Process

ISO 31000 states that the risk management process should be "fully integrated" in the organisation, that is, built into its structure, operations, and processes at strategic, operational, programme, and project levels. The processes should be tailored to suit the specific context and take into account the desired objectives, as well as the cultural and human considerations. The language used strongly echoes that of COSO's enterprise risk management guidance, confirming the degree of overlap between the two approaches.

The process represents the core of the risk management system, and as Figure 3.3 shows, at its centre is a sequence of five steps from risk assessment through identification, analysis, and evaluation, to the selection of a risk treatment. The stepped process of assessment, identification, analysis, and treatment of risks was first laid down in the original 1995 version of AS/NSZ 4360, and the current version in ISO 31000 is simply an extended form of that idea.

At an organisational level, it is the way in which the process is implemented that can make or break a risk management system. Some discussion of each of the elements of the process is therefore important, and the Airmic et al. (2010) guide provides useful detail on ISO 31000 implementation, and Leitch (2010) provides an overview and critique of its content.

Scope, Context, and Criteria

This part of the process aims to customise the risk management system to suit its specific context in terms of the organisational size and environment, the risk management objectives, and the organisational level at which it will apply (e.g. strategic or operational). Key questions to ask at this stage include:

- What is the purpose of this specific risk management system?
- How does this function/department/business interact with the wider organisation?
- What criteria are to be used to evaluate risk? Do these align with the overall organisation's attitude to risk?
- How is risk to be determined?
- Will risks be managed independently or in a portfolio-style approach?

The culture of the organisation and the attitude to risk that it engenders is very important to establishing the context within which risks will be managed. If staff are encouraged to be "risk aware" and take responsibility for the control of risks, then the system will be very different from one in an organisation where risk taking is encouraged as a way of boosting short-term profits. The general attitude to risk within an organisation and its risk appetite will commonly reflect the views of the board of directors and other senior managers and formalised in the production of documented guidance and rules on risk taking. The cases studies throughout this book illustrate very different attitudes to risk within the different organisations and serve to emphasise the significance of context within the risk management process.

Risk Assessment

Risk assessment involves three sub-elements – identification, analysis, and evaluation, which help a manager decide how to respond to a specific risk, given the context and the organisational risk appetite. Context is of definitive importance here, as the risks faced by a global airline, for example, will be very different from those faced by a supermarket chain. As we will see in the next chapter, there are common risks such as natural disasters, foreign exchange rate movements, or cyber risk that concern all businesses, but their *relative significance* will vary according to both the size and sector of the organisation.

Risk identification requires the specification of the many threats and opportunities that may impact upon company objectives. Risk identification is required at all levels of the organisation – from strategy level, through to day-to-day operational activities and special projects and may be undertaken using either a top-down or bottom-up approach. Whichever method is adopted, it is helpful to understand that risk identification is the responsibility of operating staff and not specialised risk management staff. The managers know the issues facing their business and are therefore best equipped to be able to identify the related risks. It is not uncommon, however, for risk management staff to be involved in training managers on identification techniques. A range of techniques can be used for risk assessment, including:

- Questionnaires and checklists
- Interviews and focus groups

- Workshops and brainstorming
- Flowcharts and dependency analysis
- Inspection and audits
- SWOT (strength, weaknesses, opportunities, and threats) analysis
- PESTLE (political, economic, social, technological, legal, and economic) analysis

Once identified, the risks need to be both categorised and recorded, with decisions being made about the nature and level of detail to be held on each risk. Risk registers, sometimes called risk logs, will commonly be maintained for each business area and special project, as well as at the top level for the overall organisation. The key risk register, maintained at the top level, will record only those risks seen as posing a significant threat to the overall organisation, and these risks will be regularly discussed at board of directors meetings and ideally managed or "owned" by a senior executive. The case studies in this book include examples of risk registers. A typical register, such as that illustrated in Figure 2.2, will include a brief description of the risk, the manager/person held responsible for it, the risk assessment, the decision on risk treatment, and the residual risk remaining after treatment. Frequency of monitoring or the date of the next review may also be included.

Key Learning Point

Risk identification is the responsibility of operating staff and not specialised risk management staff.

Risk analysis and evaluation involves consideration of both the likelihood and impact of the risk and the allocation of a risk rating or score. Impact and likelihood are frequently measured using either 3×3 or 5×5 matrices, which rank on a scale of low to very high, as shown in Figure 3.4.

Key risks will be numbered and marked on the squares in the matrix. The top right-hand side of the matrix indicates risks which need to be actively managed because they have both a high likelihood of occurrence and a high impact. Moving towards the bottom left of the grid represents a lower risk management priority. The levels of risk from very high (top right) to low (bottom left) are usually represented as deep red, red, amber, and green (shown in Figure 3.4 as different shading). The different shades give a clear visual profile of risk from high priority (top right) through to acceptable (bottom left). The number of squares on the grid which are coloured red, amber, or green will reflect the organisation's or business unit's appetite for risk. In the earlier case, risk tolerance is low, as only three out of twenty-five squares indicate acceptable levels of risk.

Table 3.2 Risk Register Template

RISK MANAGEMENT										
Risk Identified	Risk Owner	Risk Analysis			Risk Management Strategy		Action Plan			Risk Mitigation Status
		Impact	Likelihood	Risk Score	Mitigations/ Controls	Effectiveness	Assurance	Further Action Required	Person Responsible/ Date	
Risk Number Risk description Risk detail Risk causes Risk effects										

Note: Red/amber/green colouring in the risk mitigation column (here indicated by different shading) indicates the risk evaluation, and the risk register will include definitions of each category.

For example: red = residual risk level is unacceptable; amber = residual risk level is not unacceptable but is at a level requiring further mitigation; green = tolerable residual risk level.

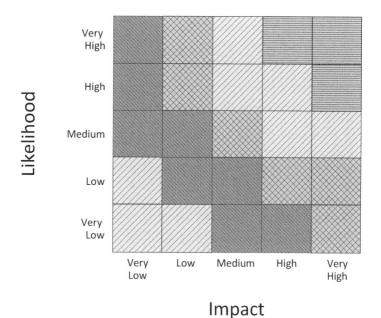

Figure 3.4 Likelihood: Consequences matrix

It is important to note that the matrix is commonly constructed based on assumptions – which may be biased – and mathematical forecasts of the probability of the different events. For example, if a business identifies flood risk as something that could interrupt their activity, then someone must forecast the likelihood of flooding at different levels of severity. Each severity level brings different consequences that will be reflected in the matrix. Any differences of opinion, biases, or assumptions that lie behind the evaluation of risks must be communicated to those who will use the matrix.

Key Learning Point

Likelihood: consequences matrices need to be interpreted with caution and with FULL KNOWLEDGE of the underlying assumptions

---

Where the likelihood of an event is uncertain, the probability estimates that underpin the likelihood estimates in the matrix are often based on probabilities that reflect past events, but the past is not always a good predictor of the future. Just think about the length of your commute to work. Even if the expected average time is forty minutes, it may vary day to day between thirty minutes and one hour, so treating forty minutes as the most likely time is potentially misleading. Furthermore, if the train line was closed in the future – even for a day – the commute may not even be possible. The lesson here is BEWARE! We will return to this topic again later in the book.

Selection of a **risk treatment** follows naturally on from the evaluation process. In ISO 31000 risk treatment refers to the activity of selecting and implementing appropriate control measures to modify the risk. As such, whilst risk control and mitigation are central to risk treatment, the terms also include risk avoidance, risk transfer, and risk financing.

From the evaluation process, any risks labelled as amber or red require a mitigating response, and so alternative options will be evaluated based on their cost and expected impact on both the likelihood and impact of the selected risk. The control needs to be both effective in reducing the risks and efficient in terms of its cost. Assuming that a risk cannot be entirely removed and the associated activity is to continue, there are four alternative treatments or responses from which to choose:

- **Risk acceptance** – do nothing
- **Risk reduction** – this may be aimed at either reducing the likelihood of occurrence (e.g. via regular maintenance of equipment to prevent breakdowns), or it could aim to reduce the impact of a risk occurring, e.g. through disaster recovery plans, provision of back-up facilities, etc.

- **Risk transfer** – for example, through the purchase of a form of risk financing such as insurance
- **Risk avoidance** – by eliminating the activities which create a given risk

Once a response has been selected, a treatment plan must be implemented. This should be documented and include the rationale for the selection, the timing of events, who is responsible and accountable for its implementation, and the monitoring procedure that will ensure its effectiveness is clearly recorded and understood.

Attitudes to both evaluation and treatment may change over time as an organisation's risk appetite alters. For example, a significant proportion of an airline's costs is made up of fuel, the price of which is set in dollars and can be subject to significant fluctuation. Traditionally, such risk is offset through hedging in the foreign exchange market, but the collapse in oil prices in 2020 and the impact of the coronavirus have led to many airlines reporting huge losses from hedging. This may affect their willingness to use this form of risk treatment in the future.

Box 3.4   Air France-KLM Hedging Losses

In 2019, fuel costs represented 23% of operating costs for the Air France-KLM Group. That year they registered a gain of $50 million on fuel hedging.

As of February 2020, Air France-KLM had hedged 65% of its estimated fuel costs for 2020 at a price of $65 per barrel of Brent crude oil. By 6 March, the market price had fallen to $45 a barrel. Even if the price fell no lower, the group would face a hedging loss of $1 billion!

Source: Financial Times 08/03/2020

The Air France-KLM case clearly illustrates how the past may not repeat itself and how some risk treatments can themselves end up increasing risks.

The process of identification, analysis, and treatment of risk is absolutely critical, and as the subsequent case studies reveal, it is usually an error somewhere in this process that triggers, at best, large losses and, at worst, disaster for an organisation. To make all three more effective, they are supported by the three components which form the edges of the circle in Figure 3.3 – communication and consultation, recording and reporting, and monitoring and review.

Communication and Consultation

Communication is concerned with informing both internal and external stakeholders about risks and how decisions are made about how they are managed. Communication of risk information should be both internal, for control purposes, and external, for reasons of accountability. Keeping stakeholders informed about the risks faced and the actions being taken to manage them will provide reassurance. In efficient markets, good risk disclosures might also be expected to reduce the cost of capital for those organisations that demonstrate effective risk management.[1]

Consultation involves the use of feedback from staff, experts, consultants, and other parties on information that can improve decision making on risks. Consultation helps management understand how well risks are being managed, how and if controls are working and where they are not, and utilise suggestions on how the process can be improved. A simple example from within an organisation might include feedback from a staff suggestion scheme on how operational or customer-facing processes might be better managed to reduce risk. An external consultation example might be the use of data from trade or industry bodies on forecast market conditions or the availability of core components as inputs into decisions on staffing to reduce the risk of staff shortages.

Combining communication and consultation ensures that stakeholders are well informed about risks and their management, but also that such management is optimised using the maximum information available from those affected. It can be likened to a doctor–patient relationship, in which the patient may behave in a way that endangers their health if certain actions are not clearly identified by the doctor as risky. Equally, the doctor cannot provide optimal advice on what to do or what not to do if the patient never speaks to him or her.

Recording and Reporting

Risk management is a structured process, the outcomes of which should be formally recorded and documented. As tools to communicate risks, documents provide both information and points of reference for staff and stakeholders whilst simultaneously improving decision making. For example, risk registers and consequences–likelihood matrices, as outlined in the previous section of this chapter, can help managers see trends in risk identification and the outcomes of their risk treatment choices. In so doing, recording and reporting provides a mechanism for accountability, which is essential to a risk management system.

Care should be taken to manage the extent of reporting to ensure that it suits the needs of the end user in terms of frequency and timeliness. Similarly, the cost–benefit calculation of different levels of granularity of reporting should be taken into account. Detail is costly and possibly unnecessary, but diversity of reporting approaches can be very unhelpful to external investors looking to compare corporate performance. This issue is discussed in depth in Woods et al. (2009). Lastly, the sensitivity of risk documentation clearly needs to be considered when determining what information should be available where and to whom. Access to who and when risk data can or should be amended or updated needs to be tightly controlled.

Monitoring and Review

If any process is to improve over time, it must be subject to continual monitoring and review. To maximise its effectiveness, monitoring should be incorporated into an organisation's performance management, measurement, and reporting activities. Box 3.5 provides an illustration of how this might happen in practice at the executive board level of an organisation.

Box 3.5 Linking Risk Monitoring to Remuneration

In the remuneration report contained in their 2019 annual report (p. 93), Zurich Insurance state that:

> "The remuneration system is closely integrated with the Group's risk management framework and is designed to not encourage or reward inappropriate risk-taking."

Line managers need to be aware that when they report upwards about performance and how risks are being managed, those reports will be part of a formal system of oversight. Simultaneously, the internal audit function will be conducting regular control reviews and reporting back to both operational and senior management on the effectiveness of existing controls. The feedback should drive both the frequency and type of control monitoring that is being undertaken and the potential redesign of existing systems. Where controls are seen to be incomplete or inefficient, more monitoring may be necessary for a while, or conversely, tight management may require less oversight.

The internal audit function plays a key role in the monitoring process, and so it is important that they retain independent judgement. Those who design internal controls should not also be responsible for their evaluation, and so managing the relationship between internal audit and risk management staff is an essential part of maintaining an effective risk management system.

ISO 31000 is complemented by ISO Guide 73: "Risk Management – Terminology," which was updated to accommodate changes in definitions used in the 2018 version of the standard and provides a collection of terms and definitions relating to the management of risk. A further document, IEC 31010:2019 "Risk Management – Risk Assessment Techniques," replaces an earlier 2009 version and provides guidance on the selection and application of systematic techniques for risk assessment. This detailed guidance is especially useful for risk managers looking for how to apply the concepts laid down in the core ISO 31000 standard. In the next chapter we will look at examples of how this all works in practice.

Conclusion

In Chapter 2 we saw that the last decade has seen a closing of the gap between US and European governance regulations and guidance. In similar vein, this chapter has illustrated a growing convergence between the US risk management standard for enterprise risk management (COSO, 2017) and the global standard ISO 31000 The similarities include:

- The view that risk management both protects and creates value
- The key role played by the board of directors and senior management in setting a precedent of good governance and a culture that is risk aware
- An emphasis on risk management being fully integrated both vertically and horizontally across an organisation
- The need for effective systems to identify, assess, and respond to risks.
- The importance of both internal and external risk management reporting
- The idea that risk management systems should dynamically evolve over time and be continually monitored, reviewed, and improved

The theory is great, but the proof of the pudding is in the eating. Does practice work as well as the theory? The remainder of this book uses case studies to suggest that it can, but often does not.

Note

1 There is an extensive academic literature in the field of risk reporting and disclosure that falls largely beyond the remit of this book, but some examples are illustrated in the end-of-chapter references. Examples and comments on annual report disclosures are also included in the case studies.

References

Airmic, Alarm, & IRM (2010) "A Structured Approach to Enterprise Risk Management and the Requirements of ISO 31000." Available for Download Free of Charge from the Websites of Each of These Organisations.

Committee of Sponsoring Organisations of the Treadway Commission (COSO) (2004) *Enterprise Risk Management.* AICPA, New York.

Committee of Sponsoring Organisations of the Treadway Commission (COSO) (2017) *Enterprise Risk Management Integrating with Strategy and Performance.* Committee of Sponsoring Organizations of the Treadway Commission, NJ.

Dickinson, G. (2001) "Enterprise Risk Management: Its Origins and Conceptual Foundation." *The Geneva Papers on Risk and Insurance*, Vol. 36, No. 3 (July), pp. 360–366.

IRM (2018) "Financial Reporting Council Proposed Revisions to the UK Corporate Governance Code Consultation Paper Dated December 2017." Response from the Institute of Risk Management (IRM), February.

ISO 31000 (2018) *Risk Management – Guidelines.* International Organization for Standardization (ISO), Geneva.

ISO Guide 73 (2009) *Risk Management – Vocabulary.* International Organization for Standardization (ISO), Geneva.

Leitch, M. (2010) "ISO 31000:2009 – The New International Standard on Risk Management." *Risk Analysis, John Wiley & Sons*, Vol. 30, No. 6 (June), pp. 887–892.

Woods, M., Humphrey, C., & Dowd, K. (2009) "Market Risk Reporting by the World's Top Banks: Evidence on the Diversity of Reporting Practice and the Implications for International Accounting Harmonisation." *Revista de Contabilidad -Spanish Accounting Review*, Vol. 11, No. 2, pp. 9–42.

Zurich Insurance Company (2019) *Annual Report.* https://www.zurich.com/en/annual-report/2019

Useful Web Links

1. www.garp.org/

    This is the website for the US-based Global Association of Risk Professionals and is a useful illustration of how this new profession has developed and created its own certification programmes and qualification system.
2. The websites of the Big Four accounting firms all have risk consultancy sections, which contain useful publications on risk-related issues and information on the type of risk advisory services they provide.

    Price Waterhouse Coopers: www.pwc.com

    KPMG: www.kpmg.co.uk

    Deloitte: www.deloitte.com

    Ernst and Young: www.ey.com

Discussion Questions

1. What, if any, are the differences between COSO 2017 and ISO 31000 in relation to:

    a. The overall vision of the role and scope of risk management
    b. The detail of how the component elements are connected

2. Look at the latest annual reports of two of the FTSE 100 companies and/or two public-sector organisations such as government departments or local councils. What do they tell you about their exposure to risk, the quality of internal controls, and the effectiveness of the risk management system? To what extent should an organisation report about risk management to its stakeholders?

4 Risk Management in Theory and Practice

Aim

The aim of this chapter is to summarise the core risks faced by organisations and explain how this knowledge is used in the designing of the risk management systems and procedures. Whilst governance and risk management regulations (as detailed in Chapters 2 and 3) encourage some standardisation of risk management systems, there remains a need for controls to reflect the specific organisational context. Using the example of Marks and Spencer as an illustration, the chapter concludes that risk management frameworks in every organisation have common features (based around the standards), but the detail of the risk architecture are variable. This conclusion is further reflected in the case studies later in this book.

The chapter is broken into the following sections:

- Principal Risks
- Building a Risk Architecture
- Conclusion

Principal Risks

The ISO guide to risk management vocabulary defines risk as "the combination of the probability of an event and its consequences" (ISO Guide 73). The definition incorporates both opportunities (upside risk) and threats (downside risk), and risk management is thus concerned with providing mechanisms through which to control the impact of both the positive and negative aspects of risk.

Such a broad definition, however, hides a mass of complexity. Organisations face a multitude of different types of risk, which also change and evolve over time. As Tom Peters observed over thirty years ago, the business environment is characterised by "unprecedented uncertainty" (Peters, 1989), and in such an environment people search for ways of managing that uncertainty. One starting

DOI: 10.4324/9781315208336-4

Table 4.1 Survey Findings of Principal Risks (2012–2020)

2012	2018	2020
Allianz	**Cambridge Centre for Risk Studies**	**Allianz**
Economic	Regulation and reporting	Cyber risk
Business interruption	Financials – revenue, profit, share price	Business interruption
Natural disaster	Security, including cyber	Legal and regulatory
Legal and regulatory	Geopolitical	Natural disaster
Reputational	Business continuity	Market developments

Sources: Allianz Risk Barometer 2012 and 2020; Cambridge Centre for Risk Studies, Risk Management Perspectives of Global Corporations 2018

point for doing so is to classify risks into categories, whilst recognising that certain categories will have varying degrees of relevance according to the business sector within which an organisation operates.

Surveys of senior executives in global corporations are regularly undertaken with the aim of identifying what they see as the key risks facing their organisations, and Table 4.1 summarises the findings of three such surveys. They include two conducted by the global insurance company Allianz and one by the Cambridge Centre for Risk Studies in Cambridge (England).

Whilst the language differs slightly between the two sources, the table shows that the principal risks remain relatively fixed over time. These risks are high-level, long-term concerns that affect an organisation's commercial and strategic viability which, when managed effectively, protect and build organisational reputation. What matters is the ability to continue operating and achieve good financial results within the existing economic, political, and technological context. New risks (e.g. cyber security) will emerge over time, and the changing global political environment can generate new risks, but the principal risks are long-standing and worthy of closer consideration.

Legal and regulatory risk appears in all the surveys in Table 4.1, and it straddles many areas of an organisation, from fundamental accounting reporting rules and competition law, through to regulations on sustainability reporting, health and safety, and legal requirements in respect of data protection. The issue is even more complex for companies operating globally across many different regulatory regimes. Systems to ensure compliance need to be established and monitored across all relevant areas, and for this reason many large companies now have compliance and disclosure committees at the senior executive level. The broad-ranging scope of regulatory risk explains why it is so highly ranked and commonly viewed as a risk requiring board-level oversight.

Regulatory Risk Example

In 2015 the US Department of Justice found the French bank BNP Paribas guilty of flouting sanctions laws laid down in the International Emergency Economic Powers Act (IEEPA) and the Trading with the Enemy Act (TWEA). BNP Paribas was accused of processing multibillion-dollar transactions in the United States on behalf of Sudanese, Iranian, and Cuban entities. The company was ordered to pay a $140,000,000 fine and forfeit $8,833,600,000 to the United States, making a total penalty of almost $9 billion.

This example illustrates how corporate ethics are intertwined with compliance, and tight risk management systems combined with an appropriate risk culture are paramount if such risks are to be avoided. This will be discussed more fully later in this book.

Business interruption risk is similarly wide ranging and may result from a multitude of either external causes, such as natural disaster, accident, or a global health scare such as the recent coronavirus pandemic, or internal failures, such as health/safety breaches or weak inventory management. Allianz report that fires and natural catastrophes are the major causes of business interruption, but the sophisticated global supply chains used by companies today also render them increasingly vulnerable to contingent business interruption arising from problems with a supplier or customer. The following example is a good illustration of this.

Business Interruption Example

In May 2018 a fire at a Meridian Magnesium Products factory in Michigan caused severe production problems for Ford, Fiat Chrysler, and General Motors. The company makes lightweight metal parts for vehicles, and around one third of its production goes to Ford.

As a result of the fire, Ford had to temporarily lay off 7,600 workers, General Motors had to cut its van production in Missouri, and Fiat Chrysler temporarily stopped production of its Pacifica minivan.

Political or civil unrest may also seriously interrupt business operations. Civil protest can often result in looting and serious property damage and losses. The Insurance Information Institute suggests that the largest losses from rioting to date stemmed from the 1992 Los Angeles riots, which were triggered by police beating a local black man. The total insurance claims for damage from the riots amounted to $775 million, equivalent to around $1.4 billion in today's terms.

Natural catastrophes such as typhoons, earthquakes, landslides, and hurricanes can also prove very costly to business. According to Swiss Re, the average global annual insured losses incurred as a result of natural and manmade catastrophes over the decade 2009–2019 equalled US $75 billion. Of 292 disasters in 2019, 193 were natural and the remainder manmade, and they accounted for $50 billion and $6 billion dollars, respectively. Globalisation and growing interdependencies of supply chains mean that the impact of natural catastrophes is no longer localized, and a tsunami in Japan can have consequences in Europe. Additionally, as concerns over climate change continue to escalate, many scientists predict that the number of extreme weather events will increase, and with it the associated risk of business interruption.

Predicting a disaster caused by the weather can be difficult, if not impossible, but risk management systems can mitigate their impact through response plans that identify ways of resolving the business interruption (e.g. switching production sites/ensuring backup of core services such as information processing). Insurance may also be available in some cases as a way of mitigating costs.

Market development/disruption risks include those coming from new competitors, market stagnation, mergers/acquisitions, and general market volatility. It can be tricky to distinguish market volatility of currency exchange rates, for example, from political risk. The ongoing exchanges between the United States and China on trade relations also illustrate how political and economic risks are intermingled. New competitors, price wars, and product developments can also pose serious threats to a business. In the highly competitive mobile phone and internet marketplace, Vodafone identifies market disruption from new telecom operators entering the market or price wars that reduce margins as one of their principal risks.

Market Development Risk Example

The discount chains Aldi and Lidl have had what can be described as a seismic impact on the UK's food retail business. Arriving in the UK in 1999, Aldi offered a new model of low prices and a limited product range. The industry's major players did not believe this would appeal to UK shoppers, but after the financial crisis in 2008 Aldi's market share began to grow rapidly, reaching 8% in 2019. This placed it just 2.3 percentage points away from becoming one of the "big four "supermarkets in the UK.

Sainsburys, Tesco Asda, and Morrisons were slow to respond to the threat caused by the discounters and were challenged by Aldi's novel competitive strategies such as "specially selected" products at premium prices and the introduction of fair-trade goods. A variety of responses from the major players has to date failed to prevent long-term loss of market share to Aldi and Lidl.

Despite heavy cost cutting to improve its profit margins, in early 2020 Tesco opted to engage in a price matching "war" with Aldi in an effort to regain some of its lost market share. The outcome remains to be seen.

This example suggests that unlike Vodafone in the telecoms market, the entry of the new players (discounters) into the UK grocery market was not seen as a strategic risk by existing key players, and their risk management focus lay elsewhere. There are lessons here for all sectors – competition is competition: don't ignore it!

Geopolitical risk appears as a principal risk in the IRM/Cambridge Institute for risk studies survey in 2018 and is also cited by the Institute for Risk Management as a risk of concern in 2019. The term refers to risks that arise as a result of social, political, and economic events at both national and global levels. Current examples include:

- The impact of the UK's departure from the European Union (EU)
- Regional stability in the Middle East and the risk of a US/Iran war
- Climate change
- Political stability in Latin America
- US–China relations, especially in the technology market and trading relations

The geographic areas of concern will reflect where an organisation operates or sources its supplies and its potential plans to move into an emerging or volatile region. Geopolitical developments are a key concern in the energy sector because of both where oil is extracted and growing concerns over climate change and the accompanying expansion of sustainability regulations. A global transition towards an increased use of sustainable fuel sources, electric vehicles, and the widespread de-carbonisation of business models poses huge challenges to this sector.

This view is made clear by the oil giant BP, which notes in its annual report that "geopolitical risk is inherent to many regions in which we operate and heightened political or social tensions or changes in key relationships could adversely affect the group" (BP Annual Report, 2019, p. 69). Failure to monitor and manage such risks can have both financial and reputational consequences.

Geopolitical events may also have huge consequences for global supply chains, and so it is often linked to business interruption risk.

However, geopolitical risk can also offer opportunities. The EU's Sustainability Development Strategy is a good example of how risk and opportunity can be flip sides of the same coin. The strategy will be seen by some as increasing the risks faced by their company, but by others as providing a chance to be ahead of the game and seize new market opportunities.

Example: Climate Change as an Opportunity

In 2019, Joe Bamford, the chief executive officer (CEO) of the UK-based construction equipment manufacturer JCB, acquired the Northern Irish bus company Wrightbus. Wrightbus, manufacturers of the new Routemaster buses so familiar on London streets, had gone into administration. JCB already owned the specialist hydrogen technology company Ryse, and Bowden took the view that increasing demands for the transport sector to cut transport emissions provided a perfect business opportunity. The aim was for Ryse and Wrightbus to work together to produce vehicles powered by hydrogen fuel cells that offer a zero-carbon alternative to both traditional and electric buses that is particularly well suited to heavy transport. Hydrogen buses are already in use in London and Pau in France, with plans for further deployment in Antwerp, Groningen, Aberdeen, and San Remo.

Cyber risk[1] is a relatively new phenomenon that is rising rapidly, both in real terms and its significance on the corporate agenda. The ever-expanding digitalisation of business processes, such as point of sales systems (POSs) and the subsequent growing reliance on information technology (IT) systems, together with a number of high-profile incidents, have all combined to increase awareness of cyber risks across organisations of all sizes. As Table 4.1 shows, it topped the Allianz risk barometer in 2020, as there is growing evidence of the rising cost of cyber incidents, which can interrupt business operations, result in regulatory penalties, and may also generate compensation claims from those adversely affected. Data breaches are a primary area of concern, where personal or confidential information is leaked either accidentally or as a result of a malicious attack. A mega data breach (involving more than 1 million records) is estimated by IBM to have an average cost of $42 million. The number of ransomware incidents is also rising and accompanied by increasingly high extortion demands.

Cyber Risk Examples

In 2019, British Airways (owned by IAG) was fined £183 million by the UK regulator for a breach in its data system in 2018 which resulted in criminals getting access to the personal details of around 500,000 customers (BBC.co.uk., 2019). The details included the passenger's name, travel plans, billing address, email address, and payment card details, including the three-digit security code from the back of the card

In June 2018 VISA, the global payments company, suffered a service failure that left customers unable to pay for transactions. The problem lasted almost a full day, and a total of 5.2 million transactions failed to process properly. Despite operating two backup data centres to take over transaction processing in the case of failure, a hardware problem with a switch meant that the backup failed to activate. The company waived all fees for merchants affected by the disruption and also offered compensation to both the outlets and the customers who suffered losses as a result – for example, additional bank charges. The Bank of England also ordered VISA to fully implement recommendations on improving its systems, identified by an independent review, and to appoint consultants PWC to oversee its implementation.

Like the other principal risks discussed earlier, cyber risk can hit any part of an organisation and, as illustrated by the British Airways example, is linked to other risks such as regulatory compliance. The VISA example illustrates how it also has the scope to interrupt the entire business and so is of strategic importance. For this reason, many companies are now appointing chief information officers at the senior executive level to take full responsibility for IT strategy and oversee the management of the associated risks.

One important risk not discussed earlier is that of *reputational risk*. In a survey of senior executives from around the world, the Economist Intelligence Unit (EIU, 2005) asked respondents to rank different categories of risk on a scale of 1–100 in terms of their significance to their business. **Reputation risk** was ranked top, but the EIU also reported that senior managers find it particularly difficult to manage, which perhaps explains why it no longer appears in the Allianz risk barometer.

Reputation is a prized asset, but it could be argued that it is not a separate risk category, and instead merely reflects a failure to manage other risks.

Reputation risk is therefore best viewed as a high-level risk, but one which reflects the quality of control over other, more easily categorised risks. Reputation risk is vitally important, because for private organisations it is a key driver of the business value. The erosion of reputation can damage future revenue streams and hence profitability, but reputation risks are high, because as Warren Buffett observed, "It takes twenty years to build a reputation and five minutes to destroy it." Preserving a company's reputation is therefore a very important dimension of risk management, and there is evidence to suggest that it not only affects customers' buying decisions but also employee loyalty and investor choices. As such a good reputation can also serve as a barrier to entry and protect competitive position.

Rolls Royce PLC

Rolls Royce makes engines for planes, trains, ships, nuclear submarines, and power stations. In 2017 this UK engineering giant was ordered to pay a total of £671 million to settle corruption and bribery cases with EU and US regulators. The firm reached an agreement with the UK Serious Fraud Office, which accused it of conspiracy to corrupt or bribery over a lengthy period and across the globe. Countries named include India, China, Malaysia, Nigeria, and Russia.

The impact of reputational damage varies, however, depending on the sector and size of organisation. This is best illustrated by two examples.

The Rolls Royce case shows how a problem that could hit its reputation in fact arose out of poor management of ethics and a failure to censure corrupt behaviour by its staff. This may have been the result of poor risk management controls and/or a weak risk culture. Interestingly, however, even if the company's reputation took a hit, the stock markets did not appear to care. On the day that the settlement was reached with the regulator, Rolls Royce shares closed 4.5% higher, as the market clearly appreciated the elimination of the uncertainty regarding the cost of the case! In effect, the market was saying that the bulk of the value of Rolls Royce lies in its physical assets and reputation is not hugely significant.

The second example shows the importance of client sensitivity to a company's reputation in a very different sector.

Facebook and Cambridge Analytica

In 2018 a row erupted between Facebook and the UK political consulting firm Cambridge Analytica. Cambridge Analytica was accused of using Facebook's infrastructure four years earlier to harvest information on over 87 million Facebook users via an external app. It was subsequently claimed that Cambridge Analytica used the information to psychologically profile US voters in advance of the 2016 presidential election and to influence the UK's Brexit campaign, but both claims were denied.

Facebook claimed that it had not given permission for the data to be used and demanded that Cambridge Analytica delete it but did nothing to confirm that this had been done. The data breach became the subject of investigation by both UK and US regulators.

In May 2018 Cambridge Analytica, despite its denials, filed for bankruptcy after it claimed that the resulting social media furore had left it with no clients and mounting legal fees. The company said that a "siege of media coverage" had driven away all its suppliers and customers and it could no longer survive.

In 2018, Facebook set aside £2.4 billion in its accounts to cover the anticipated cost of its breach of data regulations in the United States, but the final settlement reached with the Federal Trade Commission amounted to £4 billion. When news of the settlement was announced, Facebook's share price rose and closed 1.8% up on that day.

Source: Forrest (2019).

The key lesson from these examples is that reputational risk matters more in some sectors than in others. Consumer goods or business-to-business markets where customers are sensitive to brand will rate reputation risk very highly. Sectors like engineering or heavy industrials regard it as less important. The IRM/Cambridge Risk Centre survey asked respondents to rank the importance they attached to reputational risk on a score of 1–10. The results are shown in Table 4.2, and these confirm the idea that customer-facing service organisations see themselves as potentially more vulnerable to this form of risk.

These examples also highlight the importance of organisational size and market presence. In the aero engine market, Rolls Royce really has only one major global competitor – Boeing – and its engines have long lives, so customers need to remain loyal to get spare parts, maintenance contracts, etc. Similarly, Facebook is almost one of a kind, and users have a lot of their personal life history stored within their system in photos, etc. Customers who are embedded reduce the risks of reputation loss. Equally, the financial damage inflicted by the penalties, whilst high, were manageable for both companies. For Cambridge Analytica the story was very different. Data analytics is a growing field

Table 4.2 Ranking of Reputational Risk by Industrial Sector

Industrial Sector	Ranking of Reputational Risk on a scale 1-10.
Utilities	7
Consumer goods (discretionary)	7
Healthcare	6.5+
Information Technology	6.5+
Industrials	6.5+
Energy	6+
Financials	6+
Materials	6+
Real Estate	6
Public Authorities/NGOs	5+
Telecommunication services	5

of business, and their Unique Selling Point was therefore quite limited, as was their financial capacity to see business fall away. Their ruin was inevitable.

A crisis management plan is critical if companies are to survive threats to reputation, and a good public relations department is part of this. A recent illustration of its importance is in the response of one company to comments by President Trump during the 2020 coronavirus pandemic that the use of bleach and detergent products on people might be useful. The same day that Trump made his much-criticised observations, RB, the main US company producing these types of goods, issued the following press release:

> Due to recent speculation and social media activity, RB (the makers of Lysol and Dettol) has been asked whether internal administration of disinfectants may be appropriate for investigation or use as a treatment for coronavirus (SARS-CoV-2).
> As a global leader in health and hygiene products, we must be clear that under no circumstance should our disinfectant products be administered into the human body (through injection, ingestion or any other route). As with all products, our disinfectant and hygiene products should only be used as intended and in line with usage guidelines. Please read the label and safety information.

The case demonstrates how reputational risk can emerge from all kinds of unpredictable sources. What matters is that the risk management system has prepared for this and can respond rapidly to mitigate the fallout.

Establishing a Risk Architecture

The principal risks discussed earlier have two important features:

* They are high-level risks that could threaten the core strategies and future of an organisation.

- They are interlinked with one another. If a cyber attack damages a company's ability to trade, then is it a cyber risk or a continuity risk? The links could even be three-fold, such as a political risk which raises issues of changes of compliance rules that in turn threaten production capabilities.

High-level risks require regular oversight and monitoring at the most senior level and in line with the governance regulations "the Board is responsible for determining *the nature and extent of the significant risks it is willing to take in achieving its strategic objectives . . .* and should maintain sound risk management and internal control systems" (UK Corporate Governance Code, 2010). Similarly, in the Committee of Sponsoring Organizations (COSO) Enterprise Risk Management (ERM) framework, validated under US Sarbanes-Oxley (SOX) legislation, the key role for the board is one of risk oversight.

The way in which each organisation labels its principal risks and the relative importance attached to each will ultimately depend upon both the nature and scale of the business. The principal risks identified by the UK retailer Marks and Spencer include Brexit, financial performance, compliance, technology (including cyber security), and business continuity. In other words, very similar to those listed in Table 4.1. As a retailer operating in a highly competitive market, including ones threatened by regulatory change as a result of Brexit, the list might be viewed as predictable, but the aim of identification is simply to begin the process of creating a framework which can be used to monitor and manage risks. Such a framework is clearly illustrated in Figure 4.1, which is adapted from information included by Marks and Spencer, in the governance section of its 2019 annual report.

Figure 4.1 also clearly illustrates how responsibility for the classification and oversight of principal risks rests with the board, working alongside the executive directors, audit committee, and the group risk team. The audit committee is made up entirely of non-executive directors and plays a key role in providing assurance to the board on the effectiveness of the internal audit function, financial controls, internal controls, and risk management. The group risk team carries responsibility for designing the controls that will be used to mitigate the risks identified across the group. Oversight of strategic risks which are emerging but not yet current is the responsibility of the executive directors, audit committee, and group risk team. It is assumed that they will report to the board any issues which may require their attention and an updating of the existing principal risk register.

The principal risks are used in the formulation of a group risk profile, but data for the profile is also provided from the bottom up. The group's operating model divides the group into functional and business components, for which separate risk registers are compiled with input from both junior and senior staff. These risk registers are reported periodically to the audit committee, and responsibility for their management rests with the business- and functional-level boards. Individual businesses include food, clothing, and home, and M&S international functions include finance, communications, and human resources (HR). There will be some overlap in the type of risk exposures across multiple businesses and functions, and other risks will be business specific, but the ***net aggregate exposures*** need to be understood and included in the group risk profile. Such aggregation can only be done at the senior level by those with an overview of the whole group's operations.

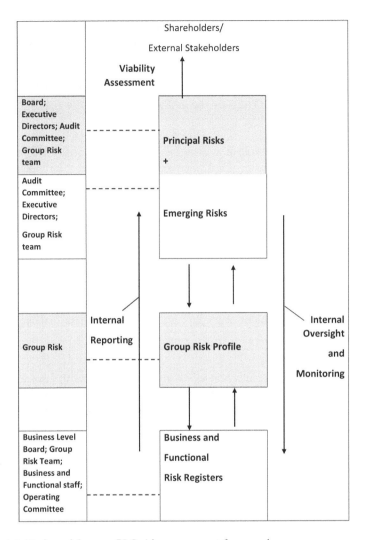

Figure 4.1 Marks and Spencer PLC risk management framework

Key Learning Point

Lower-level business/functional and operating risks are aggregated to form the organisational risk profile.

The basic framework used by Marks and Spencer reflects the core process outlined in ISO 31000, in which risk management is built into its structure, operations, and processes at strategic, operational, programme, and project levels. Whilst Figure 4.1 contains limited detail, it does indicate that:

- Risks are identified from both top down and bottom up
- Internal reporting of risks (on the left) is mirrored by internal oversight and monitoring (on the right)

In combination, these result in a looped cycle of risk identification, monitoring, reporting, and revision of risk registers as appropriate. Note also that the left-hand side of the diagram, which indicates who is responsible for which level of drafting of risk registers, shows that the group risk team is represented at all levels. This ensures that they have a 360-degree view of risk exposures that can be reported back to the board.

Key Learning Point

The board's role is one of oversight, not of day-to-day risk management.

The group team is legally obliged to report externally to shareholders on its exposure to risk, its system for their management, and the effectiveness of internal controls. Additionally, as noted in the previous chapter, under UK governance rules, a viability statement must be published in the company's annual report, stating whether the board of directors has a "reasonable expectation" that the company will be able to continue in operation and meet its liabilities as they fall due over the chosen assessment period. This period should be significantly longer than the twelve months from approval of the associated financial statements.

The viability statement should take account of a company's current position and principal risks and indicates how the company prospects have been assessed, over what time frame the assessment has been done, and why the chosen time frame is appropriate. Implicit in this requirement is that the risk assessment is forward looking, and the code suggests the use of both quantitative and qualitative analysis of risks and the application of sensitivity analysis as necessary. Marks and Spencer's viability assessment (2019, p. 30 annual report) considers the group's business model, strategy, approach to risk management, and principal risks and uncertainties. The planning time frame used by Marks and Spencer is three years, and so this is also the time period used for the viability assessment. As such it includes key events that form part of the strategic plan (e.g. a rights issue and 50:50 joint venture with Ocado for a food delivery service). The assessment is done by modelling a number of plausible scenarios relating to the principal risks (e.g. low market growth or failed strategic initiatives) and evaluating whether they threaten the viability of the company. The potential to mitigate such events is also incorporated into the assessment, which is reviewed by the audit committee prior to its consideration by the board.

A study of the annual report of any major global company will reveal similar disclosures about the role played by the board of directors in relation to risk management and the underlying risk management framework, but the level of detail is widely variable. For example, Vodafone Group PLC identifies a total of ten principal risks, which are categorised as medium, high, or critical in nature. They also include a diagram (albeit rather difficult to interpret) illustrating the interconnections between the risks. Interestingly, they also name the executive director(s) who own(s) each of the principal risks and so held accountable in the case of failure.

The governance report in the annual report of the oil giant BP identifies its principal risks, but then separates out specific ones which are prioritised for direct oversight by the board. Several board sub-committees take responsibility for oversight of a specific principal risk in a system that allows for input from a wider number of specialists. For example, a safety, environment, and security assurance committee oversees the risks linked to process and personal safety, as well as security and environmental risks.

In summary, every organisation will have its own list of principal risks and a structure through which the group risk profile is established. Similarly, the methods used to report this information externally will also be variable. These variations reflect differing organisational histories, priorities, and complexity.

Conclusion

Risk management standards such as COSO and ISO 31000 provide a framework for the creation of what is sometimes termed the risk architecture of an organisation. The term architecture refers to the structures used for identifying, recording, managing, reporting, and monitoring risks, as illustrated in Figure 4.2.

The generic example in Figure 4.2 is taken from the Airmic/alarm/IRM guidance on implementing ERM and ISO 31000 (2010).

The aim of the risk standards is not to be prescriptive, but to offer guidance on how risks can be managed in any size and type of organisation, and so not all organisations will have, for example, a group risk management committee or a disclosures committee, as shown in Figure 4.2. Nonetheless, in some shape or form, all organisations seeking to implement enterprise-wide risk management will have systems for the identification, assessment, and treatment of risks together with support for internal reporting, monitoring, and review of the risk controls. Figure 4.2 thus provides a useful starting point for designing a

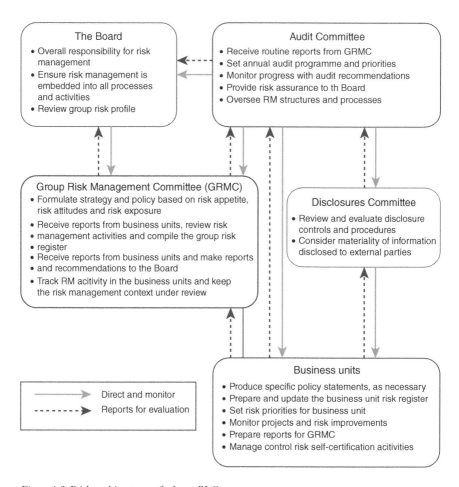

Figure 4.2 Risk architecture of a large PLC

risk architecture or critically reviewing an existing one. The case studies which follow illustrate how the risk architecture can significantly impact upon an organisation's ability to manage its risks effectively.

Most importantly, effective enterprise risk management depends upon an organisation-wide understanding of and commitment to risk management. The architecture is as dependent upon information provided from the bottom up as it is on information coming from the top down.

Note

1 This topic is discussed in greater detail in Chapter 5.

References

Airmic, alarm, & IRM (2010) "A Structured Approach to Enterprise Risk Management and the Requirements of ISO 31000." Available for Download Free of Charge from the Websites of Each of These Organisations.

Allianz Risk Pulse (2012) *Big Three Risks Trouble Companies*. Allianz SE, Königinstraße 28, 80802 Munich, Germany.

Allianz Risk Barometer (2020) *Identifying the Major Business Risks for 2020*. Allianz Global Corporate & Specialty, Munich.

BBC.co.uk. (2019) "British Airways Faces Record £183m Fine for Data Breach." Published on line July 9, 2019.

BP Annual Report and Form 20-F (2019) Available for Free Download from: www.bp.com/en/global/corporate/investors/results-and-reporting/annual-report.html.

Cambridge Centre for Risk Studies (2018) *Risk Management Perspectives of Global Corporations*. Cambridge Centre for Risk Studies at the University of Cambridge Judge Business School and Institute of Risk Management, Cambridge.

EIU (Economist Intelligence Unit) (2005) *Reputation: Risk of Risks*. EIU, London.

Financial Reporting Council (2010) *UK Corporate Governance Code*. Downloaded from: www.frc.org.uk/getattachment/31631a7a-bc5c-4e7b-bc3a-972b7f17d5e2/UK-Corp-Gov-Code-June-2010.pdf.

Forrest, A. (2019) "Facebook Data Scandal: Social Network Fined $5bn Over 'Inappropriate' Sharing of Users' Personal Information". *Independent*, July 12, London.

Institute for Risk Management. "Risk Predictions 2019." Downloaded from: www.theirm.org/news/risk-predictions-2019/.

M & S Annual Report & Financial Statements (2019) Available for Free Download from: https://corporate.marksandspencer.com/investors/reports-results-and-presentations.

Peters, T. (1989) "Tomorrow's Companies." *The Economist*, March 4, pp. 27–30.

Useful Web Links

www.agcs.allianz.com is the website of the division of the insurance company Allianz, which publishes the results of its annual risk survey, the Allianz Barometer.

A Google search of "principal risks and uncertainties" will generate multiple links to a range of company websites where they detail their principal risks. Comparison of companies across different sectors is a useful and interesting exercise.

Discussion Questions

1. Analyse your own position – either as a student or employee – and specify your medium-term objectives and list all of the risks that may threaten your ability to achieve those objectives. Group the risks into categories, identify the key risks, and try and construct a likelihood–consequences matrix for the key risks. What have you learned from this exercise?

2. What procedures does your own organisation have in place to (a) report internally and (b) manage an incident that may threaten its reputation?

3. Look at the latest annual reports of two of the FTSE 100/S&P 500 Top 50 companies and/or two public-sector organisations such as government

departments or local councils. What do they tell you about their exposure to risk, the quality of internal controls, and the effectiveness of the risk management system? To what extent should an organisation report about risk management to its stakeholders?

4. The viability assessment is relatively new to UK governance regulation, but it allows a company to construct its own model and make its own assumptions on the likelihood/severity of alternative scenarios. What does this imply about the faith that can be placed in a viability assessment?

5 Managing Technology Risk

Aim

The use of digital technologies has expanded hugely, and the risks to organisations using them to manage sales, logistics, and all aspects of their operation have grown almost exponentially. As we saw in Chapter 4, cyber risk – attacks from outside an organisation – topped the Allianz risk barometer in 2020, and organisations are increasingly concerned about how any form of technology failure can interrupt business operations, incur regulatory penalties, generate compensation claims from those adversely affected, and cause reputational damage.

Technology risk (or IT risk) is defined as "any risk of financial loss, disruption or damage to the reputation of an organisation from some sort of failure of its information technology systems" (accaglobal.com). This is a broad-ranging definition that includes both failures caused by weak internal controls and/or governance and malicious attacks originating from outside the organisation.

The problem of how to manage such risk is compounded by the technical language and specialised terminology that surrounds it:

> much of the time, computing experts live in a technical silo of their own, detached from the consumers who use their products, the corporate executives who buy these systems and the politicians who develop policies that rely on IT. And most of the time the non-experts complacently ignore what the geeks do, since it seems excessively dull and technical.
>
> (Tett, 2014)

This quote has important implications for members of a board of directors, senior management, and risk management staff, because ignoring what is going on in IT within an organisation is a risk in its own right. Good decisions cannot be based on inadequate knowledge, but a global survey in 2019 revealed that less than one in four companies felt that their quarterly board-level reporting of technology risk was "very effective" (PwC, 2019).

The aim of this chapter is to suggest a way through the technical language barrier and demonstrate how standard risk management techniques can be used

DOI: 10.4324/9781315208336-5

to identify, assess, prioritise, and respond to technology risk and establish monitoring and performance management systems that can be applied enterprise wide. Building systems for the governance of technology into the wider risk management structures helps to reduce the danger of it being siloed and reinforces the link between technology and organisational strategy and objectives.

The chapter is split into sections which will:

1. Define technology risk, why it is important, and the primary lines of responsibility for its management
2. Discuss sources of technology risk
3. Use an illustrative case study of British Airways to discuss how a data breach can occur and its potential impact on an organisation
4. Outline a governance and risk management structure for technology that incorporates:

   a. Consideration of the role of technology in the organisation
   b. Lines of responsibility and accountability for technology risk management
   c. How it is integrated into existing risk management structures and processes
   d. Incident management
   e. Minimising the financial and reputational risks

A glossary of terms is included at the end of the chapter that defines the main types of risk that are discussed.

Definition of Technology Risk and Lines of Responsibility

It is important to be precise in the use of terminology and clarify the distinction between technology (or IT risk) and cyber risk. The difference is critical because it is reflected in the governance structures used for risk management.

Operational risk includes anything that might threaten an organisation's operational capacity. Technology such as IT is integral to the operations of most businesses today, and so technology risk is a sub-category of operational risk. Threats to the effective operation of technology can come from both internal and external sources, and cyber risk is *specifically* a risk from *outside*, commonly a malicious attack to access information or data or disrupt the effective operation of systems. Cyber risk is therefore a sub-category of technology risk. This immediately gives us a hierarchy that is commonly used in organisations whereby the head of cyber risk (commonly a chief information security officer [CISO] or chief security officer) will report to the chief information officer (CIO), who is in turn accountable to the chief operations officer.

The distinction between the CIO and CISO is perhaps more easily understood by a detailed clarification of their respective responsibilities (see Table 5.1).

Table 5.1 CIO Versus CISO Roles

CIO	CISO
• Identification of IT needs to meet strategic operational requirements • Management of IT resources and infrastructure • Formulation and implementation of IT strategy • Oversight of the IT architecture and governance	• Management of the security of the physical and network-based technology assets • Maintaining the security of information (e.g. systems for data storage/ protection) • Establishing systems to manage cyber risk

In some organisations, the CIO and CISO posts run side by side, rather than in a hierarchy, but whichever structure is chosen, there is clear overlap between them. Operational risk is concerned with keeping things running, and so if hackers disrupt the ability to serve customers via a cyberattack, or some computer hardware fails and some processes cannot be completed, then operational capacity is threatened. The common thread of a need to establish systems for business continuity links the CIO and CISO, and it is common for them to work together to establish systems to ensure any disruption is minimised.

One clear point of distinction between the roles is that the CISO is concerned solely with security, whereas the CIO is also responsible for the IT infrastructure, which requires consideration of how technology might be used to achieve strategic objectives. The innovative use of new technologies can be used to create competitive advantage, and Amazon provides a useful example of this. The systems used by Amazon to monitor and analyse an individual's browsing history on their website enable them to predict the types of products that may be of interest to a specific user. It may feel spooky to have an ad appear for a product that you like but hadn't yet looked for, but it is all part of Amazon's way of using technology to boost sales and gain market share. The CIO will play an important part in advising on the way technology can help in achieving strategic aims.

Sources of Technology Risk

Risks may arise from internal and/or external sources, as shown in Table 5.2, and are best understood with illustrative examples.

Looking firstly at internal sources, poor management of technological change is a common problem. Most organisations have a mixed history of IT systems, with a mix of older legacy systems that have been "improved" by the addition of newer hardware and software, but the old and new are not always entirely compatible. Additionally, it can be very tempting to complete an update before everything is absolutely ready, and the result can be serious problems.

Table 5.2 Sources of Technology Risk

Source of Risk	
Internal	**External**
• Poor management of technological change (e.g. inadequate testing of new systems) • Technical failure – including from bought-in software • Human error • Operational failure (e.g. loss of power) • Social media	• Phishing • Ransomware • Distributed denial of service (DDoS) attack • Virus

---

Poor Management of Change: TSB Bank 2018

After splitting from Lloyds Bank, TSB opted to migrate to its own new banking platform in 2018. The platform was launched before full testing was complete, and thousands of customers found themselves unable to log in to their accounts, saw details of other people's accounts instead of their own, and spotted inaccuracies in the transactions on their own accounts. Four weeks after the IT "upgrade," some customers were still unable to obtain access.

An independent report by the law firm Slaughter and May commissioned by the bank revealed that the board failed to ask pertinent questions and did not learn lessons from earlier errors in the migration process.

The meltdown cost TSB dearly and led to an investigation by the Financial Conduct Authority (FCA) and Prudential Regulation Authority, with the FCA noting "we expect sufficient oversight and engagement from senior management before any migration occurs." By late 2019 TSB had paid out £366 million to cover the costs of the IT failure, including £130 million in compensation to customers, but it could yet be hit by a large fine from the FCA.

Technical failure is another possible source of technology risk. In December 2018 30 million O2 users in the UK lost access to 4G data services on their smartphones. The problem was caused by a glitch in software supplied by Ericsson and affected O2 and all its associated network services such as GiffGaff, Tesco Mobile, and Sky Mobile, as well as Transport for London, which uses O2 services for its bus timetabling information boards. The outage lasted for almost twenty-three hours and led to an investigation by the regulator Ofcom, which concluded that O2 had not contravened its obligations, but there were lessons to be learned for network providers in respect of hardcoded security certificates that can cause externally provided software to fail. Ofcom affirmed that O2 had an appropriate approach to risk management, an established contractual agreement with its supplier, and conducted rigorous testing of supplied software.

Most importantly, they also had the technical skills to respond immediately and restore service availability relatively quickly.

Mistakes by people are sometimes referred to as "fat finger errors" in reference to the idea that the error may be a consequence of hitting the wrong key on the keyboard, but in reality there are many causes of human error, most of which could be avoided through good risk controls. One example of this is the case of a junior employee on the foreign exchange desk of Deutsche Bank in London. In 2015, the employee paid $6 billion to a hedge fund, mistakenly paying a gross figure for a trade instead of the net amount in settlement of the whole day's trading. The desk manager was on holiday at the time, but the payment went unchecked under the "four eyes principle" whereby every trade should be reviewed by a second person prior to processing. The funds were recovered in full the next day, but the incident had to be reported to the regulators.

Importantly, funds transferred in error are not always repaid, as Citibank found to its cost in early 2021. In late 2020 the bank, acting as an agent for Revlon Company's loans, intended to make an interest payment to Revlon's creditors but instead handed over US$893 million in full repayment of a loan. This sum was 100 times larger than intended, and whilst some lenders returned the money, others did not and Citibank lost their legal case to reclaim the $500 million that had been retained. Under New York State law, a legal recipient may keep funds transferred by mistake if they pay off a debt, the recipient did not know of the mistake, and/or the recipient did not trick the sender into making the payment. Again, "four eyes" might have avoided this error. The judge's decision noted that

> the non-returning lenders believed, and were justified in believing, that the payments were intentional. To believe otherwise – to believe that Citibank, one of the most sophisticated financial institutions in the world, had made a mistake that had never happened before, to the tune of nearly $1 billion – would have been borderline irrational.
>
> (Finextra, 2021)

Internal technological risk may also result from an operational failure (i.e. failure of a non-technical operating system that results in technical breakdown or malfunction). This is one of the reasons that technology risk is seen as a subset of operational risk, and it highlights the need for back-up systems that can kick into action immediately in the event of something like a power failure. Power outages can, amongst other things, prevent staff from completing their computer-based tasks, stop customers from being able to make purchases, or result in data loss or corruption, all with costly consequences. In the healthcare sector, the consequences of a slow response could be fatal to patients (e.g. due to failure of surgical, drug supply, or monitoring equipment). Minimising such risks depends on a number of factors, including a clear understanding of the links between wider operational risks and technology risks. Ensuring this understanding and managing the implications is the responsibility of the head of operational risk and the CIO working together. Defining the nature and type of back-up systems required, specifying and testing a disaster recovery plan, and informing staff on how and when to react to problems are all tools that can help manage such risks.

The final internal factor to consider is social media use by staff. An offensive or reputationally damaging post may be wilful or accidental, but whatever the cause, it represents a risk that can be managed through ensuring that your organisation has a clear social media policy and a culture that alerts staff to the reputational threats arising from social media misuse. Employees must be made aware of the danger of publishing media content that does not align with core organisational values. Additionally, social media can be used very effectively to achieve strategic objectives by, for example, ensuring that brand promoters engage actively with influencers and brand advocates. Not exploiting such opportunities is a different form of risk.

All the internal causes of technology risk can be significantly reduced via the application of a formal technology governance system such as that described later in this chapter. The prevention of external risks crystallising is rather different and requires the deployment of very specific security systems that consistently monitor the threats and are designed to instigate rapid responses to minimise the potential damage.

The methods by which an adversary can breach or infiltrate a network or system is called an attack vector, and this may take various, sometimes overlapping, forms, including phishing, ransomware, DDoS, and viruses, all defined in the glossary at the end of this chapter. As the digitisation of business increases, so too do the number of potential entry points into an organisation's network; consequently, the cyber risk threat also rises.

The nature of the risks varies from malicious attacks aimed at preventing internal systems from functioning, through to breaches which can steal or destroy data. Data breaches are of particular concern because of the resulting costs that are incurred, which often include regulatory fines. A global survey by IBM of over 500 firms that had experienced security breaches in the previous year found that the average cost of a data breach was US$3.92 million (or $140 per data record) in 2019, but that costs varied according to the root cause. Internal system glitches or human error caused 48% of breaches, but their costs were below average. In contrast, malicious external attacks that caused 52% of data breaches incurred considerably higher average costs of $4.27 million (IBM, 2020). It is perhaps not surprising then that Jonathan Evans, the former director general of MI5 in the UK, is quoted as saying: "The Boards of all companies should consider the vulnerability of their own company to this threat as part of their normal corporate governance – and they should require their key advisors and suppliers to do the same."

Examples of Cyber Attacks and Estimated Associated Costs

- **Phishing** – In 2014 a phisher impersonated a hardware manufacturer and for 2 years sent both Google and Facebook fake invoices totalling $200 million before they were caught. Proof that even big tech companies are not immune!
- **Ransomware** – The 2017 WannaCry outbreak. Often delivered via email attachments, this worm encrypts files and prevents user access. High-profile organisations attacked by WannaCry include the UK's National Health Service (NHS) and Boeing Corporation. The NHS was brought to a standstill for several days, and the estimated cost is thought to be around £92 million. Rapid deployment of software patches meant that the impact on Boeing was short lived and minimal.
- **DDoS** – Research published in 2019 suggested that such attacks are costing the UK economy around £900 million per year when downtime costs, lost revenue, increased operating costs, higher insurance premiums, lost customers, and reputational impact are taken into account. In 2016 there was a serious attack on Dyn, which is a major domain name system (DNS) provider – a DNS translates domain names into Internet Protocol (IP) addresses that enable browsers to load Internet resources. The attack programmed devices such as cameras, printers, and smart TVs (the internet of things) to send requests to a single victim. Many major websites, including Airbnb, Netflix, PayPal, and Amazon, were seriously affected. The problem was resolved within twenty-four hours, but the motive and source of the attack were never discovered.
- **Virus** – There is often overlap between a virus and phishing, ransomware, or a DDoS. For example, My Doom is generally accepted to be the world's most costly virus. Launched in 2004 but still around today, it enters via emails, steals addresses, and messages a huge web of computers (a botnet) that then conduct DDoS attacks. The damage caused to date is estimated at $34 billion, and despite a $250,000 reward, its originator has never been caught.

This discussion shows that technology risk can arise from multiple different sources and carries potentially high costs, so it is a risk that it is essential to manage. Evidence suggests that, on average, external attacks are more costly than internal failures, and data breaches are especially expensive. A short case study will illustrate how costs can rapidly accumulate when data is maliciously attacked by an outsider.

Data Breach Case Study: British Airways

This case is of interest from a risk management perspective because it reveals three areas of control failure:

1. Failure to comply with data protection regulation
2. Failure to adequately protect the organisation from cyber attack
3. Failure to detect the attack until notified by a security researcher after two months

The data breach took place in 2018, between 21 August and 5 September, when hackers gained access to both the personal and credit card data of more than 400,000 British Airways (BA) customers via the BA website, its app, and Avios, the company's frequent flyer scheme provider. Cyber security experts believe that data access was gained by hackers – either internally or externally, but probably the latter – implanting a malicious code onto the BA website. The code meant that when customers were making a booking, their details were able to be extracted and passed on to a third party. The information stolen included the passenger's name, address, email address, and payment card details, including the card number and the three-digit CVV security code.

The Information Commissioner's Office (ICO) fined BA £20 million in late 2020 for breach of the Data Protection Act, and BA also faces civil action for compensation from affected customers seeking damages for financial loss, inconvenience, and distress.

Key Facts

1. In total, personal data from approximately 429,612 people was potentially accessed.
2. The attacker gained access via BA's CAG, which is a tool that allows users to access a website whilst working remotely. This was done by using the log-in credentials of an employee of Swissport, the cargo services provider for BA, who was based overseas.
3. The system was not protected via multi-factor authentication (i.e. the requirement to complete at least two steps before being able to gain access).
4. Once in the Swissport system, the attacker was able to then break into the rest of BA's network, including that containing the sensitive customer data, which would normally be subject to privileged access.
5. Card data was stored in unencrypted plain text – due to human error, according to BA. This gave the attacker access to the details of 108,000 payment cards.
6. From 14 to 28 August card data was copied and sent to a separate website set up by the attacker, "BAways.com." Additionally, from 21 August to 5 September, card details were skimmed and redirected to the new website as live bookings were being made.

7.   On 5 September a third party notified BA of the transfer of material to the BAways.com site, and within ninety minutes the malicious code was identified and the vulnerability contained.
8.   BA notified ICO of the data breach the following day.

Information Commissioner's Findings

The ICO report found BA in breach of Article 5 (1) (F) and Article 32 of the General Data Protection Regulation Act (GDPR) 2018. The breaches refer to BA's failure to use appropriate technical and organisational processes to ensure that personal data was processed in a manner that offered security against its unauthorised or unlawful processing, accidental damage, destruction, or loss. The report justifies this conclusion on three main counts:

• Failure to prevent initial access, such as via the use of multi-factor authentication, despite widespread advice on identity access management being freely available from bodies such as the National Cyber Security council.
• BA did not have an up-to-date risk assessment of the CAG system used to gain remote access to their network. They also failed to configure and test the CAG to mitigate against users being able to "break out" of it and access other parts of the BA network. Remote control access systems are a known risk, and guidance on their management is freely available but was not deployed by BA, who did not conduct adequate penetration testing of their network.
• Privileged areas of the network could be accessed after the breakout from the CAG because the passwords were stored in unencrypted plain text. In 2016, the Open Web Application Security Project (OWASP) had concluded that the use of this storage method meant that malicious users could be "almost certain" to gain access through the account. Clear guidance on protecting privileged access accounts had not been utilised by BA.

Conclusion

The ICO ultimately fined BA because it did not fulfil its regulatory obligations and failed to protect data using technologies that were widely available. The fine of £20 million was much lower than could have been imposed because of the impact that coronavirus had on the business in 2020, but the costs to BA go way beyond the fine and include reputational damage that could leave customers wary of using their online booking systems. Most importantly, the ICO report suggests that the problem was potentially largely avoidable if existing security advice had been put in place.

A system of governance for managing technology risk, such as that which could have been used by BA, is outlined next.

A Governance and Risk Management Structure for Technology

The Australian Standards Board first published a voluntary standard on IT governance in 2005, and in 2008 this was converted to an international standard: ISO 38500 (ISO, 2008). The aim of the standard is to provide guidance to boards and senior management to enable them to assess and monitor the use of IT in their organisation. ISO 38500 thus complements other related standards that impact on IT management, including ISO 9000 (quality management), ISO 20000 (IT service management), and ISO 27001 (security management).

The standard lays down a number of key principles that need to be considered when establishing an IT governance system, which include consideration of how IT supports the organisation; the specification of lines of responsibility for IT management; and the monitoring of IT investment, performance, and levels of compliance with relevant regulations and legal obligations. All of these issues are addressed in the governance structure outlined later, and details of a web link to assist in finding out more about ISO 38500 are included at the end of the chapter.

Defining the Role of Technology in the Organisation

Risk management is directly linked to corporate objectives, and so in the case of a governance system for technology risk, the starting point must be a good understanding amongst senior management of the role that IT plays in the achievement of objectives. The board of directors should ask the fundamental question "Are we in control of IT" and be knowledgeable about:

1. Whether technology is strategically critical or simply a support function (e.g. used to monitor customer spending patterns or simply record transactions).
2. Whether it drives innovation and, if so, in what parts of the business (e.g. as a tool to link sections of the supply chain in real time to improve logistics management).
3. The technological regulatory environment in which we operate. Is it little regulated or highly regulated? Financial services is highly regulated; retail services less so.
4. Which technology risks are and are not insurable?
5. The potential impact on the organisation if information is stolen or corrupted.
6. The extent to which technology risk management is integrated into the wider internal control system.

As noted earlier, however, many company directors lack technological expertise, and their lack of understanding is ranked by the Institute of Internal Auditors as one of the top ten technological risks facing organisations today (IIA,

2015). Additionally, directors need to be conscious of the extent to which many IT technologies are standardised and replicable, resulting in corporate success being no longer dependent upon aggressive technological advantage seeking, but meticulous management of costs and risks (Carr, 2003). At least one board member with technological expertise is therefore essential to ensuring that structures are in place to provide accountability for IT performance, investment, compliance, and security. IT governance will include processes, structures, people, policies/procedures, and a culture or set of ethics that defines expected practice.

There is a danger that the technical nature of IT risks results in a tendency for them to be siloed, but because most organisations today are using IT end to end throughout their operations, the real need is for their risk management to be fully integrated in line with the principles underpinning both enterprise risk management (ERM) and ISO 31000. One way in which this can be achieved is via the use of a standardised technology risk framework such as COBIT 2019. COBIT specifies a set of principles, processes, and tools designed to help in the governance of IT, and its effectiveness is increased when it forms part of the wider risk management system that is enterprise wide (Ettish et al., 2017). Staff trained as COBIT practitioners can help in designing a governance system, as well as offering advice on regulatory compliance, IT policies, and contractual arrangements to mitigate risks.

Two of the central recommendations within the COBIT framework specify the need to define the technological risk appetite and the adoption of a common language for the risks arising from technological use. For example, a data breach such as in the BA case should be broken down into financial risks, regulatory risks, and reputational risk. In this way, technology risks are integrated into the wider risk management system. Risk appetite is set, as always, by the board of directors and should therefore be defined in terms of the standard language. For example, the risk culture or code of ethics might include a section on social media policy, which seeks to prevent staff from making inappropriate statements that could be reputationally damaging. In this way, a technical risk (social media) is reconfigured as a reputational issue.

The board also carries responsibility for establishing the overall control structure for the management of risk, and this must cascade down through the organisation and incorporate structures to ensure that technology risks are effectively assessed, communicated, recorded, and monitored for accountability. The tools used for assessment, recording, and monitoring of technology risk are the same as those used for any other form of risk.

Lines of Responsibility and Accountability for Technology Risk Management

As already noted, at board of director level, a director of operations will carry ultimate responsibility for technology risk as part of the wider operational risk portfolio. It is common for the head of operations to be an executive committee member rather than a full board member. Nike is one example of a company adopting this approach, where the position is one level below the main board, matching the level of the chief compliance officer.

Nike, Inc.

The role of the chief operating officer for Nike is described as to "lead global technology and digital transformation, consumer demand and supply management, manufacturing, distribution and logistics, sustainability, workplace design and connectivity, and procurement."

This description of the responsibilities of the chief operating officer in Nike reveals how technology is seen as strategically important to company growth, but it is also a job concerned with the day-to-day grind of making manufacturing and logistics work well.

The precise position in the hierarchy and job title will reflect the nature of the business. For example, BP has two technology-related executive team members (sub-board level) – one who is group head of technology and another executive vice president for safety and operational risk.

Regardless of the title, these executives "own" the technology risk and must oversee its management as it cascades down the organisational hierarchy. This can be achieved by segmenting specialist areas of responsibility such as security and perhaps having a head of cyber security as well as a head of security reporting up to the executive.

Whoever owns the technology risk must take the lead on ensuring different forms of IT risk are all managed effectively. This will include decisions relating to a range of technology issues, as shown in the left-hand column of Table 5.3. The right-hand column shows that all technology risks can be translated into standardised risk consequences, which may be easier for staff to understand.

The monitoring of technology risks is therefore done in a manner identical to that of any other risk of which it forms a part. For example, an internal audit would be expected to have a set procedure for overseeing the purchase of new technology or the selection of contractors for outsourcing of its supply in order to mitigate the potential financial and compliance risks that may result. Similarly, statistics on the number of staff trained in information security, for example, will be regularly reported to the compliance committee, and breaches of financial authority guidelines also reported alongside other data used to monitor compliance.

Managers within the individual business units will carry responsibility for risk assessment and reporting, but as the technological needs of the businesses may differ widely, ideally, a strong technology governance system will include

Table 5.3 Technology Risk and Consequences If Left Unmanaged

Technology Risk	Risk Consequences If Left Unmanaged
• Lifecycle management of both hardware and software • Purchasing of new technology, including criteria for selecting between alternative sources, namely, outsourced, the cloud, insourced, or hybrid (a mix of insourcing and outsourcing) • Evaluation and monitoring of data quality • Ensuring integration of IT systems across the enterprise • Systems to enhance staff awareness of privacy regulation and ethical principles underpinning IT use • Selection of systems to ensure cyber security	• Poor ROI; temporary operational shutdown; lack of innovation • Low financial returns; compliance risk; failure to exploit opportunities • Weak understanding of operational technology needs leading to missed marketing opportunities/profits • Reduced financial returns; temporary operational shutdown; failure to exploit opportunities • Compliance risk; financial risk – fines, etc; reputational risk • Compliance risk; Financial risk – fines and compensation; reputational risk

a technology specialist on each business unit board. This director will own the technology risk for the unit and can then act as the conduit to liaise with senior management on newly emerging risks and monitor and report on the risks within their own area of business. In this way, at all levels of the organisation and across all areas of operation, there are clear lines of responsibility, but technology risk is integrated into the core risk management system and not siloed and left to "the geeks."

Integrating Technology Risk Into Existing Risk Management Structures and Processes

Table 5.3 shows the first key step in the integration process: stop seeing technology risk as something special and different – think instead of its consequences in more recognisable terms. One way of looking at technology is as a resource, just like labour, for example, that is used by the business to achieve its strategic objectives. Resources cost money and carry risks, and so attention should be paid to how technology is managed, and specifically:

1. How well if fits with strategic needs
2. If it delivers value and the required return on investment
3. Monitoring to ensure technology works efficiently and effectively

Ensuring strategic fit, value for money, and operational efficiency means that procedures need to be put in place to assess technological needs, the associated risks, and how they should be managed, reported, and monitored. The second step to integrating technology risk into ERM is thus to utilise exactly the same processes that already exist in the wider risk management system for evaluation of technology risk. Workshops and brainstorming sessions can be used to involve operational management in identifying the risk of a failure in access to technologies and resulting consequences. Risk matrices can be constructed to evaluate the likelihood and consequences of different risk events, and common reporting systems and oversight by internal audit and compliance committees used to ensure that technology is understood to be a risk enterprise wide and not just within the IT department.

Risk management staff will be involved in staff training, advising on compliance controls and the consequences of non-compliance, and ensuring that a crisis management plan is in place and has been tested in case of catastrophic technology failure. Internal audit staff will be involved in oversight to ensure that processes are in place to ensure technology meets the business needs, including specified financial, compliance, and performance targets. For example, in the same way that an internal audit will have a standard procedure for vetting property investment purchases such as a new retail site, they will be involved in auditing each stage of a technology investment. This might include standard procedures for:

1. Assessing feasibility and design requirements
2. Monitoring the programming, testing, and installation process against defined targets
3. Engaging in a post-implementation review to identify lessons learned

Similarly, both risk managers and internal audits can assist in reducing the risk of technical failure by actions that might include:

1. Monitoring of outsourced services
2. Establishing, in conjunction with managers, key performance indicators (KPIs) for vendor performance
3. Defining the lines of responsibility for all aspects of the data system
4. Undertaking a risk analysis of the cost of timeouts
5. Maintaining staff awareness of technology risks via training and guidance on correct behaviour

In summary, although it might sound more challenging, technology risk is the same as any other and can be managed using the same tools.

Incident Management

A key component in the armoury that can be used to manage any form of risk is the establishment of a plan for a rapid, clear response, aimed at minimising the consequences of any incident. Business continuity management (BCM) procedures such as ISO 25999 clearly illustrate the benefits of such forward planning. This is especially true in the case of cyber risk, as the consensus view today seems to be that an incident is close to inevitable. For a cyber or other technology incident, the response must include two dimensions – the technical – getting the system up and running again – and the managerial, which is concerned with ensuring that the impact on customers, suppliers, and corporate reputation is limited.

The costs incurred with an incident can be categorised as follows:

1. Detection and isolation
2. Notification of affected parties
3. Lost business – this may be operational downtime, lost customers, and the cost of acquiring new customers to replace those lost
4. Long-term impacts – legal fees, regulatory fines, compensation for affected parties, and reputational damage

Most costs will be incurred in the twelve months following the problem, but some regulatory decisions can take a very long time, meaning that the costs incurred in fines may not be payable until two or more years down the line.

Evidence collected IBM (2020) on the consequences of a data breach revealed that the presence of both an incident response team *and* incident response plan testing in an organisation can significantly cut the resulting costs incurred. Organisations deploying both a team and plan testing incurred average costs of $3.29 million per incident, compared with $5.29 million for those without such facilities. Clearly, being prepared pays off.

Similarly, the quicker a breach can be identified, the lower the resulting cost. This was clearly illustrated in the BA example, where the failure to spot a problem substantially increased the number of affected customers and the resulting compensation to be paid. One way of reducing the time lag is via automated security systems that use technology such as artificial intelligence (AI) data analytics and machine learning to identify breaches. The financial services sector invests heavily in such technology, and evidence from IBM (2020) suggests that the sector is much quicker than healthcare or retail and hospitality at spotting breaches. Automated security systems reduced the cost of data breaches to less than half of that in cases where they were not used: $2.45 million versus $6.03 million (IBM, 2020).

Another risk reduction technique that is increasing in popularity is the use of "red team" testing, which involves independent security teams assessing the vulnerability of an organisation's network to attack. Where an organisation has multiple legacy IT systems running together and limited in-house expertise, this style of risk management can be particularly effective.

Insurance can help to protect against some of the costs arising from an incident, most commonly the necessary legal services and victim restitution.

Being prepared for a cyberattack requires clarity with regard to who is responsible and accountable for:

1. Detection and prioritisation of an incident
2. Determining the response(s)
3. Containment

4. Recovery
5. Identifying and implementing the lessons learned from the event

Risk managers and internal audit professionals need to determine if their processes are sufficiently robust to respond to an attack in a timely manner and in a way that protects the organisational reputation whilst minimising the harm to the affected customers/suppliers.

Minimising the Financial and Reputational Costs of Technology Risks

Even risk managers who lack technical expertise in IT systems can use a checklist to test the robustness of control systems within their organisations. How good is your organisation when measured against the following list?

To minimise reputational and financial costs you should:

1. Establish clear governance requirements and guidance in respect of IT compliance, including use of social media
2. Clearly define the boundaries of the IT governance and security plan (e.g. including suppliers)
3. Invest in regular, up-to-date compliance training
4. Continually review the level of in-house expertise in IT
5. Apply a zero trust strategy in relation to the accessibility of data
6. Invest in security automation
7. Minimise the complexity of IT and security systems
8. Implement effective auditing and monitoring of compliance breaches
9. Protect sensitive data in encrypted cloud databases
10. Use technology to monitor suspicious activity on remote laptops and mobile devices
11. Establish and then test incident response plans

If an organisation can affirm that all of these measures are in place, then the board of directors is in a position to take the view that they are in control of IT. If not, then beware.

Technology Glossary

COBIT – Control Objectives for Information and Related Technology. COBIT is a framework created by the **ISACA** (Information Systems Audit and Control Association) for IT governance and management. The framework is intended to link to corporate objectives and be enterprise wide. It fits well within a wider ERM or ISO 31000 risk management framework.

DDoS – Distributed denial of service attack. Such an attack commonly uses multiple machines and IP addresses in a malicious attempt to disrupt a server or network.

Fat finger error –   Most commonly used to refer to a keyboard input error resulting from someone hitting the wrong key. Their impact on a market can be very significant.

Phishing –   Emails or text messages sent by criminals posing as legitimate individuals with the aim of gaining access to sensitive/valuable data such as credit card details.

Ransomware –   Malicious software that infects a computer or network and prevents its functioning until a financial ransom has been paid. Such software is often found in email attachments, which should always be security checked before opening.

Virus –   A malicious programme designed to alter the way in which a computer operates and to spread rapidly across multiple machines. Viruses can affect computer software and damage or destroy data.

References

Carr, N. (2003) "IT Doesn't Matter." *Harvard Business Review*, May.

Ettish, A., El-Gazzar, M., & Jacob, R. (2017) "Integrating Internal Control Frameworks for Effective Corporate Information Technology Governance." *Journal of Information Systems and Technology Management*, Vol. 14, No. 3, pp. 361–370.

FinExtra (2021) *Citi Loses Legal Battle Over $0.5 Billion Funds Transfer Gaffe*. Downloaded from: www.finextra.com/newsarticle/37489/citi-loses-legal-battle-over-05-billion-funds-transfer-gaffe#:~:text=Citigroup%20has%20lost%20a%20legal,of%20distressed%20cosmetics%20firm%20Revlon.

IBM (2020) *Cost of a Data Breach Report 2020*. Ponemon Institute & IBM, Michigan, USA.

Institute of Internal Auditors (2015) *Navigating Technology's Top 10 Risks*. IIA, Lake Mary, FL, USA.

ISO (2015) *ISO/IEC 38500: Information Technology – Governance of IT for the Organization*. International Organization for Standardization, Geneva.

PwC (2019) *Approaching Breaking Point. Global Technology Risk Management Study*. PwC Ontario, Canada, April.

Tett, G. (2014) "Beware Techies Talking Gobbledegook." *Financial Times*, January 3, London.

Useful Web Links

1. Case studies in the implementation of COBIT. These are free to download from www.isaca.org/resources/cobit/cobit-case-studies.

2. Navigating Technology's Top Ten Risks. Published by the Institute of Internal Auditors Research Foundation and free to download from www.iia.nl/SiteFiles/Publicaties/Navigating%20Technology's%20Top%2010%20Risks%20_Small.pdf.

3. A summary guide to ISO 38500 on IT governance can be accessed on the website www.itgovernance.co.uk/iso38500.

Discussion Questions

1. Does your organisation have a CIO and/or a CSO? If so, how do their roles differ and how do they overlap (if at all)? Who is the owner of IT risk in your organisation?
2. Describe and discuss your organisation's social media policy, including Twitter, paying particular attention to whether you feel it is up to date.
3. Discuss how COVID-19 and the growth of remote working has affected IT risk in your organisation and how it has responded to this challenge.

6 Enterprise Risk Management in Manufacturing

The Case of Akzo Nobel (2000–2020)

Aim

The aim of this chapter is to illustrate how one large global company has, over the course of the last fifteen years, established an enterprise risk management (ERM) system which applies the principles of corporate governance and risk management outlined earlier in this book. In Chapters 3 and 4 we discussed the core components of a risk management system and the design of an organisational risk architecture. In this chapter we apply that knowledge to analyse:

- The motivation(s) for Akzo Nobel to adopt ERM
- The links between risk management and corporate strategy
- Key components of the ERM system
- Risk identification, assessment, and responses
- Reporting and monitoring of risks
- Making risk management enterprise wide
- Is ERM working?

Akzo Nobel: Background

Akzo Nobel N.V. is a Netherlands-based paints and coatings company formed through the 1994 merger of two well-established Dutch companies with origins dating back to 1792. The company is listed on Euronext Amsterdam and uses an American Depositary Receipt programme to facilitate trading on the OTCQX platform in the United States. In 2019 it was ranked as the world's third largest company in its sector. Akzo Nobel's major competitors are the US-based Sherwin-Williams Company and PPG. The latter made an unsuccessful bid for Akzo Nobel in 2017.

The paints division supplies paint products to the domestic do-it-yourself (DIY) and professional market, with familiar brands that include Hammerite, Polyfilla, Sadolin, and Dulux. The coatings side of the business is more specialised and includes automotive refinishing products and marine, aeronautical, and industrial powder coatings. The current strategy is to focus solely on paints and coatings, but this reflects a very different position from that of Akzo

DOI: 10.4324/9781315208336-6

Nobel at the start of this case study in 2004, when it was made up of three business segments – pharmaceuticals, chemicals, and paints/coatings. Divesting its interests in pharmaceuticals and chemicals over the last fifteen years has created a more homogenous business that is less complex to manage. The case study thus tells a story of strategic refocusing that runs in parallel with the evolution of the ERM system. This strategic transition is critical to understanding the development of the ERM system and perhaps also a key reason for why it appears to have proved successful. Complex businesses have complex risks, often interconnected; simplifying down helps to reveal risks and make them more manageable.

Motivations to Adopt ERM

Regulatory Breaches

In 1997 the US courts imposed fines on two Akzo Nobel executives for their role in a cartel to fix the prices of sodium gluconate, a chemical used in the food service industry for cleaning glass and metal equipment. Other cases relating to different chemicals (and the drug Remeron) followed, including cases for civil damage, and one anti-trust case led to the jailing of an Akzo Nobel executive in 2000. It took many years to reach settlements, with the result that Akzo paid multiple fines to US and Canadian courts as well as the EU Commission and was engaged in a series of appeals for a very long time. In 2010 the annual report still included provisions totalling €158 million to cover the cost of outstanding anti-trust cases dating from a decade earlier.

Whilst the fines and damage payments were not sufficiently large to have a major impact on the company's financial position, they were damaging to its reputation. In mitigation, Akzo Nobel fully cooperated with both the US and European authorities in their investigation of anti-trust activity and was granted a 40% reduction in its EU Commission fine in return for this.

The deep need to restore confidence in the company and explicit acknowledgement of the cumulative costs arising from internal breaches of anti-trust and anti-competitive legislation led to a decision in 2000 to assert new business principles by declaring zero tolerance of anti- competitive behaviour and begin the project that culminated in the formal launch of ERM in Akzo Nobel in 2004.

Key Learning Point

The decision in 2000 to move to zero tolerance of non-compliance can be seen as both presenting a public face of intolerance of such behaviour and also as a form of risk management per se. Regulatory breaches pose a form of avoidable risk.

The period 2000–2004 was one in which both national and international governance codes and regulations were evolving, and these played a key role in motivating and shaping the risk management approach adopted by Akzo Nobel.

Regulatory Developments on Governance

Sarbanes-Oxley Act (SOX) 2002

SOX was a critical factor influencing the approach to risk management because the company's shares were listed on NASDAQ, and so compliance with the rules laid down by NASDAQ and the Securities and Exchange Commission (SEC) on SOX implementation was essential. Figure 6.1 illustrates the so-called "COSO cube," which denotes the Committee of Sponsoring Organizations of the Treadway Commission (COSO) internal control framework extant in 2004 and used by Akzo to develop their own risk management system. It is important to note that the COSO framework was endorsed by SOX as a mechanism for demonstrating compliance with Section 404 on internal controls over financial reporting. As such, its use in Akzo reinforced the message of the importance attached to regulatory compliance. Additionally, at this early stage in the ERM project, it is unlikely that the processes of control, risk assessment

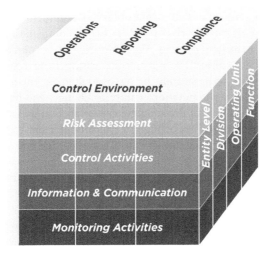

Figure 6.1 Control-integrated framework principles

Source: Poster of Internal Control-Integrated Framework Principles. ©2013. Committee of Sponsoring Organizations of the Treadway Commission (COSO). Used by permission.

and profiles, monitoring, and compliance are, as suggested in the COSO cube, fully integrated across all levels and areas of the business. Instead, the depiction denotes an ambition to move towards ERM over time.

Dutch Corporate Governance Code (Tabaksplat) 2003

The company's 2004 annual report stated that "risk management is one of the essential elements of the Company's corporate governance" (Annual Report, 2004, p. 61). This view perhaps reflects management concerns about the loss of market share and increased competition arising from the anti-trust cases it had recently lost. As already observed, poor governance generates risks.

As a large Dutch registered company Akzo Nobel had to comply with the national governance code as published in 2003. Provisions within the Tabaksplat covered issues relating to the remuneration of board members, the independence of supervisory board members, and specific requirements with respect to internal control systems. These complemented the guidelines laid down in the COSO framework.

In addition to the regulatory developments discussed earlier, in 2003 the EU Commission announced the establishment of the European Corporate Governance Forum as part of its action plan to reform company law and improve governance standards. Not surprisingly, this further increased the pressure on Akzo Nobel to instigate a programme for improved risk management and governance.

Changing Risk Arena and Shareholder Expectations

As the twentieth century ended, some observers commented on a noticeable shift in the nature of the key risks faced by major companies. In a 2005 presentation to risk managers outside Akzo Nobel, the corporate risk manager suggested that the traditional tangible risks arising from fire, employees, or environmental issues were steadily being overtaken by intangible and often uninsurable risks, such as reputation, failure to change, and business interruption. This was also an era of growing awareness and campaigning in the area of social and environmental reporting. The stakeholder net was widening, and so a company's potential reputational risks were extended beyond mere regulatory compliance. One clear example of this was the commencement of the use of corporate social responsibility (CSR) ratings, which rated businesses by the quality of their practices in the areas of social and environmental responsibility. Operating in the chemicals, paints, and coatings field, such assessments could not be ignored by Akzo Nobel – good management of environmental and social risks could be financially valuable to the company. Once the key ratings agencies such as Moody's began to take such factors into account in determining their corporate credit ratings, the management of CSR risks rose rapidly up the management agenda. Consequently, early on in their ERM project, Akzo Nobel declared its aim to be in the top performers in the chemicals segment of the Dow Jones Sustainability Index, hopefully boosting its attractiveness to the US market.

Changing Business Environment

The risks that are faced by any organisation reflect the current, constantly evolving, business environment. As a result of court cases in the United States and Europe, by 2004 Akzo had suffered significant falls in market share for some of its key products. In response, it was restructuring to reduce its complexity, divesting itself of pharmaceuticals, and rationalising its chemicals portfolio. The planned strategic changes required a rethinking of risks and internal controls, providing a further, final motivation for the introduction of ERM.

Perceived Benefits

Improvements in risk management were seen as offering four key benefits:

- Increased compliance
- Transparency of risk appetite to shareholders and stakeholders
- Improved decision making due to increased risk awareness
- Potential value creation

These four benefits are clearly interdependent, with the first three all serving to potentially increase the value of the business. Akzo Nobel's thinking thus reflects the common idea that profit-maximising firms usually consider implementing an ERM programme only if it increases expected shareholder wealth (Bertinetti and Gardenal, 2016).

The Link Between Strategy and Risk Management

Risk management is all about finding tools to assist in achieving corporate objectives, and as such it is clearly closely intertwined with strategy. Strategic changes should result in corresponding adjustments to risk management, or else there is a potential for new risks to be missed or poorly managed. Table 6.1 illustrates how the development of Akzo Nobel's ERM system runs parallel with a reconfiguration of the global businesses. Fifteen years ago, the group had three divisions spanning the pharmaceutical, chemicals, and paint and coatings sectors. By 2019 it was both smaller (in terms of revenue and employee numbers) and solely focused on paints and coatings. This simplification was good for risk management, as multiple business types carry complex and potentially unrelated risks that can be difficult to incorporate into an ERM system. The biggest challenge of ERM is ensuring that the system is truly enterprise wide, and the strategic evolution in Akzo Nobel clearly assisted this process.

The time frame for Table 6.1 is chosen to reflect the fact that the company began exploring new tools for managing its risks in 2000.

Table 6.1 Strategy and ERM (2000–2020)

Strategy	Year	Risk Management Initiatives
	2000	Begin exploring alternative new risk management tools
Expands coatings business, purchasing global marine and coatings operation from NOF Japan	2002	Pilot training workshops for senior managers as part of inititiative to develop a code of conduct
	2003	Risk boundaries defined via a code of conduct, business principles, and corporate directives and authority schedules
Sale of three chemicals businesses to reinvest proceeds in coatings	2004	Code of ethics for senior officers adopted
Acquired BASF coatings business		Annual report declared the risk management system to be compliant with the COSO ERM framework
	2005	First corporate risk manager appointed
		Upgrade of treasury/banking to create a common system group-wide
Divestment of pharmaceutical operations via sale of Organon for €11 billion	2007	Internal control officer appointed to ensure risk management processes are evaluated for effectiveness
		Annual report declares the risk management system "mature"
Purchase of ICI – becomes world's largest coating and specialist paints company	2008	Centralisation of procurement
		Compliance committee established
€50million invested in performance coatings		Commencement of integrated reporting – adding corporate social responsibility material into the annual report
	2012	Six internal processess selected where greater internal consistency required
		First move towards unified business planning system
	2014	Business Directives portal launched to give employees a one-stop website for all of the directives, rules, manuals, guidelines and procedures
Paper chemical business sold for €153m	2015	Business partner code of conduct launched
Takeover bid from PPG of €26 billion; commitment to selling speciality chemical arm as a defence	2017	Business partner compliance programme launched
Speciality chemicals arm sold for €10 billion	2018	
Sole focus on paints and coatings	2019	Policy portal launched – centralised information on policies, roles, and procedures regarding global processes

Table 6.2 Akzo Nobel (2004–2019)

Year	2004		2008		2019	
Business segments (% total revenue)	Pharmaceuticals	25	Chemicals	37	Decorative paints	40
	Chemicals	34	Decorative paints	34	Performance coatings	60
	Paints and coatings	41	Performance coatings	29		
Global employees	63,600		60,000		33,800	
Global revenue € billion	12.7		15.4		9.3	
Profit/lossfrom continuing operations € billion	0.88		(1.044)		0.555	
Earnings per share (diluted) €	2.69		(4.45)		2.52	

The strategic trajectory is further confirmed by the information shown in Table 6.2.

Table 6.2 shows a company transitioning from multiple business segments into one specialising in paints and coatings. The revenue share earned from paints and coatings shifts from 40% in 2004 to over 60% in 2008 and then 100% by 2019. From 2004 onwards Akzo Nobel slowly sold off unwanted sections of its chemicals businesses, ended its involvement in pharmaceuticals in 2007, and in 2008 purchased the UK giant ICI in a move aimed at strengthening its global position in the paint sector and affirming its leading role in the coatings business (Reuters, 2008).

A simplified business model creates an environment better suited to ERM, but Table 6.1 shows that developing an effective risk management system is a long, slow process. Key stages are worth highlighting.[1]

Stage 1: Building a Risk Culture (2000–2004)

Over this period the focus was on developing tools to improve the ethical behaviour of employees and establish risk boundaries. This was a direct response to the need to eradicate the risk of further breaches of anti-trust/anti-competitive regulation of the type that had blighted the company's recent history.

The view was taken that a culture of appropriate behaviour could not be imposed by edicts from above. Risk controls and techniques complement and reflect corporate culture, and so all training was managed in house. The training, which was rolled out in a top-down manner, had two objectives:

• Define a staff code of conduct
• Establish a set of business principles

The result was a code of conduct that defined staff responsibilities and was complemented by other tools to define risk boundaries: a set of business principles, corporate directives, and authority schedules together with a statement on sustainability.

In 2003 a fully operational risk management department was established, and the annual report (p. 46) declared:

> We foster a high awareness of business risks and internal control procedures, geared to safeguarding transparency in our operations.

The role of corporate risk manager was created in 2004, and the annual report declared that the risk management framework was compliant with the COSO ERM system.

The first corporate risk manager, Dick Oude Alinke, was appointed in 2005. He was an existing Akzo employee who had previously worked as an insurance broker and claims manager at ABN Amro Bank.

Stage 2: Streamlining and Refining Risk Management Tools (2004–2008)

The focus now shifted to the creation of a detailed risk architecture. The message went out: "Unidentified risks are a threat; identified risks are a managerial issue."

Managers at all levels were held personally responsible for risk management and needed to understand the business; clarify their objectives; and identify, assess, and respond to risks in a consistent and integrated way. Group-wide consistency in the tools used to identify, assess, and report risk was viewed as essential.

The development of common systems to ensure consistency across crucial processes was seen as key to reducing risks. For example, the business principles guided corporate-wide decision making on matters such as child labour and activities in politically sensitive countries and was complemented by a code of conduct for vendors. Similarly, a corporate audit protocol established a system of five yearly health and safety audits of all sites, with the aim of matching audit records across Asia, Europe, and North America.

In 2007 an internal control officer was appointed to ensure internal oversight of risk management processes, and the same year the system was declared "mature." The term "mature" is difficult to define, except as an expression of confidence. For the purposes of this case study, it is seen as a statement of a shift from initial development of core risk management systems into a period of continuous improvement.

Stage 3: Continuous Improvement (2008–2020)

At the heart of the continuous improvement era are three interlinked themes:

- Continuing streamlining of operations in line with long-term strategies
- Ongoing standardisation and centralisation of processes and systems
- Redefining of enterprise boundaries in terms of risk management

In acquiring ICI, Akzo Nobel became the world's largest paint/coatings and specialist chemical company, but the same year it also recorded losses of over €1 billion. Streamlining of operations and improved efficiency were essential to recovering future profits. For example, procurement was centralised, and the figure soared from €0.5 billion to €6.5 billion, resulting in savings from both economies of scale and improved decision making.

Risk management systems were also streamlined. Risk workshops were used to integrate the businesses acquired from ICI, using existing approaches to risk identification, reporting, and assessment to build enterprise-wide alignment of risk management, compliance, and internal control processes.

A call for "integrity and compliance in all our actions" was embedded in the code of conduct, and both the anti-bribery and competition law compliance manuals were updated. The objective of providing training to all staff on the code of conduct by 2009 was declared, and a compliance committee was established aimed at fostering awareness of, and compliance with, the newly updated code of conduct.

In 2012, six processes, covering recurring risk categories, were codified to ensure greater consistency. These were:

- People, product, and process safety – with a special focus on safe behaviour
- Operational control cycle – regular standardised meetings established to review performance and produce quarterly rolling forecasts
- Continuous improvement
- Innovation
- Procurement – supplier selection processes
- Talent management

This codification was the first step towards the development of a unified business planning (ERP) system that is still ongoing.

Complementing the standardisation and streamlining of processes during this period, Akzo Nobel was also actively extending the boundaries of its definition of enterprise risk. For example, integrated reporting (IR) was introduced in 2008, long before the International Integrated Reporting Council was set up in 2010. IR is a way of improving company reporting by incorporating information about the value created by a business in terms of non-financial resources such as human, social, and intellectual capital as well as financial capital. It is underpinned by a recognition that an organisation's activities have an impact on society at large (e.g. via climate change). Such impacts may be redefined as risks, which can be managed to add value to the business. In a linked extension of the boundaries of the ERM system, codes of conduct and decision-making guidelines were introduced for business partners in 2017 and 2018.

All the annual reports from 2004 to 2019 include a statement that the risk management system in Akzo Nobel complies with the ERM framework in COSO and SOX. The summary of how the system evolved over time is useful to understanding the link between strategy and risk, but the detail of how the system works is of particular interest. The remainder of this chapter is therefore devoted to an in-depth analysis of the core components of that system.

Core Components of the ERM System

Governance and Culture

Governance

In line with Dutch law, Akzo Nobel's board structure is two tiered. A board of management, composed solely of executive directors, works alongside but takes precedence over a supervisory board made up entirely of non-executive directors. The two boards are independent of one another, and both are accountable to shareholders. The executive board oversees the work of lower-level management boards, which in turn monitor the work of, and receive reports from, the heads of the related business units. The precise format of the sub-executive boards has evolved over time, but the principles remain consistent. The governance structure conforms with the Dutch Civil Code and the Dutch Corporate Governance Code.

The work of the supervisory board includes reviewing corporate strategy, objective setting, and design of the internal control and risk management system, and so they have a key role to play in relation to the implementation of ERM. One important way in which they are involved in risk management oversight is via the audit committee, which is a permanent sub-committee of the supervisory board and responsible for monitoring the quality and integrity of risk management and internal control practices.

The executive committee is directly responsible for establishing and ensuring an effective risk management and compliance framework, and a number of board sub-committees assist in this process:

- Integrity and compliance committee – investigates violations of laws, regulations, and internal rules
- Risk control and compliance committees – monitor the effectiveness of internal controls and associated breaches
- Human rights committee – oversees implementation of the corporate human rights programme
- Privacy committee – supervises privacy controls and breaches of those controls

An integrity and compliance function is responsible for the day-to-day management of risk, reporting directly to the general counsel (company secretary) and with direct access to the chairman of the audit committee. The role of the function includes training and provision of support and guidance across the group. Integrity and compliance managers can also be found in each major business hub, where they are responsible for risk identification and response, training, support, and monitoring. In 2019, the heads of the integrity and compliance, internal control, and internal audit functions met monthly to discuss findings and trends and to ensure a consistent approach.

Integrity and Compliance

Akzo Nobel's decision to use the term integrity and compliance function instead of risk management function appears to be a purposeful indication of where board priorities lie. The language encourages individuals to feel *personally* responsible. If staff follow the rules and behave with integrity, risks will be identified and managed.

In their 2019 annual report, Akzo Nobel depict the integrity and compliance framework as a pie chart made up of ten components, with governance at the top, but at the heart of the framework is culture. This depiction recognises the centrality of corporate culture to the effective management of risks, and efforts to instil an ethical mindset began back in 2004.

Culture

The Institute for Risk Management defines risk culture as "a term describing the values, beliefs, knowledge, attitudes and understanding about risk shared by a group of people with a common purpose, in particular the employees of an organisation or of teams or groups within an organisation" (IRM, 2012, p. 7). Risk culture is reflected in the behaviour of staff and their attitude(s) to risk, both of which are influenced by the underlying organisational culture. A clear board policy on risk, which defines the organisational risk appetite and risk boundaries, is thus the cornerstone for the construction of a culture of ethical behaviour in which staff are both risk aware and utilise common language in relation to risk.

A strong risk culture is important in ensuring that individuals behave in a manner that coincides with organisational objectives, principles, and codes of behaviour. In contrast, an inappropriate risk culture can encourage mavericks to behave in ways which create financial or reputational risks for their organisation. As discussed earlier, Akzo Nobel's adoption of ERM was in part motivated by a weakening performance resulting from regulatory breaches – in other words, a weak risk culture. Akzo Nobel needed a full-scale revision of its risk culture that introduced strong and consistent ethical principles. Coinciding with the decision to adopt ERM, the human resources (HR) department in Akzo Nobel declared its decision to develop a performance-based culture.

The transition from the corporate culture of 2004 to what it is today can be usefully divided into two phases, as illustrated in Figure 6.2.

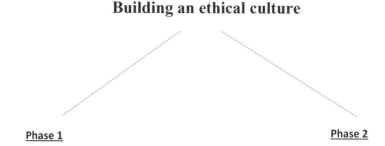

Building an ethical culture

Phase 1

- Policy declaration of core principles
- Ethical awareness workshops & training
- Development of a code of conduct

Phase 2

- Clarification of risk boundaries
- Specification of managerial responsibilities for risk management

Figure 6.2 Building an ethical culture

The starting point in Phase 1 for creating a risk-aware culture was a board-level policy statement of core principles of behaviour that included bans on bribery, harassment, child labour, and political donations. This was accompanied by a board commitment to fair competition policies in relation to product marketing.

But what exactly is bribery and/or harassment? How is "fair competition" defined? Is there a universal definition of child labour?

Ensuring ethical behaviour by staff demands their engagement with the issues, and training is cascaded from the top down. In initial training, executives used role playing to discuss work-related ethical dilemmas such as those posed earlier. Six business unit managers then ran pilot workshops for 200 senior managers, with the aim of establishing a new set of business principles and code of conduct. In turn, those senior managers began to run workshops for their middle managers in order to filter down the concepts and principles. As the process moved out into the wider business via risk workshops, junior staff most likely to be exposed to such dilemmas (e.g. in sales and purchasing) were the next to be trained. By the end of 2004 it was finally rolled out to all staff,[2] and the system continues today.

Typical questions addressed at business unit–level workshops might include:

- Are there any countries where we should not do business?
- When does a facilitation payment become a bribe?

- A customer requests frequent flyer tickets in exchange for an order. Nobody could find out, and no money is exchanged. Is such an arrangement ethical?

Staff are told "if in doubt, discuss with more senior management," and if it is agreed that an action flouts business principle, then it should not be done.

An internal survey of ethical awareness amongst staff indicates that the training has been very effective. In one business unit, 88% felt able to identify warning signs of unethical conduct, compared to 40% pre-training, implying success in "trying to bring it down to a level where people understand it" (Maitland, 2003). Part of the explanation for this may lie in the use of Akzo Nobel's own staff to conduct the training, as there is better understanding of each party's respective position.

In combination, the board's policy statements and the ethical principles formed the foundation for the development of a code of conduct for all 67,000 staff spanning eighty countries. The code of conduct was intended to convert understanding of the principles into full compliance with them by staff. When initially drafted, it focused solely on employees, and it was expanded in 2005 to include a privacy code to protect data on employees, customers, suppliers, and others.

Akzo Nobel regards the code of conduct as "one of the critical foundations of good corporate governance" (Annual Report, 2005, p. 69), and the code, which is now available in thirty-two languages, sets the boundaries of what is seen as acceptable behaviour. Staff are expected to read and understand the code and confirm their compliance as part of the annual performance review process. If a situation cannot be clarified as compliant, staff are encouraged to talk directly to their line manager or the group's legal department.

Key Learning Point

A code of conduct that is part of the formal performance appraisal process provides a tool for risk control across all staff. That does not necessarily mean that all staff understand its role and its significance.

Reflecting changes in risks and the business environment, the code of conduct has been regularly updated, and a copy of the current version can be found using the web links at the end of this chapter. Today, the code applies to both employees and contractors, and there is a parallel code for business partners such as suppliers.

One way in which the code has evolved is that it has progressed from addressing primarily ethical issues, encouraging staff to "do the right thing," to one that now incorporates non-negotiable behaviour in three core areas: safety, integrity, and sustainability.

The summary of core principles outlined in Table 6.3 could be argued to be very broad ranging and hence difficult to implement in practice. Wearing a seatbelt for safety is easy to understand, but "we protect personal and confidential information" is far more complex. Without systems to help staff interpret and understand the principles, efforts to establish a risk-aware culture may flounder. Communication of issues and offering scope to debate risk boundaries is vital. Today this is done via e-learning packages which are mandatory for all staff, further details of which are discussed in the section on communication and reporting of risk later in this chapter.

The addition of principles of safety and sustainability to the code of conduct reflect both the nature of Akzo Nobel's business and the evolution of core organisational objectives, which create new key risks. Paints and coatings manufacturing and distribution is a potentially dangerous business, and safety concerns must be prioritised. Akzo Nobel's 2019 annual report (p. 17) states their aim is "zero injuries, waste and harm through operational excellence." Such objectives can never be met without massive staff engagement. In relation to sustainability, Akzo Nobel pays close attention to external benchmarks such as Sustainalytics, Excellence Global, and the Ethibel Sustainability Index, that monitor corporate performance in this regard. Additionally, referencing the

Table 6.3 Three Core Principles: Safety, Integrity, and Sustainability

Code of Conduct

Safety	*Integrity*	*Sustainability*
Lifesaving rules: • Work with a valid work permit when required • Use fall protection when working at height • Obtain a permit for entry into a confined space • Make sure moving machinery is guarded • Check equipment is isolated before work begins • Obtain authorisation before disabling safety equipment • Wear a seatbelt in motor vehicles when provided • Do not use alcohol or drugs at work	• We compete in a fair and honest way • We follow trade restrictions carefully • We protect personal and confidential information • We keep a clear line between business and personal interests • We look after company property and use it appropriately • We keep records in accordance with company policies • We are alert to fraud and report suspicious activity • We communicate in a professional way	• We recognise human rights and treat people with dignity and respect • We recruit and manage employees fairly • We reduce the environmental impact of what we do • We address the concerns of those affected by our operations • We give back to communities we operate in • We work with business partners who share our principles

demands of the United Nations' Sustainable Development Goals forms part of the company's agenda.

The requirement to confirm adherence to the core principles and the associated guidance means that they are effectively recast as a tool of risk management control.

From the beginning, there has been a strong emphasis on reporting breaches of the code, with assurance that the individual reporting the breach will not suffer as a consequence. Today, a separate Speak Up! website exists to facilitate such reporting. More details of how this works in practice and how its effectiveness is measured are covered in the section on risk monitoring later in this chapter.

The key point to note is that codes of behaviour have little value if they are not followed, and other aspects of the risk management process serve to complement and reinforce the power of the risk culture. The governance structure, principles, and code of conduct outlined earlier provide a bare skeleton around which a more detailed ERM system can be constructed, as detailed next.

Strategy and Objective Setting

The objective of risk management is to provide reasonable assurance that business objectives can be achieved, and so clear strategic objectives provide a reference point for risk analysis. Strategic planning is a board-level responsibility, and in Akzo Nobel, strategic direction is determined by the board of management, with oversight from the supervisory board. As we will see later, strategies reflect inputs from business unit boards that take into account current market conditions and risks. Overall, therefore, strategies are determined through a process that is both top down and bottom up in style.

The objectives cover financial, operational, and sustainability issues, as well as innovation, which is regarded as a driver of long-term value creation. This approach mirrors the philosophy that underpins ERM: "value is maximized when management set strategy and objectives to strike an optimal balance between growth and return goals and related risks."

Core strategies are discussed in depth in the annual report, and as of 2019–2020 these can be summarised as follows:

- Focus on the paints and coatings sector
- Value over volume – improving profit margins
- Integration of the supply chain – exploiting scale economies
- Standardisation of processes, systems, and planning
- Innovation in products and supporting technologies – see example that follows
- Sustainability – reducing the environmental impact of products

These objectives largely reaffirm the strategic trajectory that has been pursued since 2004. Innovation is important to Akzo Nobel, as it is a way of maintaining their leading position in the paints sector. Keeping ahead of the game helps preserve and increase market share.

An Example of Innovative Strategies

In 2019 Akzo Nobel launched its Colorsensor technology. This portable device can be used by decorators to scan an object's colour. The data can then be linked to a mobile phone app to provide an exact match.

The innovation helps decorators and architects reduce the risk of not quite matching a client's colour specifications, whilst also extending the market for a potentially unlimited palette of colours. The key to the innovation being successful is to then ensure colour mixing is totally accurate but costs are kept low to ensure continued profitability.

Similarly, sustainability reflects the organisation's sensitivity to evolving stakeholder demands on the environmental impact of its products. For example, in addition to the standard financial objective of return on investment, Akzo Nobel aims to achieve a target of more than 20% of sales derived from products rated highly for their ecological performance. Incorporating sustainability into the objectives has a dual effect. Firstly, it makes an organisation think more broadly and consider how non-financial capital – both within the business (e.g. employees) and outside the business (e.g. global climate) – is affected by strategies. Secondly, it explicitly acknowledges investor sensitivity to sustainability, and in so doing can increase shareholder value.

The strategies at the board level are cascaded down across the business units and central services, with ongoing two-way debate ensuring regular review(s) at all levels. When the ERM programme was in its initial phase fifteen years ago, the corporate risk manager Oude Alink declared: "successful risk management depends on the complete alignment of day-to-day business planning, reporting and management, as well as strategic vision" (Protiviti, 2007, p. 3).

Matching strategic vision at the plant, business unit, and board level is facilitated by a business planning cycle that has steadily been integrated company wide. The plan covers demand and supply across the full product portfolio. The result is that operating plans and financial forecasts are revised and integrated on what is now a monthly basis, allowing rapid adjustment to newly emerging risks.

Risk management is all about establishing systems to aid in the achievement of objectives, and central to such systems are tools for the identification and assessment of risk.

Key Learning Point

Integration of strategies and objectives across all levels of the organisation is an important feature of ERM. A centralised planning system helps to facilitate this.

Risk Identification, Assessment, and Response

The system used in Akzo Nobel to identify and manage risk, whilst led from the top down, is interactive, utilising bottom-up information to inform the planning process. The process owner is the risk and integrity function, which also carries responsibility for risk awareness training and support. Risk and integrity staff organise ERM-style workshops across the organisation, with the aim of getting managers directly involved in self-assessment of risks in the areas under their responsibility. The objective is to personalise the process and maximise the use of employee knowledge and experience when it comes to risk identification and management. Emphasis is placed on the risks that need to be actively managed, with less importance given to the risks that can be accepted.

Risk profiles are drafted across seven different levels within Akzo Nobel, as illustrated in Table 6.4, with each one reporting the top ten risks plus the chosen responses up to the next level of management. The risk profiles are reviewed annually, and separate profiles are drafted for important strategic changes such as acquisitions. In the case of the board of management, key strategic risks and the group's aggregate risk profile are subject to review and oversight by the supervisory board.

The major risk factors affecting Akzo Nobel identified by the board of management and executive committee thus incorporate the risks identified at lower levels, but also add a group-wide perspective, taking into account broader strategic factors. The key risks are outlined in the annual report and have evolved

Table 6.4 Risk Profiling Levels

Level	Objectives/Risks Assessed	Responsible Party
Group	Strategic	Board of management (BM)
Business unit	Operational	BU board chaired by BM
	Financial	member
Sub-business unit	Compliance	Senior managers
Process		Senior managers
Site (main)		Site manager
Plant		Plant manager/director
Corporate functions		Functional head/director

EXTERNAL – STRATEGIC
*Global economy and geo-politics

*Strategic moves in our value chain

INTERNAL – STRATEGIC
* Organic growth

* Innovation and identification and successful
  implementation of major transforming
  technologies

EXTERNAL – OPERATIONAL
*Information technology and cyber security

INTERNAL – OPERATIONAL
*Management of change

*Analytics and big data

EXTERNAL – COMPLIANCE
*Complying with laws and regulatory
  developments

 Risk has been assessed as increasing

 Risk has been assessed to remain fairly stable

Figure 6.3 Akzo Nobel key risks (2019)

Source: Annual Report, 2019, p. 60

over time, with those assessed to be increasing or stable relative to the previous year clearly indicated. The principal risks, as shown in Figure 6.3, are very similar to those discussed in Chapter 4.

External strategic risks such as geo-political trends in relation to climate change require ongoing monitoring of political developments and their incorporation into strategic and operational plans. Similar monitoring of competitor activity is used to help manage strategic risks across the value chain. The inclusion of innovation and the need for successful implementation of new technologies as a key risk is interesting, as it demonstrates how risk and opportunity are flip sides of the same coin. Unexploited or failed opportunities are risks in themselves. Compliance risks are broad ranging and include competition law, environmental law, anti-bribery, fraud, and data protection.

Key Learning Point

Key strategic and operational risks are determined, in part, by using input from managers across all levels of the organisation.

As part of the business planning cycles, the key risk register is regularly updated in response to feedback from business unit boards and other senior management. One element of the updating emerges from enterprise risk management workshops, which are held regularly – eighty-four in 2017, for example. Their aim is discussion of a variety of risk scenarios suggested by management teams and functional experts. The intended outcome is a clear risk action plan with identified action owners and due dates. The workshop results are then used in risk profiling and trend analysis and shared by managers across the company at different levels.

The risk workshops are complemented by regular self-assessment of risks across the seven levels of management. This process, depicted in Figure 6.4, is central to the risk management system, and extensive training is used to ensure that managers are familiar with the process and their associated responsibilities.

Stage 4 of the process is a matrix of four quadrants depicting the impact versus likelihood of the identified risks. The circles indicate specific risks (e.g. loss of personal customer data, life-threatening accidents), and their precise position in the matrix is determined in stages 1 to 3 of the self-assessment process. Asking managers to self-assess the risks for which they can be held responsible not only helps to embed a risk management mindset enterprise wide but also makes valuable use of their specialist knowledge to reduce risk.

The arrow running from bottom left across the diagram illustrates areas of risk where it is deemed appropriate to maintain current levels of control, although in quadrant B, where both impact and risks are high, additional controls may be needed. Quadrant A is an area where impact is high but likelihood low, so it may be tempting to undercontrol the risks here, and that question is also important to debate. Similarly, in quadrant D, although likelihood is high, the impact is relatively low, so maybe these risks are being overcontrolled. Enforcing this process of risk assessment in a uniform manner across the organisation is seen as a way of building a robust and integrated ERM system.

Key Learning Point

Good risk management involves identification not just of the risks themselves but also the appropriate level of control.

The matrix in Figure 6.4 thus serves to focus managerial attention on the risks that need to be managed versus those that are less important and can be accepted.

Once risks have been identified, there is a need for managers to decide how to respond, and responses can be summarised by the four Ts:

- Take – accept the risk and fund the consequences if it crystallises
- Terminate – revise objectives; pull out/divest, or reduce the scale of activity

Stage 1: Rating the Potential Impact

What is the potential impact of the risk on our plant/business unit/department's ability to achieve its objectives? (Excluding all existing control measures)	Impact Score 1-3: low 4-6: medium 7-10: high

Stage 2: Likelihood of Occurrence

How likely is the risk to arise within the next three to five years? (taking account of existing risk controls)	Likelihood Score 1-3: low 4-6: medium 7-10: high

Stage 3: Control Effort

What effort is being made to manage the identified risk, assuming that the effort is effective?	Control Effort Scale 1-3: low 4-6: medium 7-10: high

Stage 4: Outcome. Impact versus Likelihood Matrix

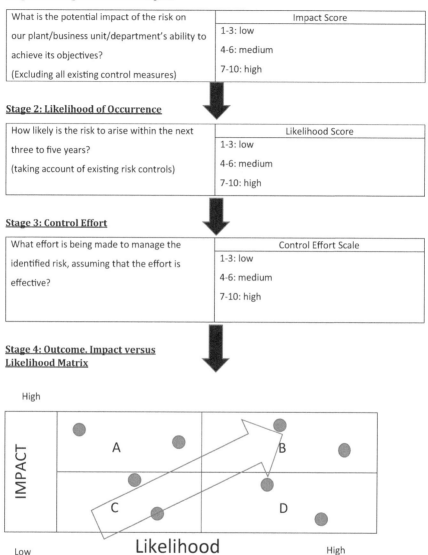

Figure 6.4 Components of the risk self-assessment process

- Transfer – sharing; contracting out/outsourcing; joint venture; diversify; hedge
- Treat – manage risk through cultural change and reorganisation; monitoring

The choice of response is dictated by the organisational risk appetite. Risk appetite is set by the board of management to reflect stakeholder requirements, other strategic objectives, and the types of risks encountered. Risk is a regular item on the board agenda, and the tolerance level for different categories of risk varies:

- Strategic risk – the company is prepared to take considerable risk to achieve innovative growth
- Financial – the aim is for prudential financing and cash management
- Operational – minimisation of the downside risk from failures
- Compliance – zero tolerance of breaches of the code of conduct

Risk appetite is managed by requiring management compliance with risk boundaries, which determine the freedom of action or choice in terms of risk taking and risk acceptance. The boundaries are detailed in position statements and an array of guidance that includes business principles, the code of conduct, authority schedules, policies, and corporate directives. This material is available in nine languages and is complemented by both face-to-face and online training programmes on integrity and compliance available to all employees.

An example of the guidance given to staff in relation to the requirement to apply integrity in business relations is shown in the following box.

Code of Conduct Extract: Integrity

Honest Business Conduct

We are committed to applying the highest ethical and legal standards. We conduct business fairly and with integrity. We don't make, offer, or authorise bribes or conduct any other form of unethical business practice. We do not make facilitation payments.

We believe in competing on the merits of our products. We each have a responsibility to ensure that we base our dealings with business partners on objective decisions and are not influenced by gifts or entertainment. All gifts and entertainment given or received must be of modest value and appropriate to the business relationship. We seek approval for our actions.

For further guidance, please refer to: Directives Portal Anti-Bribery, Gifts & Entertainment

---

Incorporating a direct link to the relevant directives portal (requiring an employee to sign in) helps make the system easy to negotiate whilst simultaneously emphasising the link between the code of conduct and other guidance on principles, etc.

Position statements cover specific issues, such as zero tolerance of bribery; authority schedules detail what each level of management can and cannot do in terms of decision-making powers; and the corporate directives detail internal rules and procedures in relation to six processes that are seen as recurring risk categories. The processes covered by corporate directives are:

- People, product, and process safety
- Operational control cycle
- Continuous improvement
- Innovation
- Procurement
- Talent management

An illustrative example provides a useful aid to understanding the day-to-day application of the directives. Process safety is a key concern for Akzo Nobel, given the nature of its products and scale of manufacturing operations, and details of how process risks are managed can be found in the annual sustainability reports. Risk management in this area is critical for both regulatory compliance purposes and as a way of promoting good operating practice.

The US-based Centre for Chemical Processes Safety (CCPS, 2010) defines process safety management (PSM) as:

> a disciplined framework for managing the integrity of hazardous operating systems and processes by applying good design principles engineering and operating practices. It deals with the prevention and control of incidents that have the potential to release hazardous materials or energy. Such incidents can cause toxic effects, fire or explosion and could ultimately result in serious injuries, property damage, lost production and environmental impact.

The discipline of the safety management process outlined in Figure 6.5 is reflected in the feedback loop that is embedded in the four stages. Once an event is defined and indicators of events are specified, then monitoring of process safety can be undertaken, with greater attention being given to those sites and plants with the greatest potential risk. The consequences of events can range from catastrophic (Tier 1) through to errors of omission, for example, with minimal impact, but if risk is to be reduced long term, then all levels must be managed effectively.[3] For the risk manager, it is important to note that the lower tiers serve as leading indicators of potential and more serious events further up the line. The bottom tier is that of culture and management discipline: staff awareness and engagement with safety issues will help to reduce not only the absolute number but also the severity of process safety breaches. Learning from mistakes and rethinking how processes can be improved mean that the risk assessment for sites is then revised accordingly. In process safety, as in all

Framework

Definition of a process safety event:	A loss of primary containment (LoPC), unsafe release, or an undesired event/condition that could have resulted in a LoPC. Undesirable conditions include imperfect controls or disciplines.
Specification of key performance indicators (KPIs)	Leading: Inadequate controls or discipline (e.g. poor staff recognition of "line of fire" scenarios, where a material release might occur). Lagging: An LoPC event

Categorisation of:
• **Sites**
• **PSE events**

Sites

Categories A to C, based on the RESIDUAL risk of an event, taking into account existing controls and performance

A is the highest risk category

PSE Events

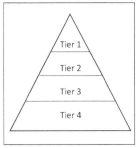

Monitoring of events and responses	• Logging and reporting of events by category Tier 1–4 • Rate-adjusted measurement of incidents (e.g. number of Tier 1 events per 200,000 working hours) • PSM capability benchmarking • Employee training (e.g. hazard awareness, line-of-fire awareness) • Revision of practices to ensure continual improvement, including regular reviews of KPIs

PSE EVENTS KEY:

Tier 1: Most critical. Potentially catastrophic, leading to possible loss of life or major environmental consequences.

Tier 2: Less critical and may be leading indicators of Tier 1 events. Technical specifications on the range of material released are used to define a Tier 2 event.

Tier 3: Low-level consequences such as small spillages and near-miss incident indicators. Used as a leading indicator of possible Tier 2 events.

Figure 6.5 Process safety management

elements of ERM, establishing clear rules and behaviour guidelines is critical to success.

The outcome of the risk assessment and treatment process is that at seven levels of management, a risk action plan is generated, with clearly identified risk and action owners and specified dates for the required actions to be completed. The risk profiles are shared with managers across the organisation, and around 20% of the risks are likely to be taken up to the next level for reassessment and inclusion in the risk consolidation process.

Risk Reporting and Monitoring

The board of management (executive committee) is responsible for the establishment and adequate functioning of the system of governance, risk management, and internal controls. Governance regulations also require that the board of management undertake an annual review of risk management and internal controls to ensure their ongoing effectiveness, although they are not required to report their findings. They are supported in this by an integrity and compliance committee, which is responsible for providing assurance on risk management and legal, regulatory, and ethical compliance. The committee provides recommendations to the board of management and reports directly to the supervisory board, which, in conjunction with the audit committee, ensures independent oversight of control effectiveness.

The governance structure as described reveals two complementary components of risk reporting and monitoring:

- The design and implementation of systems for internal oversight, including risk reporting and tools of internal control.
- The *independent* assessment of the effectiveness of the controls. Those involved in the design of controls should be independent of those who assess their efficacy.

As seen in the previous section, responsibility for the development of risk management tools such as the code of conduct and corporate principles, and for staff training, rests with the integrity and compliance function, whose managers are embedded across all core business functions and operational activities. Their work is overseen by the integrity and compliance committee, which formally monitors compliance and undertakes an annual review of effectiveness. The committee's work is supported in practice by the internal audit function, which operates a rolling programme of audits to assess risk management and internal controls across all areas of the organisation. The audit plan is risk based, taking into account past compliance findings. The annual summary report from internal audits forms part of the annual review of internal control effectiveness, which is subject to approval by both the board of management and the audit committee. The heads of internal control, integrity and compliance, and internal audit meet monthly to review developments and plan joint responses.

Staff in the integrity and compliance function, the committee of the same name, and internal audit are all employees of the business, and so independent evaluation of control efficacy is still required. The audit committee, reporting to the supervisory board, performs this independent role.

The system of risk reporting and oversight is depicted in Akzo Nobel's 2019 annual report as being a two-way tiered process, as illustrated in Figure 6.6. Reporting is a bottom-up process, whereas oversight is top-down.

The reporting process is interlinked with the risk self-assessment described earlier, with the top ten risks identified in Stage 4 of the self-assessment being reported upwards.

Reporting risks from the bottom up serves two functions:

- Risks are identified by those closest to them in practice, making good use of management experience.
- Replication of risks from different sources alerts senior managers to their significance, but also facilitates the development of systems to consolidate and reduce them at the corporate level.

Each business unit and major function has its own risk and compliance control committee (RCC), which annually reviews key compliance risks and mitigating

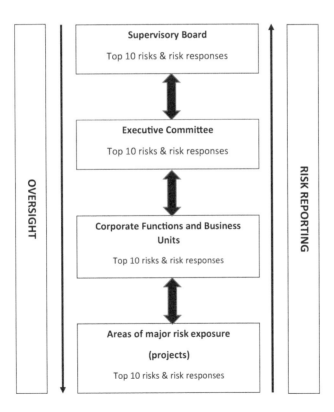

Figure 6.6 Risk management reporting

actions within their function and reports to the integrity and compliance committee on key compliance risks and breaches in relation to anti-bribery, fraud, data protection, and environmental and competition law. Additionally, within each business area, a management team member is appointed as the "compliance focal point" or "risk champion," taking responsibility for rolling out compliance projects and monitoring compliance with the code of conduct. Taking risk oversight down to the business level helps ensure that risks are monitored where they arise, and so resolving control weaknesses may be both easier and quicker.

Reporting extends right down to the level of the individual via the Speak Up! whistleblowing process, through which employees, business partners, and members of the public can raise matters of concern relating to compliance with the code of conduct. The system, introduced in 2009, is well embedded and enables confidential complaints to be made via a manager, the HR function, telephone, or the internet. Akzo Nobel states that in operating Speak Up! it applies a strict standard protocol that ensures anonymity, non-retaliation, and objectivity, as well as the right to be heard. In 2009, 198 violations of the code of conduct were reported, and these resulted in 66 employment contracts being terminated. In 2019, 164 Speak Up! reports were recorded, of which 82 were concluded to be unsubstantiated and 4 dismissals resulted from the reports.

In the same way that risk reporting starts with the individual and goes right up to the supervisory board, and ultimately the shareholders, via the annual report, the oversight of risk starts at the supervisory board level and runs back down to each member of the staff. The tools used for oversight include both internal audit and the formal committee structures outlined earlier, as well as systems which are used to reinforce and monitor both management and individual responsibility for internal controls. These different elements are illustrated in Table 6.5.

The committee structure in the left-hand column is headed up by the audit committee, made up entirely of non-executive directors (members of the supervisory board). The audit committee is responsible for independent monitoring of the quality and integrity of risk management and internal control practices across the whole organisation. This includes oversight of the internal audit function. The committee receives reports on compliance issues from the general counsel – the company's primary legal officer – the director of integrity and compliance, and the head of internal audits.

Responsibility for the day-to-day monitoring of new risks and compliance breaches rests with the integrity and compliance committee, which uses the RCC reports from the individual businesses and functions to identify material violations of laws, regulations, and internal controls and to provide updates to the executive level on material Speak Up! reports. The committee is also responsible for deciding appropriate disciplinary measures and recommending to the executive level what it believes are the actions necessary to improve controls. Since 2019, there have been monthly reports to the executive level on material breaches currently under investigation.

Table 6.5 Tools for Risk Oversight and Monitoring

Committees	Audit	Individual Oversight
• Audit committee • Compliance and control committee • Risk and control compliance committee	Internal audit – risk based	• Non- financial letters of representation • Performance evaluation

Risk-based internal audits that embrace both operational and functional parts of Akzo Nobel are central to the monitoring process. The audits provide a regular independent perspective on the adequacy and effectiveness of risk management and internal controls, and the head of internal audit reports twice yearly to the board of management and the audit committee. Internal audit findings form part of the input to the annual assessment of the quality of internal controls.

The role of individuals in risk management cannot be overstated, and mechanisms to ensure managerial and personal accountability are therefore fundamental to the ERM system. As Table 6.4 shows, accountability and compliance are managed using two tools which reflect levels of responsibility. The first is non-financial letters of representation, which are required to be completed annually by all members of management teams in both business units and major functions. The requirement to complete such letters has been in place since the ERM system was introduced in 2004. In signing the letter of representation, a manager confirms compliance with laws and internal rules. All exceptions must be reported, and the responses planned and documented. The results of the process are given to the executive level and form part of the annual compliance report that is submitted to both the audit committee and the supervisory board. The compliance report is also given to the external auditor.

Individual accountability is achieved through the requirement for all members of staff, as part of their annual performance review, to affirm their understanding of and compliance with the code of conduct and the associated directives. Familiarity with its content is achieved through mandatory e-learning packages for employees that cover the code of conduct, lifesaving rules, competition law, anti-bribery, fraud, and information security and privacy. As an integral part of the broader corporate directive framework, the code of conduct specifies codes of behaviour in relation to safety, sustainability, and integrity. Additionally, staff exposed to competition laws are separately required to confirm their compliance with such laws and regulations. The latest published figures show that in 2018 over 10,000 employees signed the competition law declaration.

In summary, the reporting and monitoring processes for risk and internal control combine to form a control loop that, in principle, should ensure that risk profiles are continuously revised and updated. As new risks are reported, changes to controls should be introduced, whilst the regularity with which staff are required to confirm their compliance with both internal and external rules and regulations helps to maintain a risk-based mindset organisation-wide.

Making Risk Management Enterprise-Wide

One of the biggest challenges for large organisations is how to make ERM truly enterprise-wide. The language sounds good, but putting it into practice is hugely challenging. In Akzo Nobel's case, evidence suggests that the shift from what was described in 2007 as a "mature" ERM system to the much broader-scoped system that exists today has been achieved through:

- Centralisation and standardisation of:
  a. Operational processes and support systems
  b. The core elements in the ERM system – culture and systems of risk identification, assessment, and monitoring
- Redefining enterprise risk boundaries
- Efforts to interlink and aggregate risks across the enterprise

Centralisation of operational and business support systems has been ongoing since a 2005 project to centralise and simplify the treasury function across Akzo Nobel, enabling advantage to be taken of natural hedges whilst also reducing the risk of poorly monitored individual risk taking. Since then, other support services have been centralised, including insurance, procurement, and the introduction of a single enterprise resource planning system for use across all businesses. This centralisation of services aids risk management in two ways:

1. Reducing the scope for managers behaving independently and potentially breaching codes of behaviour (e.g. in negotiating sales contracts)
2. Reducing the possibility of risk siloes that could go unnoticed at a senior management level

The standardisation of risk management tools complements the centralisation of business processes, and in a very direct way serves to extend ERM across the whole enterprise. As already seen, Akzo Nobel continuously emphasises the importance of the code of conduct as a way of ensuring that employees (and suppliers) have a common understanding of what risks are and are not tolerated and how they are to be identified and managed. This is complemented by the Directives Portal, which details codes of practice in relation to six core risk areas, and the Policy Portal (launched in 2019), which explains key policies and procedures relating to individual boundaries of responsibility. In combination, these three tools are aimed at generating a common enterprise perspective on risk and individual accountability, which is continuously reinforced via the use of simple, repeated messaging:

- "We must always stop work if conditions or behaviour are unsafe."
- "It's about doing the right thing."
- "Unidentified risks are a threat, identified risks are a managerial issue."

Standardised monitoring of breaches of the code is facilitated through the internal whistleblowing service Speak Up! which was launched in 2009. Serious breaches – those having a financial impact of greater than €0.5 million; involving senior management; or relating to competition law, export controls, or bribery – are dealt with by the corporate compliance committee. Other matters are decided by the RCC committees within the individual businesses or functions.

The risk workshops, which were central to the initial launch of ERM in Akzo Nobel back in 2004, remain a common feature of risk assessment and management across the whole enterprise, along with the resulting risk reporting systems. Standardisation of procedures is a tool for generating a common ERM perspective on risk.

Redefining enterprise risk boundaries is a development which has been most evident since 2007 when ERM was declared to be "mature." There are two interconnected strands to the redefining of boundaries. The first strand relates to who and what is deemed to be part of the enterprise in terms of the boundaries of compliance with codes of conduct and core principles. The second strand involves rethinking the meaning of enterprise risk in relation to who and what is impacted by the actions of Akzo Nobel.

In 2009 a key supplier management programme was developed, aimed at getting suppliers to sign up to agreed sustainability targets reflecting Akzo Nobel's own eco-efficient objectives. Within three years the supplier obligations had been extended beyond sustainability to require suppliers to sign the Akzo Nobel vendor policy embracing business integrity and compliance with Akzo Nobel's code of conduct. Since 2015, all new business partners have been required to sign a code of conduct verifying their compliance with the law and Akzo Nobel's core principles of safety, integrity, and sustainability or to apply their own equivalent business principles. Within Akzo Nobel, therefore, the term "enterprise" now includes Akzo Nobel itself and all associated joint ventures, etc., plus suppliers, distributors, and agents.

The broadening of the definition of enterprise and the resulting shifts in the definitions of enterprise risks appear to be a result of a growing sustainability agenda within Akzo Nobel, which requires a "cradle to grave" understanding of the environmental and social impact of an organisation's activities. The same year that the ERM programme was launched (2004) Akzo Nobel became a signatory of the UN Global Compact and a member of the World Business Council for Sustainable Development, composed of 170 multinational companies taking a leadership role in sustainable development. Simultaneously, Akzo

Nobel began to develop a formal review process to measure their CSR performance. In 2005 they issued their first CSR report and were listed in the top ten firms in the Dow Jones Sustainability Index, used as a global benchmark by investors.

CSR involves recognising that an enterprise's activities can create climate, environmental, safety, and human rights risks for the broader community. To be truly enterprise-wide, ERM must evolve to reflect these changes, and Akzo Nobel's 2008 adoption of IR was part of this evolution.

Evidence from academic research suggests a degree of complementarity between ERM and IR. The integrated thinking required for ERM, and associated understanding of how risks interact at the enterprise level, is very similar to that required for IR, and researchers found that companies simultaneously deploying both ERM and IR performed better in terms of value creation over the long term (Bertinetti G. and Gardenal G., 2016). The complementarity of IR and integrated thinking is similarly acknowledged in research conducted by Deloitte into reporting by major global companies, although they recognise the challenges faced in collecting consistent, comparable non-financial information (Deloitte, 2015).

Efforts to aggregate risks are implicit in integrated reporting, which recognises that financial returns to shareholders are interlinked with returns to other stakeholders. An illustrative example is the connection between profitability and the efficient use of resources. Increased efficiency will have a positive effect on profits but can also have a positive impact on sustainability through the preservation of scarce resources. In recent years Akzo Nobel has undertaken what they term an annual materiality assessment, which aims to recognise the interdependence between key risk categories and how these link back to strategic priorities. The risk categories illustrated in the 2017 annual report are:

- Sustainability
- General business risks
- Financial and regulatory

The report (p. 30) includes what Akzo Nobel calls an integrated materiality diagram, which shows the links and overlaps between these categories. To an outsider, the diagram is difficult to interpret, but it shows connections between, for example, economic performance and global growth rates and foreign exchange risks and the value of the company pension fund. Many connections are blurred – perhaps purposefully for reasons of confidentiality – but the general principle is important: ERM acknowledges the interdependence of financial and non-financial risks.

Is ERM Working?

Ultimately, this is a question that only Akzo Nobel's supervisory board and board of management can answer. The extent to which ERM is working can only be measured against the organisation's declared objectives within a chosen time frame. At a basic level, however, it is possible to evaluate the impact of the long-term ERM programme against Akzo Nobel's declared priorities – sustainability, integrity, and safety. Assuming that strategies are selected with the aim of preserving and building these priorities, ERM's success can be measured by comparing AN's performance in each of these three areas today with its performance pre-ERM. Value creation for shareholders is the other key measure of success, as COSO itself declares that ERM is a practical way to create and protect value.[4]

Table 6.6 summarises Akzo Nobel's performance in integrity, sustainability, safety, and finance over the period 2005–2019. The year 2005 is the chosen start date, as it allows twelve months from the formal launch of the ERM programme. The specific measures used to assess performance in each area represent key performance measures used internally within Akzo Nobel but are clearly open to debate. The figures should be interpreted with some caution, as it is difficult to assume that ERM is the sole explanation for the observed trends.

ERM's impact on integrity measures is clear. ERM was initiated in response to regulatory breaches in North America and Europe, and the high level of anti-trust provisions in the first decade of the twenty-first century reflects the financial penalties subsequently incurred. From 2010 onwards, the financial statements no longer include specific figures on anti-trust provisions, and by 2019 they are not mentioned at all. The number of Speak Up! complaints relating to integrity issues is another lower key indicator of the effectiveness of compliance measures. More specifically, the number of dismissals for breaches of the code of conduct has fallen dramatically post-2010, suggesting a high level of staff awareness and compliance. In summary, the figures suggest that both regulatory and internal compliance rules are being heeded, and in this respect ERM can be seen to be successful.

The figures on sustainability suggest a similar trend, although changes in measurements make it less certain. Both greenhouse gas emissions and provisions for environmental clean-up costs have fallen substantially over the time frame, and hazardous waste levels appear to also be falling. Clarity of the position on hazardous waste is muddled, however, by changes in the definition and measure, which make it appear that between 2010 and 2019 there was a progressive fall in the amount of hazardous waste. Figure (a) of 3.3 kg per ton shows a reduction in the 2010 level. In 2018, however, the figure for 2015 is restated as 10.74 (figure b), which then facilitates a further drop in levels through to 2019.

Taking an external perspective, from 2005 ff, Akzo Nobel stayed in the top ten of the Dow Jones Sustainability Index until 2017, recording a top three position for several years. Within Europe, they were first listed in the FTSE 4 Good in 2006 and continue to be viewed as an industry leader in the field by external benchmarking bodies such as Sustainalytics and Corporate Knights.

Table 6.6 Impact of ERM on Key Performance Measures

	Integrity		Sustainability			Safety		Shareholder Value	
	Anti-trust provisions €M	Speak Up! reports and dismissals	Hazardous waste (1)	Greenhouse gas emissions (2)	Provisions for environmental costs €M	People (3)	Process (4)	ROI % (5)	Share price € Year end (6)
2005	204	n/a	n/a Adopted 2008	n/a Adopted 2009	268	1.5	Tiers 2 and 3 used 2009ff Tier 1: 15	19.4	39.15
2010	158	Total and category breakdown: n/a Dismissals: 115	3.9	267	419	0.72	Tiers 2 and 3 (total): 22 Tier 1: 10	11.6	46.49
2015	n/a	Total: 224 Safety: 6 Integrity: 123 Treatment of staff: 95 Dismissals:52	3.3 (a) 10.74 (b)	221	305	0.32	Tiers 2 and 3 (total): 12 Tier 1: 0	14.0	61.68
2019	n/a	Total:164 Safety: 5 Integrity: 59 Sustainability: 100 Dismissals: 4	9.1	75	75	0.24	Tier 3: 970 Tier 2: 64 Tier 1: 3	14.1	90.69

KEY
1. Kg per ton of production
2. Kg of CO_2 per ton of production
3. Total reportable injury rate per 200,000 working hours
4. Tier 3 process event is of lowest severity; Tier 1 is most severe, involving a threat to life
5. ROI quoted is from Akzo Nobel's own calculation of adjusted operating income/invested capital
6. 30 March was selected as a random date, given that prices will vary throughout the year

Both the people and process safety records in Table 6.6 show substantial improvement. They suggest increased awareness of safety issues and compliance with good practice. The rise in the severe Tier 1 events in 2019 shows that continuous improvement is difficult, but the raw figures do not reflect the changing business size and profile.

The same story holds true for financial performance. Return on investment (ROI) levels are still much lower than in 2005, but the organisation itself is very different. It would be useful to compare ROI with other leading paint and coatings companies as an alternative measure of success. Share price has clearly risen, but again the raw figures may not take account of changes in the size of issued share capital. The annualised compound growth rate of 6.2% also ignores the impact of inflation, but it still suggests strong performance.

In summary, although other factors will clearly have played a part in the results shown in Table 6.6, it provides initial tentative evidence that ERM is working. Most significantly, it is working across a wide range of both financial and non-financial risks. There are clearly lessons to be learned by companies seeking to improve their risk management.

Notes

1 Details of the culture, training, and risk management systems will be discussed later in the chapter.
2 A more detailed discussion of this training process can be found in Maitland (2004).
3 A four-tier event classification is standard across many industries that deal with hazardous substances. A useful source of additional information and detail on risk management of processes can be found on the Centre for Chemical Process Safety website or in their publication *Guidelines for Hazard Evaluation Procedures*, 3rd edition. Wiley, New York, 2008.
4 A discussion of current evidence on the impact of ERM on company value is included in the final chapter of this book.

References

Akzo Nobel Annual Reports 2004–2019.

Bertinetti, G., & Gardenal, G. (2016) "Enterprise Risk Management and Integrated Reporting: Is There a Synergism?" In Mio. C. (eds.), *Integrated Reporting*. Palgrave Macmillan, London.

CCPS (2010) *Centre for Chemical Process Safety. Guidelines for Process Safety Metrics*. John Wiley & Sons, Hoboken, NJ.

Deloitte (2015) *Integrated Reporting as a Driver for Integrated Thinking?* Deloitte, Netherlands.

IRM (2012) *Risk Culture Under the Microscope, Guidance for Boards*. Institute for Risk Management, London.

Maitland, A. (2003) "How Do We Make Companies Do the Right Thing? We Delegate. Ethics: Trying to Impose Codes of Conduct from Above Is Doomed to Failure, Hans Wijers, Akzo Nobel Chairman Tells Alison Maitland." *Financial Times*, July 10, London.

Maitland, A. (2004) "How Do We Make Companies Do the Right Thing? We Delegate." In Wickham, P.A. (ed.), *Management Consulting: Delivering an Effective Project*. 2nd edition. FT Prentice Hall.

Protiviti (2007) *Enterprise Risk Management in Practice. Profiles of Companies Building Effective ERM Programs.* Downloadable from: www.protiviti.com/sites/default/files/japan/insights/erm_in_practice_e_0.pdf.

Reuters (2008) *Akzo Nobel Completes ICI Takeover.* Downloadable from: https://uk.reuters.com/article/uk-ici/akzo-nobel-completes-ici-takeover-idUKWEB129220080102.

Useful Web Links

The Akzo Nobel code of conduct can be found https://www.akzonobel.com/en/about-us/governance-/policies---procedures/code-of-conduct.

The Akzo Nobel sustainability factsheet can be found by typing this phrase into Google or any similar internet search engine.

7   Risk Management in Retail

Tesco PLC (2004–2019)

Aim

The aim of this chapter is to illustrate how a very specific approach to risk management in one of the world's largest retailers failed to halt a crisis that caused major reputational damage and how the company, and the risk management function, has responded and recovered from the crisis. The case study, covering the period 2004–2019, shows that risk management practice is closely linked to corporate strategy and culture, which can themselves be sources of risk.

The last fifteen years have been something of a roller coaster for Tesco, with a decade of rapid growth, followed by an accounting scandal that resulted in the group reporting losses of £6.5 billion in 2015. The scandal influenced thinking about risk management, and so the case study is split into two time frames: 2004–2014 and 2015–2020. Post-2015 was a period of retrenchment led by a new senior management team that includes a declared commitment to start building a roadmap for enterprise risk management (ERM). The two time frames illustrate the significance of the culture at the top as a driver of behaviour and its impact on risk exposure.

After a brief historical background on Tesco, the case study will:

- Detail the strategy, culture, and approach to risk management before the accounting scandal of 2014
- Discuss the origins of the scandal in the context of internal control and risk management systems at the time
- Summarise the immediate consequences and Tesco's response to the crisis
- Detail the strategy, culture, and approach to risk management post-2014
- Summarise the lessons to be learned from the case

Tesco: Background and Key Facts

Tesco was founded by Jack Cohen, who started out as an East End market trader. After visiting the United States, Cohen decided to introduce the self-service supermarket approach to food retailing, and the first Tesco branch in this style was opened in 1947.

DOI: 10.4324/9781315208336-7

The early 1970s saw Tesco re-brand itself as an "aspirational" mass retailer and saw a deal between Tesco and Esso, which by 1991 made them the country's largest independent petrol retailer. In the 1980s Tesco rationalised and reformatted its distribution systems, launched its first "out-of-town" large stores, and began introducing its own product lines to compete against traditionally branded products.

By the 1990s Tesco had 371 stores in England, Scotland, and Wales, and its further expansion was through the introduction of the Tesco Metro format of mid-sized stores (around 1,100 m²). By 1995 Tesco was ranked the number-one food retailer in the UK, and the same year it became the first UK retailer to introduce a loyalty card. The "Clubcard" has since proved a valuable source of information on customer spending patterns, as well as a useful marketing tool.

The 1990s also marked the start of Tesco's international expansion, with investments in France, Poland, Slovakia, and the Czech Republic. Eastern European investments paid off relatively quickly and were followed by moves into Southeast Asia through acquisitions and joint ventures in South Korea, Thailand, Malaysia, Taiwan, Japan, and China. By early 2004, at the start of this case, Tesco's retail selling space outside the UK was close to that of the home market, although sales and profit per square metre remained lower.

Tesco operates a wide range of store sizes from small one-stop shops to out-of-town hypermarkets. Standard large supermarkets, Tesco Superstores, account for the bulk of the company's UK floorspace with an average size of 2,900 m². Its main UK competitors are J. Sainsbury, Morrissons, Asda, Aldi, and Lidl. Its shares are listed on the London and Euronext stock markets.

Risk Management in Tesco: Phase 1 (2004–2014)

To understand how Tesco ended up facing a major scandal that seriously damaged both its finances and its reputation, we need to look at the mindset and organisational structures in the years leading up to 2014.

The four key features of management strategy and style in Tesco over this decade were:

- **Aggressive growth** involving international expansion and a broadening of UK business interests (i.e. moves into non-grocery operations)
- **Performance-based control** structured around the "steering wheel" (a form of balanced scorecard) in which targets were king and accountability was expressed in terms of performance targets
- **A values-driven culture** dominated at lower levels of the organisation by "Tesco Values" as the determinant of staff behaviour and the key tool for reducing risk
- **High-profile leadership** by chief executive officers (CEOs) who led with "cast iron fists" and oversaw an authoritative system that has been said to have engendered "a culture of fear from head office to shop floor" (Neville, 2014)

Aggressive Growth Strategy

International growth was high on the strategic agenda, and Sir Terry Leahy, who was appointed CEO in 1997, was a big supporter of this strategy. The timeline shown in Table 7.1 shows the new businesses purchased or launched by Tesco during the era of Leahy's reign.

The table clearly reveals both an internationalisation of grocery operations and a shift into non-food sectors in Tesco's core UK market. Nonetheless, retailing remained the core business segment, facilitating a relatively simple internal control system, focused on management of the five key processes of:

- Buying products from suppliers
- Sending them to a distribution centre
- Transferring goods from the distribution centre to the stores
- Taking cash
- Banking the receipts

In essence, operational issues dominated thinking. The simple business format was complemented by a simple triangular organisational structure, with only five levels in the management hierarchy. The top two grades encompassed just 200 people, out of half a million global employees. This flat structure offered

Table 7.1 Purchases and New Business Launches

Date	Sector	Type of Transaction
1997	Financial	Launch of Tesco Personal Finance (now Tesco Bank)
1998	International food retail	Purchase of stake in Lotus store chain in Thailand
1999	International retail	Partnership with Samsung to manage Homeplus stores in South Korea
2004	International food retail	Purchase of a share of Chinese-owned hypermarket chain
2006	UK online non-food retail	Launch of Tesco Direct
2007	International food retail	Launch of Fresh and Easy chain in the United States
2008	UK non-food retail	Purchase of Dobbie's garden centres
	Financial	Buyout of Royal Bank of Scotland's share of Tesco Personal Finance
	International food retail	Opening of the first wholly owned Tesco store in China
2011	UK non-food retail	Purchase of Blinkbox video streaming
	International online sales	Launch of virtual Homeplus stores in South Korea
2012	UK online non-food retail	Purchase of Mobcast digital book platform and We7 music streaming
		Merger of digital video, book, and music streaming into Blinkbox Entertainment
2013	UK non-food retail	Purchase of Giraffe (UK) restaurants
		Purchase of Harris & Hoole Cafes

good opportunities for staff to progress through the hierarchy and helped with staff retention. Sir Terence Leahy's profile is evidence of this.[1]

The flat hierarchical structure combined with relatively simple processes made it easier to identify accountability for risk, defined in terms of failure to meet performance targets. Targets were defined in the steering wheel, introduced by Leahy himself in 2005.

Performance-Based Control

The steering wheel – Tesco's version of a balanced scorecard – was used for performance measurement and management against targets laid down in the group's five-year rolling plan and lay at the centre of the performance-based control system. The 2012 annual report highlights how the steering wheel helped monitor delivery of group strategy, and the targets were also used to determine short-term bonus payments to members of the board.

The 2012 annual report identifies performance risk as a principal risk and states: "All business units have stretching targets based on the Steering Wheel balanced scorecard system; performance against budgets and KPIs are monitored continually and reported regularly to the Board" (2012, Annual Report p. 40).

The steering wheel used by Tesco is reproduced in Figure 7.1. Its composition in terms of both categories and targets changed little over its life until its abandonment in 2014. The one key change was the addition of the fifth dimension of community in 2006.

The steering wheel provided a tool for both setting and monitoring performance at all levels within Tesco. In the text of annual reports, there is regular reference to key risks and the way that the steering wheel is used to control these risks via monitoring of performance outcomes.

The five-year plan established targets for the overall group, reflecting the core long-term aim of "creating value for customers to earn their lifetime loyalty." More specific UK and international strategies were then used to generate plans and performance targets for each of the separate geographic and business segments. At all levels of Tesco – from group, through the business segments, national and regional operations, right down to the individual stores – targets were also expressed in terms of the five perspectives of the steering wheel. At the store level, the steering wheel was linked to the objectives of individual members of staff so that group-level strategies connected back to day-to-day work.

The five separate perspectives of customers, operations, people, community, and finance in the steering wheel were aimed at ensuring Tesco put "appropriate balance" into the inevitable trade-offs between the stakeholders. The principle was that shareholders benefited from a balanced approach because the combination of operational efficiency and customer care together improved sales, profits, and investor returns. Company-wide, it seemed to be accepted

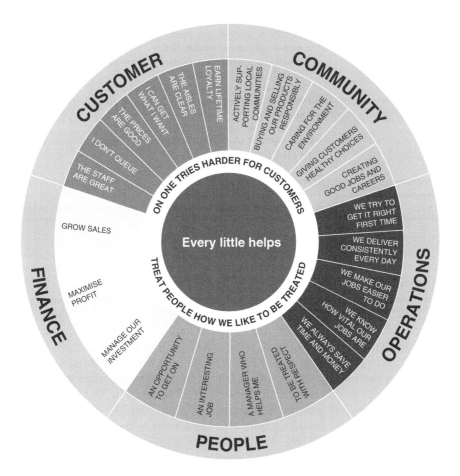

Figure 7.1 Tesco steering wheel

that if the business was performing well in the eyes of the customer, then it would also be performing well for other stakeholders. As one interviewee phrased it: "the biggest barometer we've got is our customers . . . how can we earn their lifetime loyalty?"

The emphasis on customers came from Sir Terry Leahy, who believed that customer needs take priority over worrying about the competition. This view matches the thinking of Kenichi Ohmae, a former partner in McKinsey & Company and a man widely described as "Mr Strategy." Ohmae argues that "before you test yourself against the competition, strategy takes shape in the determination to create value for customers" (Ohmae, 1988).

The idea that an improved financial performance is dependent upon good management of customers, operations, and people mirrors the ideas of Kaplan

Table 7.2 Key Performance Indicators by Steering Wheel Segment

Finance	• **Growth in underlying profit before tax**
	• **Return on capital employed**
	• **Growth in underlying diluted earnings per share**
	• **Total shareholder returns**
Customer	• **Doing the "right thing" for customers**
Community	• **Percentage of pre-tax profit donated to charities/good causes**
	• **Positive scores from supplier surveys**
	• **Over 70% of suppliers should regard themselves as being treated respectfully by Tesco**
	• **Cut CO_2 emissions by 5% per year**
Operations	*Not available*
People	• **Target retention rate for staff**
	• **Percentage of staff being trained up for their next role**

and Norton (Kaplan and Norton, 1992), who first promoted the balanced scorecard. The academic argument is that better understanding of the inter-relationships between the different scorecard perspectives can help managers to be forward looking, rather than backward looking, in their decision making. Some hold the view that increased customer loyalty is the single most important driver of long-term financial performance (Norreklit, 2000).

Key performance indicators (KPIs) were set for each of the steering wheel segments, but unsurprisingly, only a few of these were published externally. A summary of those known to be in use in 2012 is shown in Table 7.2.

The frequency of monitoring against targets was variable. Trading figures were (and still are) reviewed both daily and weekly and individual business performance quarterly. The steering wheel target KPIs for the group were also reviewed quarterly. The result was that both revenue and capital spending budgets were continually revised in response to changing market conditions.

When KPIs were not on track, systems in place at every level of the organisation facilitated investigation into why and helped to plan corrective action. Quarterly performance reports were submitted to the board of directors and a summary report also sent to the group's top 200 managers for dissemination to staff. The result was an internally focused organisation, with a culture that prioritised performance.

Governance

The UK Corporate Governance Code (FRC, 2010, p. 1) describes the purpose of corporate governance as being "to facilitate effective, entrepreneurial and prudent management that can deliver the long-term success of the company." Directors are responsible for determining the nature and extent of the significant risks the company is willing to take in achieving its strategic objectives and for overseeing the maintenance of "sound risk management and internal control systems."

The governance structure through which the Tesco group was directed and controlled pre-2011, as explained by an interviewee, is illustrated in Figure 7.2. Note that the steering wheel sits at its heart, and the overall system was designed to serve the long-term performance aims defined in the wheel.

The primary lines of accountability show the board of directors overseeing the work of the executive committee and boards of the various national subsidiaries, who in turn oversee the management teams in each country. The retail council, made up of around forty people, was responsible for aggregating all the key decisions taken by the board and the associated committees and cascading that information down through the business. By using the retail council as the single conduit for core decisions, the risk of inconsistent messages is avoided.

Several committees at both board level and below, each had a specific remit. The board of directors met nine times a year. The executive committee[2] met weekly and held responsibility for implementing group strategy and policy and monitoring performance and compliance.

Board-level strategic and regulatory committees dealt with issues which are fundamental to strategic success and the protection of Tesco's reputation. The committees met at least quarterly, and members were a combination of executive directors and senior management.

Below the board level, operational committees implemented the group's strategies and regulatory commitments at the country level. The committee titles offer insights into areas where it was felt that risks needed careful management, namely trading, people, property, and information technology (IT).

The governance structures covering international operations mirrored those covering the core UK market. This approach has two potential merits. Firstly, it ensures consistency across the whole group, and secondly it facilitates the movement of staff across different geographic areas (e.g. from Asia to Europe or vice versa) because the systems are common. In this way the valuable asset of senior staff can be utilised to maximum effect.

Overall, the committee structures and reporting systems within Tesco over this period were similar to those in other major companies and fully compliant with the UK's Combined Code. Strategies were clearly defined, and performance targets specified, but governance structures are also closely intertwined with the tools used to control the risks of poor performance.[3] It was in the operation of its risk management that Tesco differed markedly from other organisations.

Linking Risk and Performance Management

CIMA's Official Terminology (CIMA, 2005, p. 20) defines performance measurement as "the process of assessing the proficiency with which a reporting entity succeeds . . . in achieving its objectives." The same terminology (CIMA, 2005, p. 53) defines risk management as the "process of understanding and managing the risks that the entity is inevitably subject to in attempting to achieve its corporate objectives."

It would therefore seem that it is difficult, if not impossible, to talk about risk management without simultaneously talking about performance management – the two go hand in hand. This integration of risk and performance thinking is straightforward in theory but not so easy to implement in practice. Nonetheless, it formed the blueprint for Tesco's approach to risk management. In the words of one interviewee:

> One of the reasons we are a successful company is because of risk management- people do it without actually knowing they are doing it, it's part of their accountabilities. They are held to account. We monitor things on such a micro level.

The view was expressed that

> having a risk management function probably gets in the way of actually managing the risks because people are thinking about the risks as opposed to thinking about the customer, so all we are worried about is serving the customer and what can go wrong with that. . . . This is about culture and terminology . . . we don't want risk management to get in the way of what is a successful company, but we need to get risk management to dovetail into what we are trying to do.

The approach that Tesco used to achieve this dovetailing was a system overseen by internal audits that focused on process management and placed a strong emphasis on performance that was managed and enforced through cultural norms. As we will see, the focus was primarily internal, and the cultural pressures created problems for staff, particularly at the senior level.

Roles and Responsibilities for Risk

At the heart of the risk management system is the specification of roles and responsibilities for risk throughout the group. There were three distinct levels of responsibility – the board of directors and senior management, the internal audit function, and line management and other staff. We will look at each of these in turn.

THE BOARD OF DIRECTORS AND SENIOR MANAGEMENT

The board of directors held (and continues to hold) overall responsibility for risk management and internal control and their role was three-fold:

- **Setting the Group's Risk Appetite**
  Risk appetite is determined by the directors' views about market and shareholder requirements, global economic conditions, and the existing

business mix. Balancing risks and opportunities, the aim is to maintain internal controls that accurately reflect the risk appetite.

- **Identifying the Key Risks Facing the Group**

  Key risks are those which threaten core strategies. The key risk register, maintained by internal audits, is built up and revised through regular discussion between members of the board of directors, the executive committee, and other senior managers. In addition, one annual board meeting was dedicated to a review of strategic risks. The risk register contains information on the nature of the risk(s), as well as their potential impact and likelihood, and it is regularly updated through feedback from multiple sources, including the steering wheel. All risks are allocated a named "owner," and the controls and procedures used to mitigate them are identified.

  Key risks detailed in the annual reports from 2004 to 2014 cover several categories:

  - Strategy and finance
  - Reputation, operations, and people
  - Regulation and the external environment
  - Financial services/Tesco Bank
  - Corporate social responsibility (CSR)

- Since 2007 the reports have also included information on the type of risks (which have evolved over time) and how they are managed. Process risk management was seen as vital: "The Tesco philosophy is 'the customer is king': without the customer we don't exist. Every part of the process is customer oriented. . . . What that means is that the things that we would be looking for is . . . we would be watching the service-supply chain."

  Examples of important processes include:

  The acquisition and development of new sites for stores, either at home or overseas.

  Product safety from suppliers through to on the shelf in stores.

  IT systems used for both procurement, delivery, and sales (e.g. logistics planning and barcode scanning).

  Problems across any of these processes could affect the ability to trade, and therefore represent key risks.

- **Overseeing the group's risk and internal control system**

  The board is responsible for the overall system of internal control and for reviewing its effectiveness. Group-wide processes establish the risks and responsibilities assigned to each level of management and the controls to be implemented and monitored. The control system seeks to mitigate against the risk of not achieving objectives, rather than eliminate the risk of failure, and it is acknowledged that some risks are outside the board's control.

  The effectiveness of the internal control systems is reviewed annually by the audit committee, meeting quarterly and reporting directly to the board. The audit committee can also be more proactive in their management of risks and will sometimes directly inspect operations to gain an on-site view of internal control. The committee, chaired by a non-executive director, receives regular reports from the head of internal audits on internal control effectiveness and also has the power to take action to call senior line managers to account if it believes they are failing in their risk management duties.

Two other senior management committees also play an important role in monitoring the exposure to risk and the effectiveness of internal controls. Regulatory risk is the responsibility of the compliance committee, meeting four times a year, with its membership made up of two executives, the company secretary, and three senior managers. This committee also oversees the work of specialist functions such as trading law and the technical and company secretariat, which provides assurance and advice on health and safety and regulatory social and environmental issues. The CSR committee, also meets quarterly, with its membership drawn from senior management across the group, together with the company secretary. Financial risks and the treasury function are managed by the finance committee, which also sets the treasury limits.

INTERNAL AUDIT

The internal audit function, accountable to the audit committee, is independent of business operations, and its remit is to evaluate and monitor the internal control and risk management processes across the entire group. The staff see their role as facilitators, engaged in assuring the board that risks are adequately identified and controlled in line with the board's declared risk appetite.

Internal audit plans are risk based and largely focused on the core processes that influence strategic success. For each audit, all the potential risks of the chosen process are identified, together with information on what controls are in place to mitigate those risks. Auditors are then able to test control effectiveness.

Certain issues are audited automatically (e.g. new ventures, third-party risks) in an approach that fits with the work of Selim and McNamee (1999), who found that the assets, projects, and processes deemed key to strategic objectives are the things that drive the audit system. Other areas chosen for investigation are dictated by managerial experience and intuition – "at the end of the day it is people's experience and how you feel" (head of internal audit). This matches research by Helliar et al. (2002), who found that judgments on what to audit were commonly based on experience rather than probabilistic measures of risk.

Around 25% of activities and processes are audited each year, and the resulting reports clearly specify any corrective steps to be taken and who is responsible. Reports get sent to the relevant responsible board member, and the internal audit is commonly returned to check that actions have been taken as required. Line management remuneration, and sometimes survival, is dependent upon them doing what is requested.

The detail of how the internal audit works is best understood via a more detailed example. As already noted, the effective selection, development, and management of property assets is central to Tesco's success as a retailer and is

TESCO GOVERNANCE MODEL

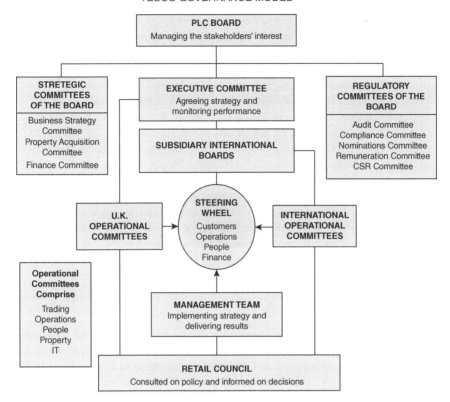

Figure 7.2 Governance model

Source: Internal documentation provided by an interviewee

seen as a way of creating long-term shareholder value. The process of site selection is therefore a source of risk that warrants attention from internal audit. The stages of the audit of a site acquisition in a central European country are detailed in Box 7.1.

Box 7.1: Internal Audit of Overseas Site Acquisition

"An auditor will pick up an area, site acquisition in X, for example. We have a property specialist put together the typical risks that you would get in a property process, so he would put together an overall risk thing, the auditor will go and have a talk to senior management and to the people involved in the process and will then adjust the risk model to reflect the risks specific to that country's business, anything that could go wrong. He then goes along to the business and literally starts working through.

First of all tell me what you do and how you do it, then show me what you do and show me how you do it and he'll actually look at the documents and everything else. So he would say in the case of 'failure to identify all potential sites of interest on the market' – so how do you ensure that you do identify all of the potential sites on the market? And they will say 'oh well we do a strategy review of this, we do this, we do . . . so on and so forth. You'll then be talking to some of the property specialists in Hungary who are outside of the business and saying 'Right, is there anything the company isn't doing?' The auditor can then report back on whether he thinks it is adequately controlled or not. A recommendation then comes out, which it is the responsibility of the line manager to implement.

If a risk is deemed significant enough, it may appear on the key risk register, and is reported to the Board as well as the Audit Committee."

Source: Interview with a member of an internal audit

Staff in internal audit come from a mix of backgrounds, some are Chartered Institute of Management Accountants (CIMA), Association of Chartered Certified Accountants or Institute of Chartered Accountants in England and Wales qualified, and others hold Institute of Internal Auditors qualifications. The churn rate within the department is quite high, and this is seen as beneficial because when staff move into other areas of the business, they take an awareness of risk management with them.

The head of internal audit reports directly to the head of the audit committee (a non-executive director) and also attends all the committee's meetings. In addition, he or she reports to an executive manager – the finance and strategy director – on a day-to-day basis.

LINE MANAGEMENT AND OTHER STAFF

International CEOs and the local boards maintain their own risk registers and carry responsibility for assessing their own control systems. In addition, the local CEOs/business heads are required to sign annual statements of assurance of compliance with the board's governance policies. The same process also applies to the key central functions (e.g. HR and finance).

In some, but not all, joint ventures (e.g. Tesco Personal Finance pre-2008) the board's assurance is dependent upon the internal control systems of the partner and their respective obligations relating to control effectiveness.

At a national level, several key groups carry significant responsibility for risk management, particularly the operational committees – trading, operations, people, property, and IT – each with a remit to manage a specific area of risk.

Performance against steering wheel targets and the findings of internal audit reviews are reported to these committees, although the ultimate responsibility for controlling the relevant risks rests with line management.

At the lower levels, every store has a steering wheel, and risk is defined in terms of not hitting the steering wheel targets. When performance is below expectations, the wheel is marked red, and when asked about the extent of risk awareness amongst store staff, the following exchange with one interviewee was very revealing:

INTERVIEWEE: "I don't think the word risk there is one. I think how far is there an awareness of things possibly going wrong, and then how do they control things going wrong."

RESEARCHER: "And that extends to the shelf fillers?"

INTERVIEWEE: "Yes it does, yes, even if it's just that they know that they don't meet the five o'clock clear up time or something."

This reaffirms the earlier observation that risk management was *redefined as performance management* in Tesco and held to be the responsibility of all staff, reflecting the organisation's commitment to a performance-based control system.

Risk Assessment, Communication, and Monitoring

This work is done by line management, using a risk and materiality matrix which classifies risks as green, amber, or red dependent upon a combination of likelihood and consequences. The categorisation is based upon experience and "gut feeling" rather than detailed risk modelling but provides a basis for clarifying which risks warrant greater or lesser monitoring. For example, in terms of financial control, the finance manager may identify the risks faced as including:

- Cash management
- Investment appraisal
- Balance sheet control
- Financial information systems
- Skill risks (shortage of key people)
- Managing "the City" (investors)
- Compliance with accounting standards
- Financing (e.g. illiquidity)
- Refinancing
- Interest rates
- Foreign exchange
- Counterparty credit
- Tax

All of these risks are assigned owners, and all are classed as green, amber, or red. Red implies the risk is a glaring problem. Amber means "we aren't comfortable with where we are at on the risk scale but we do have a plan to tackle it. Green is that we are comfortable with the risk that we are taking." The risk owner is required to take action to bring the risk level down to green wherever possible, and advice on how to do this will be provided by internal audit.

The direct involvement of operational managers in the identification of risks helps to broaden the understanding of risk across the whole group and fits with De Haas and Kleingeld's (1999) suggestion that participation is vital to the effectiveness of a control system.

The risk registers, allocation of risk ownership, and action plans all form important parts of the risk management process, but ultimately risks are only managed if the process is continuous, and this requires that the risks and action plans are the subject of regular review. The frequency of monitoring reflects the level of significance of the risk.

Figure 7.3 portrays the lines of communication used within Tesco PLC.[4] The arrows indicate the direction of the information flow, with upward arrows showing reporting lines, whilst downward arrows show the communication of objectives or priorities. Risk issues are reported to the specialist monitoring committees and internal audit. Internal audit reports to the audit committee, the members of which may also initiate internal audit investigations or take senior managers to task if there are signs of inadequate controls over risk or if performance targets are missed. If, for example, a national CEO

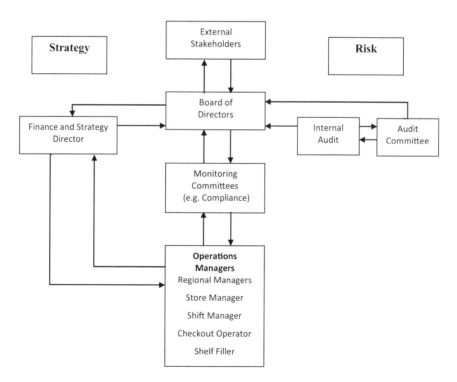

Figure 7.3 Lines of communication in Tesco

has been a bit slower in managing risk than the audit committee considers desirable, they may be flown over for a meeting to explain what is happening and why. Such meetings were described by an interviewee as "a bit like being in the headmaster's study," suggesting a level of fear and trepidation of possible punishment. Jobs could be lost, and valuable careers were potentially on the line.

The organisational structure, with only five grades of staff top to bottom, served to assist the risk communication and monitoring process. Formal lines of communication were augmented by informal systems. For example, one interviewee observed that "many years ago we decided on a strategy of trying to improve the controls of the business by getting as many people as we could [who] trained through audit [to] spread the message about risk."

The system described here is one in which all risks are owned and exposure is clear under the traffic light system. Consequently, because the risk reporting lines go right through from line management up to the board of directors, no business or individual escapes scrutiny. Whilst such a system sounds good in theory, how the scrutiny is exercised and consequently influences people's behaviour is also critical. Organisational culture is central to this issue.

A Value-Driven Culture

The five-tier structure meant that the link between the national sales/profit results could easily be traced down through regions and into single stores, facilitating tight performance monitoring. Throughout Tesco, converting the fear that might be induced by performance monitoring into genuine staff commitment to the steering wheel targets was achieved in two ways. The first was by training staff in "Tesco Values," representing the group's culture and goals. The values are summarised as:

- **No one tries harder for customers**

    - Understand customers
    - Be first to meet their needs
    - Act responsibly for our communities

and

- **We treat people how we like to be treated**

    - Work as a team
    - Trust and respect each other
    - Listen, support, and say thank you
    - Share knowledge and experience

    . . . so we can enjoy our work

The simple language made the messages both easy to understand and memorable. They are also non-contentious, encouraging compliance.

Tesco Values and the accompanying code of conduct set the terms for a code of behaviour towards customers, colleagues, and suppliers that, when followed, would reduce reputational risk, discourage fraud, and encourage regulatory compliance. Fraud and theft risks were further managed using standard accounting and access controls.

The second way of nurturing staff commitment to targets was via schemes that rewarded them according to the financial performance of the group. The schemes operated at all levels, although the incentives were higher for senior management.

- At the executive director level – direct links between remuneration and personal and group performance targets (e.g. the executive bonus scheme offered both long- and short-term bonuses of cash/share options linked to the achievement of targets on Earnings Per Share (EPS) growth, return on capital employed (ROCE) growth, total shareholder return, and other specific, but confidential, strategic goals).
- For all employees – a profit-sharing scheme for all staff with more than one year's service. The profit share is calculated pro rata to base salary, up to a maximum £3,000 annual tax-free limit. Staff may also opt into a savings-related share option scheme and a partnership share plan.[5]

Directly linking staff behaviour (Tesco Values) and the achievement of performance targets with the remuneration system "allows the business to be operated with due regard for all stakeholders" (head of international audit).

Serving stakeholder interests, however, does not necessarily mean that risks are being well managed. Whilst behavioural soundbites such as "every little helps" were widely recognised, the monitoring of compliance with the code of conduct appears to have been limited. The values remained unchanged for over a decade, and this may also have served to diminish their impact.

A whistleblowing service – Protector Line – was established in 2003, which should have helped to encourage ethical behaviour, but staff discussion forums suggest that it was poorly publicised and awareness of it very limited. The service dealt with issues of commercial security, bribery/fraud, and breaches of trading law. Personnel issues were primarily resolved by line management or human resources (HR) if a grievance process is instigated. Evidence from online forums suggests that some whistle blowers have expressed a lack of confidence in Protector Line's early effectiveness in protecting confidentiality and enforcing change. Usage of the line increased over time, however, suggesting some improvement, with 1,700 calls reported in 2009; in 2011 an email contact system was added to further improve access.

In summary, most Tesco staff interacted with risk management via efforts to do the right thing in terms of the customer, with their work monitored through in-store steering wheels. The informal and strongly promoted Tesco Values encouraged a customer-focused mindset, but the tight performance monitoring also had other effects. As already noted, a performance-based control system reinforced by a values-driven culture were key elements of Tesco's approach to management.

High-Profile Leadership: A Culture of Fear

The hierarchical system and continuous performance monitoring served to engender a culture of fear and machismo. A former employee based at Tesco's HQ in Cheshunt has been quoted as saying

> Food retailers are run through a combination of fear and motivation. . . . Staff at night fear the 6am or 7am walk with the store manager . . . the store manager will fear the regional director and they would fear head office. Power matters.
>
> (Neville, 2014)

Many employees may make similar comments about their workplace, but Terry Leahy was well known for exercising his power and upbraiding staff in front of colleagues. When business is good, targets are achievable and a performance-focused culture is easier to tolerate, but for Tesco, when the markets conditions got tough, the hard-line pressure to hit targets created a huge problem.

Managers who face a serious dressing down, miss bonuses, or lose their job if targets are not hit will respond in ways to protect themselves, especially if they have some discretion over the figures they report. From around 2010 onwards, the strategy of focusing on customers was failing to generate the desired profitability for Tesco, and huge investments in expansion both at home and overseas added to costs. Although sales almost doubled from £30.8 billion in 2004 to £64.1 billion in 2014, the key financial KPIs of operating margin and ROCE were falling. ROCE dropped from 19% to just 10% over the period of Sir Terry Leahy's tenure as CEO (Vincent, 2017), and pressure on managers was mounting. Expansion was eating up capital, causing debt to rise, and core shareholder returns were falling.

The internal control system within Tesco at the time was so focused on internal performance monitoring, and the fear of failure so embedded, that the result was a crisis.

Origins of the Scandal

Throughout the first decade of the new millennium, the emphasis on customer care served the business well. Tesco's share of the UK grocery market expanded from 22.6% in 1997, when Leahy took on the CEO role, to a peak of 30.6% in 2012, before falling to a ten-year low in early 2015. At the same time, the market capitalisation of Tesco in 2004, the year before the steering wheel was introduced, was £19.77 billion, and by 2014 it equalled £27 billion before the effects of the accounting scandal hit.

Terry Leahy retired as CEO in March 2011, but his replacement, Philip Clarke, adopted a very similar management style. Like Leahy, Clarke was a Tesco "lifer" with thirty-six years of service with the company; he had begun work as a shelf stacker and was steeped in the corporate culture. Clarke continued to promote expansion into the non-grocery sector, overseeing the purchase of the online video streaming service Blinkbox in 2011 and resisting pressure from analysts to close the loss-making US operation Fresh and Easy. In an effort to reinvigorate the UK core of the business and respond to the growth of the discount chains Aldi and Lidl, Clarke initiated a £500 million price cutting campaign in late 2011, but this did not stop Tesco from being forced to announce in January 2012 its first profit warning in twenty years. The share price fell by 16% in a single day.

A £1 billion turnaround plan in 2012 failed to stem the decline in performance, and in 2013 Tesco declared its first ever fall in annual profits, with huge write-downs, including a £1 billion charge caused by the decision to quit the US market. By early 2014, the group faced its lowest share (28.7%) of the UK market for a decade, and further price cutting efforts did not halt continued falls in the share price. In April 2014, just days before the annual results were announced, Tesco's long-serving finance director Laurie McIlwee resigned, and the subsequent results revealed a further 7% drop in profits. Three months later, following yet another profit warning, Clarke himself resigned, although he stayed in his post until his replacement took over in September 2014.

In appointing the new CEO, Tesco broke with its ninety-five-year practice of appointing from within and chose Dave Lewis from Unilever. At Unilever Lewis had gained a strong reputation for his "turnaround" skills within the group's toiletries division, and although he lacked retailing experience, analysts saw him as a man who could "win price wars and perhaps that is the big issue now facing Tesco" (Rankin, 2014). He faced a massive task, made bigger just weeks later by a huge slump in shares and a big reputational hit caused by accounting errors that forced the admission that the previous year's profits had been overstated. A crisis was unfolding as the share price fell 12% in one day, wiping £2 billion of the value of Tesco.

The Legacy Paper

Tesco's stock market announcement that the previous year's profits had been overstated was triggered by what has become known as the "legacy paper," first seen by Dave Lewis on 19 September 2014 and authored by a whistle blower in the finance department. Frustrated at not getting a response when he first drew attention to the irregularities when Philip Clarke was still the CEO, the whistle blower, a senior accountant, ultimately reported the problem to the group's legal officer.

The legacy paper claimed that commercial income was being pulled forward from future periods in order to enable Tesco to hit internal profit targets. The challenges of accounting for commercial income had already been raised within the finance department some years earlier. In 2012, Laurie McIlwee emailed staff warning them of weaknesses in the company's financial controls after problems in its Polish business. The message to finance staff was clear: "You should be in no doubt as to the seriousness [of] misdeclarations" and said that accounting for profits early was forbidden "where [the profits] cannot be justified" (Ahmed, 2015).

The whistle blower in 2014 was clearly responding to McIlwee's earlier advice and took the view that the practice was in breach of existing accounting standards. The *Financial Times* (Croft, 2017) reported that several senior staff had resigned because they "felt so compromised" by the practice. A senior project manager had turned down a promotion and left Tesco because of his concerns, claiming at his exit interview that others were "too scared" to speak out for fear of losing their jobs, and accounting staff were "in tears" about being asked to misreport profits and breach professional accounting guidelines (Croft, 2017). The recognition of commercial income (i.e. the point at which it is reported as income in the accounts) is both problematic and judgmental for the retail sector, as explained in Box 7.2.

Box 7.2: Accounting for Commercial Income in the Retail Sector

Commercial income is the term used to describe the income received by large retailers from the huge multinationals that supply many of their products. In the UK, this income is estimated to be worth around £5 billion per year to the top four supermarkets.

In competitive markets such as the UK, suppliers and brands want to occupy the premium spaces on supermarket shelves and therefore pay retailers such as Tesco to list their products. The payments may be for shelf space and location but will commonly linked to "rebates," which are incentive payments made to the retailer if specific sales volumes are achieved or exceeded.

For example, the Kellogg Company may offer Tesco a 2% rebate on its purchases of breakfast cereals if sales exceed X million cartons. If Tesco is seeing its market share falling, however, then it faces the risk of not selling enough Kellogg cereal to hit the target and earn the rebate.

Standard practice midyear is for Tesco's central finance department to email individual managers asking them to estimate the rebates expected from suppliers in respect of the half-year's trading. They do not have to provide evidence to support their estimates, and if the rebates are linked to bonuses or commissions, there could be a temptation to be overly optimistic.

If income in the form of rebates is overestimated in Period 0, then profits for that period will be overstated, and when income is retrospectively corrected to the true level in Period 1, then the profits will have to adjusted back down. Repeated use of the pulling forward technique therefore creates a hole in the accounts that increases over time. Simultaneously, managers and accounting staff on the ground are faced with dealing with the conflict between the pressure to keep performance figures high and compliance with the ethical guidelines laid down in Tesco Values and the code of conduct, as well as broader professional rules of practice.

In a subsequent investigation by Deloitte into the affair, commissioned by the Tesco board, it was concluded that Tesco staff were "unduly and persistently" optimistic about future sales and rebate levels over the course of several years. The company auditors PwC had noted that commercial income was a big determinant of profit and possibly subject to manipulation, but their concerns were placated by the audit committee (FT, 2014).

The scope for managerial judgement in estimating the level of commercial income explains why it is unsurprising that the original estimate of an overstatement of £250 million for the first half of 2014 was corrected just one month later to £263 million. Ultimately, it was revealed that the practice of reporting income not yet earned had been going on for some time, with around £75 million of the overstatement relating to pre-2013 accounts. This persistence over several years suggests the company had been in some distress and board oversight was not as effective as it should have been.

Further evidence of weak governance is reinforced by a subsequent investigation by the government-appointed Groceries Code Adjudicator, Christine Tacon, who found that Tesco had mistreated suppliers in pursuit of their efforts to maximise commercial income. Her report observed them "failing to correct erroneous records, issuing duplicate invoices and failing to make payments, in some cases for years after acknowledging the debt" (Thomas, 2014). The Groceries Code Adjudicator also found that Tesco sometimes made unilateral deductions from suppliers' invoices to compensate for making less money than hoped on their products – internal financial targets appeared to dominate their relationship with suppliers. Unsurprisingly, Tacon recommended that such unilateral deductions be stopped, and any proposed deductions were open to challenge by the supplier.

The gravity of the accounting errors in Tesco is reflected in the fact that they not only represented a breach of the UK's Grocery Supply Code of Practice (2010) but also led to investigations by the Serious Fraud Office and the Financial Conduct Authority, the suspension of eight executives, and a criminal trial in which three senior executives were ultimately acquitted. Clearly something had gone wrong with both governance and internal control systems.

The root cause of the commercial income issue lay in the culture of prioritising short-term performance targets above all else and the linking of managerial and executive pay[6] to their achievement. Worsening financial results, combined with failings in governance at a senior level, engendered behaviour both "unreasonable" to suppliers and confusing to investors. Table 7.3 illus-trates how the continuous trajectory of sales growth from 2004 to 2012 then begins to stagnate and vital financial performance figures such as operating margin, profit before tax, and earnings per share all start to fall. Both profit before tax and operating margin fell by almost half between 2012 and 2013.

Importantly, in its core UK grocery market, sales per employee fell from just under £208,000 in 2012 to £200,000 in 2014, as Tesco saw its market share squeezed by the discount retailers Aldi and Lidl despite several price cutting campaigns over the same period (see Table 7.4).

With lower prices not working to generate the desired profits, Clarke revised the strategy to seek growth via multichannel sales, and some observers have suggested that the culture also changed under his leadership. One senior source told the *Sunday Telegraph* in 2014 (Thomas, 2014) that there had been "a cor-ruption of virtues" amongst Tesco staff.

It is interesting that the problems with accounting for commercial income coincide exactly with this period of decline (2012–2014). One possible expla-nation is that the failing performance resulted in the most senior level losing sight of the customer – the driving force behind its culture for decades – result-ing in suppliers being seen as an alternative source of profits. The increased frequency of short-term promotions to encourage sales provides some support for this idea, as such promotions invariably generate commercial income.

This raises fundamental questions about the composition of the board and why and how it allowed managers to "push the boat out" in terms of recognis-ing revenue not yet earned and cut costs by failing to pay suppliers or adjusting invoices downwards. Where was the oversight? Aggressive accounting aimed at carefully timing both income and costs is acceptable within limits, but one

Table 7.3 Steady Decline (2011–2014)

Performance Measure	2004	2009	2011	2012	2013	2014
Group revenue (exc. Tesco Bank) £m	30,814	47,135	60,255	63,497	62,946	63,146
Profit before tax (£m)	1574	2954	3917	4038	2057	2259
Operating margin	5.9%	5.9%	6.4%	6.5%	3.7%	4.1%
Market capitalisation (£m)	19,966	29,107	32,672	25,486	29,981	27,000
Return on capital employed	10.4%	12.8%	12.9%	13.3%	12.7%	12.1%
Earnings per share (pence)	16.45	28.92	36.26	40.31	33.74	32.05
Revenue per employee in UK (£)	162,459	196,436	202,850	207,931	204,319	200,637
Weekly sales per square foot (UK £)	22.48	25.34	24.95	24.86	24.15	23.33

Source: Tesco annual reports

Table 7.4 Yearly Average Supermarket Share (%) of UK Grocery Market (1997–2018)

Supermarket	2004	2008	2012	2014	2018
Tesco	28	31.1	30.6	29.1	27.8
Asda	16.6	17.0	17.3	17.2	15.2
Sainsbury	15.7	16.2	17.0	16.4	16.2
Morrison	6.6*	11.4	11.9	11.1	10.6
Aldi	2.2**	2.9	3.2	4.8	7.4
Lidl	1.8	2.3	2.8	3.5	5.4

KEY
* Excludes Safeway stores bought in 2004
** 2005, as 2004 not available

Source: Based on data extracted from fooddeserts.org

might expect internal controls (and both internal and external audit processes) to prevent excesses in an organisation the size of Tesco. A crisis that is only revealed by a whistle blower at a senior level suggests a clear failure of governance, and Tesco was forced to admit to the events in 2014: "The Control Environment has not been fully effective in the year. This has manifested itself primarily in the events around commercial income and the resultant impact on the financial statements" (Tesco annual report, 2015, p. 39).

Seven Failures of Governance and Control

It is evident that Tesco was legally compliant in its reporting practice in relation to the UK's Combined Code and that it also, as required by the code, operated a whistleblowing policy to enable problems to be confidentially reported. Nonetheless, the control system failed to stop the misreporting of income, suggesting underlying problems of governance that, whilst legal, were insufficient. Several issues can be identified that may shed light on what went wrong.

The Balance Between Independent and Executive Directors

Following the global financial crisis in 2008, the prevailing view in governance debates has been to "treat the board as a supervisor/monitor of senior managers. Consequently, the board of directors tends to focus on the control of management behavior and monitoring of the company's past performance and sustainability" (OECD, 2018, p. 4). Central to this monitoring process is a balance between executive and non-executive board members.

On three occasions – early 2009, from mid-2010 until the end of the financial year in February 2011, and across several days in early 2012 – Tesco breached the Combined Code's recommendation that at least half of the board of directors, excluding the chairman, should be independent non-executive directors (NEDs). Tesco correctly reported the code breaches on all occasions.

The remaining time the balance was exactly 50:50 until in 2014, when the appointment of several new NEDs shifted the balance in their favour.

The logic behind the 50:50 requirement is to ensure that executive powers are matched by that of the NEDs, thus avoiding "groupthink." If there are strong characters amongst the executives, however, and this is perhaps combined with new or inexperienced NEDs, then executives may dominate and their views scrutinised or questioned less closely than is desirable.

NED Experience

One of the limitations of the Combined Code is that it does not require NEDs to have relevant experience in the particular field of business. The NEDs in post at Tesco in 2014 were noticeably lacking in relevant experience – none had worked in the retail food sector. Given the specialist nature of the issues surrounding accounting for commercial income – a peculiarity of retailing – it is possible that existing NEDs did not feel equipped to question existing practice. The appointment of Richard Cousins (former CEO of the catering firm Compass) and Mikael Ohlsson (former IKEA CEO) helped assuage stock market concerns in October 2014, but there remained pressure to increase both the number of posts and the breadth of NED experience.

EXTERNAL EVALUATION OF BOARD PERFORMANCE

The Combined Code lays down various requirements in relation to board evaluation, most notably:

- B.6.1. The board should state in the annual report how performance evaluation of the board, its committees and its individual directors has been conducted.
- B.6.2. Evaluation of the board of FTSE 350 companies should be externally facilitated at least every three years. The external facilitator should be identified in the annual report and a statement made as to whether they have any other connection with the company.

In the case of Tesco, on two occasions (2010–2011 and 2014–2015) the independent evaluation was delayed for a year due to changes in senior management. Such delays leave open the possibility that scrutiny is below the desired level.

The Organisation for Economic Co-operation and Development (OECD) (2018) recommends that evaluation should not only be external and independent but should also address several interlinked issues:

1. Quality of the monitoring and risk management role
2. Quality of the strategic and other business-related advice
3. Board dynamics and board members' proactive participation
4. Diversity of the board

There is no guarantee, however, that external evaluation is effective, as there are a limited number of firms who conduct such work in the UK. They have been criticised for evaluations that are over-reliant on questionnaires, as well as the scope for potential conflict of interest because several are also executive search firms deployed to appoint boardroom directors. A government-commissioned review by the UK's Chartered Governance Institute has resulted in a recommendation that a voluntary code of practice be introduced requiring reviewers to publicly commit to standards of independence, integrity, and competence (Thomas, 2021). No decision has yet been made in respect of the recommendation.

THE ROLE OF THE EXTERNAL AUDITORS

The Financial Reporting Council investigated the work of PwC in relation to the preparation, approval, and audit of the financial statements of Tesco PLC for the financial years ending February 2012, 2013, and 2014. The investigation was closed in 2017 when the FRC executive council concluded that there was "not a realistic prospect that a tribunal would make an adverse finding against PwC."

In the 2014 financial statements, the external auditor's report included the comment that commercial income was an area of focus in their work "because of the judgement required in accounting for the commercial income deals and the risk of manipulation of these balances" (Annual Report, 2014, p. 66). Reports suggest that this was the third time that PwC raised questions with Tesco about how the income was recognised in the accounts, but the audit committee successfully placated their concerns.

THE ROLE OF THE BOARD AND AUDIT COMMITTEE IN RELATION TO THE ACCOUNTS

Both the main board of directors and the audit committee have a duty to ensure that the accounts give a fair and balanced reflection of the company's financial position. Given the queries from the external auditor, the issue of commercial income was clearly on the agenda of the audit committee, but the 2014 committee report states, "It is the Committee's view that whilst commercial income is a significant income for the Group and involves an element of judgement, management operates an appropriate control environment which minimises risks in this area."

Given the need to correct the earnings figures for three consecutive years, their judgement appears to have been impaired. In the eyes of one *Financial Times* reporter "The board – especially the non-executive directors, and members of the ethics and audit committees – seems either to have been derelict in its duties, ignored the problem or turned a blind eye" (Wilmott, 2014).

Possible explanations for this include:

1. PwC were the external auditors for Tesco from 1983 to 2014. Such a long-standing relationship may affect the capacity of audit committee members to challenge the work of the auditors. Interestingly, a revised version of the Combined Code required that from 2014 onwards the external auditors should be rotated every decade. The aim is to avoid any risk of bias or subjectivity in the audit. Within Tesco, the audit committee agreed to put the audit out to tender in 2015, and the new contract was awarded to Deloitte.

    Of the directors on the board at the time the errors were announced (excluding the newly appointed CEO and chief financial officer [CFO]) two formerly worked for PwC. Mark Armour, an NED appointed in 2013, was a former partner at the accounting firm and, significantly, Ken Hanna, the chair of the audit committee, was also a PwC alumnus. Challenging former colleagues is extremely difficult from either side of the fence.

In the view of Wilmott (2014), the arrangement between the auditors and audit committee is "brilliant. . . . Neither group considers itself guilty of incompetence or impropriety. Yet collectively they presided over a serious failure of oversight."

AUDIT COMMITTEE RESPONSIBILITIES IN RESPECT OF WHISTLEBLOWING REGARDING FINANCIAL MISDEMEANOURS

Under the terms of the Combined Code, responsibility for ensuring that employees can confidentially report concerns over financial wrongdoing rests with the audit committee. The audit committee must have been aware of the email sent in 2012 by the CFO to employees explicitly forbidding accounting for profits early except when fully justified, and as such one might have expected closer scrutiny of financial controls in this area. More worryingly, the fact that finance and other staff resigned over the issue before the senior accountant finally had his voice heard in the legacy paper is very significant. Were staff not being listened to, or were they too afraid to raise concerns? Who knew what about the numbers, and why did it take so long for someone to have the courage to blow the whistle?

THE ROLE OF THE REMUNERATION COMMITTEE IN SETTING BONUS TERMS FOR SENIOR EXECUTIVES

The remuneration committee report in the 2012 annual statements declares that "at the heart of Tesco's remuneration arrangements is a performance focused culture" (p. 64). At this point, 70% of the executive directors' annual bonus (worth up to 200% to 250% of base salary) was dependent on achieving a specified rate of annual profit growth, and the remaining 30% was linked to the achievement of short-term strategic objectives. Half of the annual bonus was payable in cash and half paid in shares deferred for three years, with clawback provisions applicable to the latter portion. In 2011–2012 the short-term profitability target was not met, and two of the six strategic targets – like-for-like sales growth and ROCE – fell below the threshold required to trigger bonuses. The remuneration report includes five-year charts of remuneration for each executive director, which clearly show a substantial drop in 2011–2012.

In 2012–2013 the profit target was again missed, and so no related bonuses were paid. The ROCE performance was also below the required level, thus failing to trigger part of the short-term strategic bonus. The remuneration committee reviewed the short-term bonus payment terms and revised them with effect from 2013 to 2014. A key change was that the strategic component of the bonus was split into financial and non-financial components representing 26% and 24% of the bonus, respectively. Additionally, *no bonus relating to strategic measures could be earned if the profitability target was not met.*

This change further ramped up the pressure to hit profit targets, and if targets are passed down the hierarchy, then non-executive senior managers would feel under increasing pressure. The pressure was further enhanced by the fact that targets had already been missed for two years.

The bonus system that operated in the years leading into the accounting crisis, whilst perhaps motivated by a recognition of the need to keep shareholders happy, nonetheless offered huge bonuses for executives when short-term profit targets were hit. Furthermore, the remuneration committee's report in 2013 makes no mention of questioning the underlying validity of the targets, and the changes only served to add to already heavy pressure on management. Was the remuneration committee unable to truly challenge the board's financial targets and, if so, why?

Corporate governance regulation and guidance require that the remuneration committee be composed of NEDs to ensure objectivity in decision making. As discussed earlier, however, the power of the executive versus NEDs may be unequal, and it could be the case that the committee felt fundamentally powerless to question the performance targets set by the wider board, of which they themselves are members. This is perhaps an example of apparently good governance principles having unexpectedly adverse consequences.

Seven Consequences

The consequences of the trading statements made in September and October 2014, adjusting the announced profit figures for the first half of the year, had direct and immediate consequences. The impact was felt both financially and in terms of reputation and can be summarised as follows:

1. **A critical report from the UK's Groceries Code Adjudicator** which declared that Tesco had "acted unreasonably" towards its suppliers and ordered Tesco to make significant changes to its dealings with suppliers. The company did not incur any financial penalty, as the events took place

before the adjudicator was granted powers to fine retailers up to 1% of turnover for breaches of the code. Nonetheless, the report was damaging to the corporate reputation.

2. **Resignation of the chairman**, Sir Richard Broadbent, and the suspension of eight executives, pending further investigation. By the end of 2016, the CEO, CFO, and chairman were all new to the job.

3. **Drop in share price.** Tesco's share price in 2014 saw its worst performance since 1989. From a price of 330.05p on 2 January, the price fell to a low of almost half that figure – 164.8p – mid December, before recovering slightly to 189p by the end of the year. Such a large drop in the market value of the business has a significance well beyond the individual investor, because as an FTSE 100 member, Tesco shares will be held in the portfolio of many institutional investors, including major pension funds. There is therefore a social consequence to the events that extends beyond the business itself.

4. **An investigation by the city watchdog the Financial Conduct Authority** (FCA) into the accounting irregularities was later dropped after intervention by the Serious Fraud Office (SFO). In 2017 the FCA, in a joint press release with the SFO, announced that Tesco PLC and Tesco Stores Ltd. had committed market abuse by issuing a trading statement which gave a false or misleading impression of the value of publicly traded Tesco bonds or stock. Using its powers under Section 384 of the Financial Services and Markets Act (2000), the FCA ordered Tesco to pay up to £85 million in compensation to investors who bought shares or bonds on or after 29 August 2014 and still held these at the date of the trading statement on 22 September 2014. Investors received compensation equal to the inflated price paid, plus interest.

   In 2016, the SFO charged three Tesco executives with false accounting and fraud by abuse of position, alleging that the men had done nothing to alert senior management about the false income figures. The first trial ended after the defendant suffered a heart attack, the second was halted by the judge on the grounds that the evidence was too weak, and the third ended with the acquittal of the defendant after the SFO offered no evidence against him. In other words, no individuals were found criminally liable. In 2017, whilst the trials were still ongoing, the SFO entered into a deferred prosecution agreement (DPA) with Tesco Stores Ltd. which stated that the three men were "aware of and dishonestly perpetuated the misstatement of figures" (Croft and Eley, 2019). The DPA enabled Tesco to escape criminal prosecution in return for payment of a £129 million fine, despite the subsequent acquittal of all three executives. This led to criticism that Tesco had thrown them "under a bus" in order to draw a line under the scandal.

5. **Civil lawsuits by institutional investors.** In an effort to claim compensation for being misled as to the value of Tesco shares, several institutional investors brought two claims against the retailer, valued at more than £200 million. One claim was settled by mutual agreement, and the

remaining one was dropped just before it came to trial. Tesco had clearly forfeited a degree of market trust by its actions.

6. **Record loss of £6.4 billion for the 2014–2015 financial year.** This loss was the largest incurred by a UK retailer and stood in sharp contrast to the record profit of £3.8 billion reported just three years earlier. A significant proportion of the loss was the result of a revaluation of 3,000 UK stores, the value of which was reduced by £4.7 billion.

   Commentators have suggested that the scale of the losses reported in 2015, and their causes, indicated that Dave Lewis, the new CEO, was intentionally bundling all problems together with the aim of then enforcing a turnaround. The losses placed a marker to say things are going to change.

7. **Impact on staff morale.** The staff most affected by the scandal were those in the finance and internal audit departments. As noted earlier, several accounting staff resigned before the legacy paper finally led to senior management action, either through fear for their job or the conviction that they would not be heard. Rebuilding staff confidence in the integrity of the governance and control system is very challenging indeed.

In responding to the scandal, and picking up the pieces, one of the first things that was required was an admission of failure in the internal controls:

> The Control Environment has not been fully effective in the year. This has manifested itself primarily in the events around commercial income and the resultant impact on the financial statements.
>
> The business has invested significant time and resource to understand, evaluate and remediate the control weaknesses. Clear control improvement plans are in place.

> (Annual Report, 2015, p. 39)

The stage was then set for a turnaround, which included significant changes to the approach to internal control and risk management.

Risk Management: Phase 2 (2014–2020)

In stark contrast to the previous decade, this era is characterised by consolidation and active divestment to take Tesco away from international and non-grocery activities and refocus on its core UK retail operations. It is also a period during which huge effort was made to rebuild trust – from both customers and suppliers – as a means of increasing footfall, sales, and competitive position. The aim was to offer simple, stable prices accompanied by outstanding customer service. Three strategic priorities were identified:

- Regaining competitiveness in the UK by reducing prices
- Protecting and strengthening the balance sheet via reduced debt and capital expenditure and a review of the group portfolio
- Rebuilding trust and transparency through "empowering colleagues"

Senior Management and Strategy

The scope for strategic change was significant, given the arrival of the new CEO, Dave Lewis, in September 2014. Lewis was an "outsider," moving in from Unilever (one of Tesco's largest suppliers), and he therefore had no cultural baggage to influence his decision making. Additionally, a new CFO – Alan Stewart from Marks and Spencer – was appointed almost simultaneously. A new chairman, John Allan, was then appointed the following month. This new team of three at the very top of the group's management hierarchy could rethink the strategic agenda.

High on the list of priorities was refocusing on UK grocery retailing and the sale of loss-making or poorly performing businesses. Table 7.5 shows how swiftly this strategy was implemented.

In addition to selling non-grocery businesses and exiting several international markets, forty-three unprofitable UK stores were closed and capital expenditure reduced, with the aim of reducing levels of debt. Shareholders felt the pain, with huge dividend cuts in the 2014–2015 and 2015–2016 financial years.

A revised management style was instigated by both replacing a significant number of very senior managers and revising and simplifying the store management structures. The declared business model was to refocus the business, develop multichannel selling, and pay close attention to both customer and supplier needs, and these strategic priorities were reflected in the overhaul of the executive committee under Lewis. The committee of

Table 7.5 Rationalisation and Business Closures

Date	Sector	Type of Transaction
2013	International food retail	Chinese operations converted to joint venture
		Sale of Fresh and Easy
2015	UK non-food retail	Sale of Blinkbox entertainment
	International online retail	Sale of Homeplus South Korea
	International food retail	Completion of divestment in China, sale of remaining 20% joint venture stake
2016	International food retail	Sale of Turkish store chain
	UK bon-food retail	Sale of Dobbie's Garden Centres
		Sale of Harris & Hoole cafes
		Sale of in-store opticians to Vision Express
		Sale of Giraffe restaurants
2017	UK food wholesale	Purchase of Booker Cash and Carry
2018	UK online retail	Closure of Tesco Direct

seventeen members in 2013–2014 was cut to eleven, of which four were new in post. The new faces were the CEO, CFO, CEO for the UK and Republic of Ireland, and chief product officer. Several positions disappeared from the committee, four new ones were created, and some had minor changes to job titles.

Table 7.6 clearly shows the changed focus, as national managing director posts are replaced by a single international CEO, and the strategy of emphasising the customer experience and product offering is reflected in the new posts of chief customer and product officers. Similarly, positions in areas that had caused headaches for the group – commercial income and property – disappeared, ensuring wider board oversight of such matters. Most significantly, the three most senior executive positions – CEO, CFO and UK and Republic of Ireland CEO, plus the chairman – were all occupied by individuals new to Tesco. The new blood was well balanced, however, by long-serving Tesco staff, including the chief product officer, who started in the business as a graduate trainee in 1990, and the international CEO, who had worked at Tesco since 1979.

Key Learning Point

Getting the right balance of experience in the business versus the inspiration that may come from new management is a challenging issue for good governance.

Under the leadership of both Terry Leahy and Philip Clarke, the steering wheel had been central to the governance structure and performance system within Tesco. The new management team ditched this on the grounds that, with in excess of forty performance metrics, it had become overly complex. Lewis announced it would be replaced by the "Big Six," a more focused set of

Table 7.6 Changes to Executive Committee Composition (2015)

Positions Removed	New Posts
Chief Marketing Officer	Chief Product Officer
Group Property Director	Chief Customer Officer
Group Commercial Director	Group Strategy Director
Group Business Planning Director	International CEO
Managing Director (UK)	
Managing Director of Central Europe and Turkey	
Chief Information Officer	
Company Secretary	

measures that would emphasise the prioritisation of customer service and be easier for staff to understand. The shift marked not only a way of distancing the new management from the old regime but also a mechanism for simplifying the business. Simplification involves not just focusing on specific areas of business but also about management systems themselves.

In outlining the new approach, the 2015 annual report declared:

> It's about alignment and focus: if we give our colleagues more power to choose the right actions, we'll do a better job for customers and achieve greater success for our business.
>
> (Tesco Annual Report, 2015, p. 10)

The Big Six marked a huge rationalisation of core performance measures, and the details are included in Table 7.7.

The KPIs clearly reflect the strategic priorities, and comparing the Big Six with the steering wheel, the most noticeable change is the disappearance of operations from the KPIs. No explanation is given for this, but it may simply be that management were confident that operationally the business was run efficiently and that nurturing customer, staff, and supplier relationships was more important to financial recovery.

The simplicity of the Big Six suggests that its selection was influenced by the Objective Key Results (OKR) approach to performance management, which gained fame when it was adopted by Google in the 1990s. OKR seeks to generate an accelerated improvement in performance by encouraging staff to work together in a performance-focused environment in which they are involved in the defining and monitoring of targets.[7] The Big Six and other linked KPIs are therefore used by the directors and management for performance analysis, planning, reporting, and incentive-setting purposes. This not only fits with

Table 7.7 Rationalisation of Tesco Performance Metrics: From Forty to the Big Six

Big Six	Measured By
Group sales	Excludes sales made at petrol stations to provide a performance measure of core retail operations
Group operating profit	Operating profit before exceptional items and amortisation of acquired intangibles
Operating cash flow	From retail operations only (i.e. excluding Tesco Bank)
Customer loyalty	The frequency with which individual customers shop at Tesco and their average weekly spend
A great place to work and shop	The percentage of staff who would recommend Tesco as a great place to work and shop
Supplier satisfaction	The percentage of suppliers across the group who responded positively when asked if they were satisfied with their relationship with Tesco

Tesco's aim of empowering colleagues but also references back to the sound-bites so integral to the culture of "every little helps" and the performance-based focus of the steering wheel. Cross-functional team working is implicit in such a system, alongside the transparent sharing of objectives and performance at all levels of an organisation. What is most important is that headline strategic objectives are clear and quantitative measures established to evaluate their achievement. Interestingly, OKR grew out of a concern for overcomplexity in the balanced scorecard, which was the foundation of the Tesco steering wheel. Lewis's apparent motivation for shifting to the Big Six appears identical.

Simple Messaging for Cultural Change

Attention to customer needs was traditionally seen as a key strength of Tesco, and the Big Six brought the customer back as the centre of attention, based on a belief that happy customers would yield good financial results. The organisational structure whereby most staff are in customer-facing roles meant that if they could be persuaded to support and understand the Big Six, then a successful turnaround was possible. Support was sought by reviving the core Tesco values that were so familiar to employees.

Importantly, the philosophy underpinning the use of OKR-style performance management is transparency of targets and staff involvement in target setting. At the store level, this was translated into KPIs that were easily measured and understood but could be fully integrated into group KPIs, as illustrated in evaluating customer loyalty.

Translating Group Targets Into Store Targets

If the group objective is "customers recommend us and come back time and again," then at the store level this is converted into average spend per customer and, using loyalty card information, the frequency of visits by individual customers and their average spend. Performance targets that link stores into regional, national, and group-wide targets can then be defined.

The cascading down of targets was similarly applied to financial measures such as cash flow from operations and combined with a new regimen of weekly calls between store managers and senior management, helping to ensure local problems and opportunities were identified quickly.

The Big Six approach was effectively a return to a culture in which performance management and risk management were integrated, with risk aversion expressed in terms of doing the best one can for customers. One simple example of how this works in practice is the "one in front" promise, first introduced in 1994, which promises that no customer will have to queue behind more than one other in waiting for service at the checkout. Queues represent a risk that a customer will either walk out without buying or wait but then be reluctant to return. Risk is thus defined in very simple terms, and this simplicity offers an interesting contrast to the textbook view that risk management is a control system commonly underpinned by multiple layers of bureaucracy.

As described in the first edition of this book, published in 2011, this simple approach worked well for many years. This case has shown, however, how the system broke down and revision of the risk management structures became essential. Central to the turnaround process initiated by Dave Lewis, therefore, were some fundamental changes to internal controls to complement the reinvigoration of a risk-conscious culture.

New Initiatives in Risk Management

In 2015 an external evaluation of board effectiveness concluded that there was a need to strengthen risk management procedures group-wide. Combined with the ongoing investigations by the SFO and the Groceries Code Adjudicator, this was a wake-up call that demanded an immediate response.

Top of the list for consideration were the controls over commercial income, which represented a substantial proportion of group revenue. Two risk management problems required overhaul – the financial controls over how commercial income was recorded in the accounts and the controls over relationships with suppliers. In response, the following actions were taken:

- **Simplification of Commercial Income Procedures**
    Group audit and assurance (GAA), formerly known as internal audit, as the party responsible for providing reassurance on internal control effectiveness to the audit committee and board, instigated a review of commercial income procedures and made changes to both processes and controls. The system was simplified down from what had been approximately twenty different variations in payments terms relating to items such as volume rebates, provision of marketing material, and promotional positioning. Additionally, GAA examined controls around other areas that required significant accounting judgement.
    The impact of the changes were also subject to investigation by the external auditors, who performed detailed testing of commercial income recognised in the 2014–2015 period, paying particular attention to whether the income was recognised in the correct period and the appropriateness of accrued commercial income at the period end. The external auditors' report did not identify any matters for concern in this area.
- **Supplier Payment Transparency**
    UK payment terms for suppliers were published 2015 ff.

- **Increased Financial Disclosure**

  The board decided to increase the financial disclosures in the annual report to include the effect of commercial income on the group balance sheet.
- **Corporate Compliance Programme**

  A compliance programme was launched to widen understanding of the requirements of the Groceries Supply Code of Practice (GSCOP), and compliance officers (first appointed in 2005) and code auditors provided compliance training for buying teams and developed an e-learning training programme.
- **Management Reorganisation in Commercial Income**

  New managers were put in place in commercial income, a supplier engagement team was appointed, and the incentive structure for members of the commercial team was revised.

Further protection for suppliers was provided by reconfiguring the Protector Line (for whistle blowers and complaints) to include suppliers, as required under the GSCOP. The hope was that, in combination, these measures would prevent any repeat of the commercial income debacle that had marred 2014.

Complementing the specific efforts relating to risk management of commercial income and supplier relations, the board initiated a group-wide communication programme emphasising the importance of culture, integrity, and ethics. In 2015 the code of conduct was revised and relaunched with a group-wide training programme. The new code incorporated behavioural guidelines that defined minimum expectations for staff and specific guidance on key risk areas such as health and safety, trading regulations, and information security. An accompanying information campaign on "how to, when to" speak up accompanied the revised code, increasing staff awareness of the confidential Protector Line.

New starter training programmes were run alongside annual compliance training, and revised policies covering bribery and corruption, fraud, and gift and hospitality arrangements introduced. Compliance now became a key factor in performance management and reward, and training on responsible product sourcing methods and modern slavery was also introduced. The new code of conduct directly referenced Tesco Values as a way of encouraging staff to go beyond just following the law and instead trying harder for customers and suppliers. Familiar soundbites such as "no one tries harder for customers" and "we treat people how they want to be treated" were reinforced with the message that "every little help makes a difference." This was the thinking so strongly emphasised by Terry Leahy that had brought Tesco growing success for many years, and so staff could easily relate to the ideas and did not have to learn anything new. The overall aim was to reset the culture as a means of reducing risks.

Not everything worked quite as it should, however. A new cyber security team was established in 2015 and a group security director appointed to oversee not just cybercrime but also a fraud prevention strategy, business resilience, and crisis management, as well as to improve the Protector Line. Unfortunately, however, these moves failed to prevent a cyberattack on Tesco Bank in November 2016, when attackers exploited deficiencies in internal controls that allowed the attackers to generate virtual debit cards with authentic account numbers that netted the attackers £2.26 million. The FCA fined Tesco Personal Finance PLC (Tesco Bank) £16,400,000 for failing to exercise due skill, care, and diligence in protecting its personal current account holder.

Unsurprisingly, in 2017, the annual report (p. 17) declared that the transformation programme would now include

> the implementation of a roadmap setting out a staged process to achieve a more advanced level of risk management maturity. Transformation programmes are intended *to increase the overall level of control environment maturity and improve consistency across the Group.* The ongoing implementation of the technology transformation programme will further strengthen IT general controls.

It was clear that the changes to date had not been sufficient, and in early 2018 Tesco advertised for a group risk manager tasked with the job of developing and implementing an ERM roadmap and developing processes to bring maturity to the risk management process. Whilst the post was new, the holder would still be located within the GAA function at group HQ. The appointment marked a twofold change in thinking:

- Firstly, a shift towards a more structured approach to risk management, rather than one heavily dependent upon informal cultural messages and internal audit.
- Secondly, explicit recognition that risk management thinking and controls needed to be fully integrated group-wide – the move towards ERM had begun.

The Beginnings of ERM?

In 2016 the Big Six performance indicators were complemented by a set of six strategic drivers, which the board considered essential to transforming the group, recovering trust from customers and suppliers, and improving financial strength. The strategic drivers were:

- A differentiated brand
- A three-year plan to reduce operating costs by £1.5 billion
- The generation of £9 billion of cash from operations over three years
- Maximisation of the product mix to achieve an operating margin of 3.5% to 4% group-wide
- Maximise value from property
- Innovation – particularly in products and channels as well as operations

Details of performance against these six drivers has been included in the annual report from 2017 onwards, and principal risks were redefined as those factors that might affect the achievement of the six strategic drivers. The direct link between risk and strategy was therefore made clear. The challenge was to reconfigure the risk management system to identify and manage these risks effectively.

Three Lines of Defence

Tesco chose to adopt a risk management framework that uses a "three lines of defence" approach to manage the core components of (1) risk identification and assessment, (2) the implementation of controls to manage risks, and (3) the use of monitoring and audit tools to provide assurance that controls are working effectively. The three lines of defence model has been widely used in the financial services sector for many years, but more recently has become increasingly popular and is supported by the Institute of Internal Auditors, which published a report in 2013 (IAA, 2013) offering guidance on its implementation. The internal audit function plays a key role in the defence system, a factor which helps explain why the IAA is highly supportive, as the model encourages good resourcing for internal audits.

The three lines of defence are depicted as shown in Table 7.8.

The basic premise is that the operational, risk-facing staff will be aware of day-to-day risks and be in a position to identify and manage them, but their capacity to do so is enhanced by the presence of controls that establish fixed procedures and policy guidance on behaviour. The control and compliance function thus forms the second line of defence. However, the controls need to be effective, and this is achieved through monitoring by internal audits, which provide the third line of defence. The three tiers complement each other but play fundamentally different roles.

In Tesco pre-2014, the risk management system appeared to rely heavily on just two lines of defence: line management and internal audit.[8] Internal audit was an influential insider in terms of risk management, advising on risk identification and control issues, but their approach was very risk based, rather than compliance based. Controls over compliance do not appear to have been as important as internal audit, undermining control effectiveness, at least in relation to commercial income. The adoption of the three lines of defence model therefore required the introduction of tighter compliance procedures and controls.

Table 7.8 Three Lines of Defence Model of Risk Management

First Line of Defence	Second Line of Defence	Third Line of Defence
Operational management (e.g. business/functional heads, store managers, buyers, etc.)	Compliance and control functions (e.g. health and safety, product safety, finance)	Internal audit (in Tesco this is GAA)

The need for greater focus on compliance is evidenced by the fact that the accounting problems relating to commercial income indicated a clear failure to comply with GCSOP, together with weak controls over the estimating and reporting of commercial income and apparent weaknesses in the whistleblowing system. This was not, however, the only example of historically inadequate controls. Others include:

- A scandal in 2013 when horsemeat was found in burgers being offered for sale by several large retailers, including Tesco. The common source was a supplier based near the Irish border which, in turn, sourced its meat from a Dutch company. Whilst there was no suggestion that public health had been threatened, the affair indicated weak management down the supply chain that undermined consumer confidence and temporarily pushed Tesco's share price down. Further investigations by Tesco revealed that some of their other ready-made foods such as lasagne and spaghetti Bolognese were similarly contaminated.
- In 2014 over 23,00 litres of petrol escaped from a filling tank at a Tesco petrol station in Lancashire. The Environment Agency concluded that the incident resulted from Tesco's failure to address a known issue with part of the fuel delivery system and an inadequate alarm system; the problem was compounded by poor emergency procedures. Tesco was fined a total of £8 million – £5 million for the health and safety offence and £3 million for the environmental offence.
- In 2015 a 91-year-old man fell and suffered multiple hip fractures after slipping on a wet floor caused by fluid leaking from refrigerator units in Tesco's Hemel Hempstead store. The liquid was unable to drain away due to a blocked drain in the floor, and at a court hearing the management were found guilty of not implementing sufficient action to mitigate a risk that was recurring over more than one month. As a result, the company was fined £733,333 for breach of the Health and Safety at Work Act 1974.
- The FCA concluded that the cyberattack on Tesco Bank in 2016 was a consequence of their failure to comply with regulations on two separate counts. Firstly, a failure to exercise due skill, care, and diligence in protecting their personal current account holders, and secondly systems that did not portray the resilience required to protect customers. "The attack was the subject of a very specific warning that Tesco Bank did not properly address until after the attack started. This was too little, too late. Customers should not have been exposed to the risk at all" (FCA, 2018).

These examples indicate that the existing risk management system was not working as it should, and one of the key tasks for the new head of group risk management was to tighten up compliance.

Table 7.9 shows the governance structures used to manage compliance in Tesco post-2018.

Table 7.9 Compliance Governance in Tesco

Party	Responsibility Regarding Compliance
Board Level Board of directors	• Set group risk appetite regarding compliance (e.g. zero tolerance of fraud/regulatory breaches) • Ensure management maintains effective controls over compliance
Risk and compliance committee	• Set and monitor the implementation and effectiveness of risk and compliance standards across the group on behalf of the executive committee • Report biannually to the audit committee
Executive Committee Level Group general counsel	• Ownership of compliance risk • Oversight of the regulatory and compliance functions
Business Units/ Functional Level Unit compliance committee	• Set and monitor the implementation and effectiveness of risk and compliance standards within the business unit • Report to group risk and compliance committee
Senior management	• Implement staff training on compliance • Cooperate with GAA staff on reviewing and strengthening compliance procedures • Identify newly emerging compliance risks and report breaches to the unit's compliance committee • Oversee receipt of staff annual declarations of compliance and also sign their own regarding the unit
Staff Level Staff – in stores, warehouses, offices, etc.	• Undertake training as required (e.g. anti-bribery and corruption) • Sign annual declaration of compliance with the code of conduct that includes compliance guidance • If working with suppliers, staff members must sign a declaration of compliance with the GCSOP

The table shows a clear line of accountability directly from store/warehouse or office staff through to the board of directors. All staff must undertake mandatory training on the code of conduct that includes provisions on compliance, and depending on their specific role, there may also be annual refresher training. Staff working with suppliers must also sign an annual declaration of compliance with the GCSOP. In the first line of defence, the management within business units are responsible for ensuring the requisite training is undertaken and declarations signed (i.e. confirming that the second line of defence is being implemented). Compliance committees at both the unit and executive level monitor breaches of compliance and instigate further investigation and corrective action by the GAA, as well as impose penalties as required. The committees also report to the audit committee on the effectiveness of current compliance controls. The audit committee provides the third line of defence, receiving regular reports from the GAA as well as the compliance committee. Ultimate oversight of the first line of defence is the responsibility of the general counsel, who carries executive responsibility for compliance risk and reports to the board on such matters. The board has a duty under corporate governance regulation to report that the internal control system is effective and receives reports from the audit committee that inform this process.

The accountability and monitoring across the three lines of defence work in similar ways across different categories of compliance. For example, in relation to health and safety matters there are business unit–level health and safety committees that report to the group risk and compliance committee and oversee regular store safety audits and compliance reviews. Similarly, product safety compliance is managed through sometimes unannounced supplier audits, complemented by staff training on hygiene controls and a defined procedure for dealing with non-compliant products.

The system is organisation-wide in its scope and characterised by:

- Common rules group-wide (e.g. code of conduct)
- Common procedures and reporting lines (e.g. business unit compliance committees)
- Tighter controls requiring staff to confirm compliance (e.g. statements of assurance)
- Simplicity which helps staff understand what is required

The Revised Risk Management Framework

The development of new and tighter compliance controls, combined with the introduction of the three lines of defence and revisions to the committee and governance structures, means that the framework for risk management post-2018 is very different from that of pre-2014 as depicted in Figures 7.2. and 7.3. The new framework is shown in Figure 7.4.

Figure 7.4 clearly portrays the collective role played by the three lines of defence in managing risk. Most importantly, of the seven components, five are related to controls, indicating that this aspect of risk management is now being emphasised much more than previously. Controls include clear governance (i.e. a system led from the top), in which risk appetite and rules are obvious to all. Policies come second – documented points of reference so that people can check exactly what they are supposed to do. Standards, procedures, and guidance control, by the very fact of their standardisation group-wide, eliminate the risk of unanticipated individual behaviour. Communications and training get the messages about risk across to everybody, and investigations and sanctions demonstrate that breaches of control will not be tolerated. Tesco is still at an early stage on its journey towards a new style of risk management, and so the

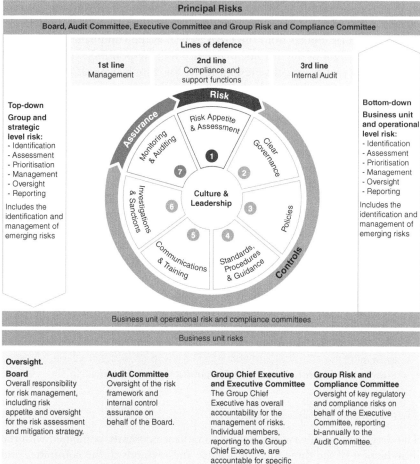

Figure 7.4 Risk management framework (2020)

Source: Tesco Annual Report 2020 (p.13)

scope and volume of documented controls can be expected to increase over time, but there is clearly progress.

Figure 7.4 also depicts an ERM-style approach insofar as it highlights the involvement of all levels of the organisation in each of the core elements of the risk management process as defined by the Institute of Risk Management (IRM). Risk assessment, treatment, monitoring and reporting apply both top down and bottom up. Significantly, culture and leadership sit at the centre of the figure, reflecting the importance attached to corporate culture as a tool for risk management. The 2020 annual report references "an unrelenting focus on safe colleague behaviour as a culture across Tesco" (p. 22) that complements efforts to use direct controls to strengthen operational routines.

Culture is denoted by the core values, which aim to ensure that all staff understand what matters and how to behave:

- No one tries harder for customers.
- We treat people how they want to be treated.
- Every little help makes a big difference.

These messages are identical to those embodied in Tesco values pre 2014 – the objective now is to reinvigorate them, emphasising the message that meeting customer needs is the key to success.

In the same way that the cultural values remain unchanged, other elements of the risk management system are also like those that existed pre-2014. These include central governance structures (e.g. board and senior management responsibilities and the role of the audit committee), the systems and training used to help managers to identify and assess risk, and the risk-based focus of the audit work done by GAA. In summary, the main changes post-2014 relate to increased controls and formalised risk management procedures, a tighter system of accountability (e.g. the introduction of declarations of compliance for all staff), and a commitment to move to an ERM-style approach by widening the scope of risk management.

Redefining the Organisation for ERM

In Chapter 3 we saw that the 2017 Committee of Sponsoring Organizations (COSO) ERM Framework confirms the link between ERM and stakeholder expectations and explicitly connects ERM with performance, arguing that "risk influences and aligns strategy and performance across all departments and functions." In Figure 7.4 the principal risks are those which threaten the achievement of core strategies, and the three lines of defence provide the structure through which these risks are managed. At the centre of the figure is culture and leadership, which serves as the pillar around which risk assessment, control, and assurance revolve. In principle, therefore, culture acts as the "glue" that binds the framework together across the entire organisation.

It is no coincidence that in seeking to redress the control problems that emerged in 2014, the board chose to begin by reasserting Tesco values as being at the heart of Tesco's culture. Behavioural benchmarks and standards that straddle the whole organisation form the foundation for risk management. The Akzo Nobel case in Chapter 6 is identical in looking to culture as the starting point for moving on from significant regulatory breaches.

Also central to ERM is the idea of a system that is truly organisation-wide in its scope. One of the noticeable features of Tesco's approach, particularly post-2014, is the way in which it defines the Tesco organisation and now integrates that wider definition into its risk management processes. One simple example of this is the development of common governance processes for technical failures, disaster recovery, and business continuity that apply across all businesses, including Tesco Bank. Consistency aids staff understanding and makes for easier monitoring.

If risk management is about hitting performance targets to achieve strategic objectives, then understanding the stakeholders that you serve is critical. Tesco currently identifies itself as serving five stakeholders: customers, colleagues, suppliers, shareholders, and the community.[9] ERM requires that all of these parties are integrated into both the performance management and risk management systems.

Keeping customers happy is the central mission, as if this works, then all other stakeholders also benefit. A group communications director holds responsibility for building trust in the brand, and KPIs measure customers' overall levels of satisfaction and perception of brand and product quality, which are monitored via regular surveys.

The welfare of colleagues is overseen by the chief people officer, common to all organisations, and staff surveys are used to monitor their views on whether Tesco is a great place to work and shop and if they feel that they can see a clear link between their work and Tesco's purpose. This latter measure helps in evaluating the level of staff risk awareness. The risk of unhappy staff is reduced by measures such as twice-yearly colleague contribution panels, chaired by an NED, that discuss staff concerns, and the provision of not just the whistleblowing line but also a mental health support service that provides 24/7 support to staff feeling anxious or in need of support.

The events of 2014 highlighted the need to ensure that suppliers are treated fairly, and surveys are used to monitor their satisfaction. Additionally, supplier behaviour can create other risks for Tesco and impede their achievement of other objectives such as product safety, continuity of supply, or sustainability targets. A chief product officer on the executive committee carries responsibility for product planning, sourcing, and supply, and his or her work is complemented by oversight from the corporate responsibility committee. Corporate responsibility issues include animal welfare, human rights, and working with suppliers to reduce plastic packaging levels.

Community matters fall under the remit of the corporate responsibility committee, and the KPIs and risk controls are wide ranging. For example, tools to identify and manage climate-related risks are well defined, and the link between climate change and responsible sourcing and supply is widely acknowledged. The aim is to reduce carbon emissions across all operations by 60% by 2025 compared to 2015–2016 levels, and performance against this target is reported annually. Similarly, in conjunction with World Wildlife Fund, Tesco has set up a metric to measure the environmental impact of a typical shopping basket and aims to half this impact over time. Local community measures include efforts to reduce food waste in line with the United Nations Sustainable Development Goal of halving global food waste by 2030. As part of this process, with the objective of preventing any food fit for human consumption going to waste, Tesco has been very active in donating food to charities and community groups. In the light of the economic hardships caused by COVID-19, this has had a powerful impact on communities.

The interests of shareholders are targeted through specific financial objectives such as operating profit and free cash flow that are closely monitored. Strengthening the balance sheet was also specified as a key objective, and progress on this is assessed by measures of both free cash flow and total indebtedness.

Inevitably, serving the interests of this wide range of stakeholders has meant that performance targets for risk management and control purposes far exceed the Big Six that were headlined in 2015. There is a need to distinguish between KPIs for reporting purposes and KPIs for internal control, as they frequently do not exactly match. Headlining just six KPIs sends out a message of simplification, which was clearly needed, but the reality is more complex. The challenge is to ensure that the day-to-day performance targets help, rather than hinder, staff understanding of the organisation's overall objectives.

Recognition of the interdependence between different sources of risk is fundamental to ERM, and whilst there is little information about how this is managed internally, it is clear that the issues are recognised. One example of this is the Little Helps Plan, set up in 2017, which redefined how the organisation defined value and what can improve the business: "The value we provide today isn't just about what's good for shopper. It's what's good for our colleagues, good for our farmer and supplier partners, and the communities our colleagues and customers live in" (Tesco PLC Little Helps Plan Update 2018/19, p. 2).

Further details on the Little Helps Plan are readily accessible online and provide a valuable illustration of how issues of social responsibility can be integrated into strategic planning and risk management.

In many ways, the transition towards ERM that has begun in Tesco is not hugely different from its historic use of the steering wheel, which also had five areas of focus: customer, community, people, operations, and finance. The difference lies in the way the risks are being managed and controlled. Governance, especially control, is now tighter, and the interdependence between risks is more clearly acknowledged. Pre-2014, for example, it appears that the financial controls over recognition of commercial income were being managed independently of the controls over supplier contracts, even though they proved strongly connected.

Is It Working?

The acid test of the strength of the new approach to risk management is whether strategic objectives are being achieved. The 2020 annual report declared "turnaround delivered," with KPIs against all stakeholder targets substantially improved relative to 2014–2015.

Given the low starting point, it is very impressive to see that in 2020 Tesco was awarded the title of Grocer of the Year – Britain's favourite supermarket

(The Grocer, 2020). In addition, Tesco won the award for best customer service for the second year in succession. Returns to shareholders have also recovered, with ROCE exceeding 11% in 2019 compared with just 4% in 2015, and the market capitalisation increasing from just £13 billion in October 2014 to £22 billion six years later.

Performance against the Big Six from 2014 to 2020 is summarised in Table 7.10.

The figures confirm that there has been substantial improvement on all counts. Sales have increased by 16.8%, cash flow from retail operations has more than doubled, and operating profit before exceptional items has more than trebled. The statistics covering softer measures of consumer, staff, and suppliers' satisfaction are also positive, but perhaps more difficult to interpret, as the definitions are very specific. The rise in customer satisfaction levels (albeit now falling slightly) reflects Tesco's revamp of its Clubcard loyalty scheme, which has proved a useful weapon in a very competitive marketplace.

Table 7.10 The Big Six Performance (2014–2015 to 2019–2020)

KPI	2014–2015	2015–2016	2016–2017	2017–2018	2018–2019	2019–2020
Sales (a) £ billion	48.35	48.4	49.9	51.0	56.9	56.5
Operating profit (b) £ billion	0.94★	0.985	1.28	1.646	2.607	2.959
Cash flow (c) £ billion	1.86	2.08	2.28	2.77	3.64	4.24
Customer satisfaction (d)	n/a	2	7	12	17	14
Great place to shop (e)	77	41	48	49	50	46
Great place to work (f)	70	81	83	83	83	82
Supplier satisfaction (g)	58	70	76.5	74.9	77.5	77.8

★ Note this is a profit only because of the definition used, which excludes exceptional items. In this year exceptional items of £6.69 billion were charged to the accounts, leaving Tesco with an operating loss of £5.75 billion.

KEY:

a – Sales (excluding fuel)

b – Operating profit before exceptional items and amortisation of acquired intangibles

c – From retail operations only (i.e. excluding Tesco Bank)

d – The definition changed in 2015–2016 to percentage of fans minus critics answering the question "How likely is it that you would recommend Tesco to a friend or colleague?"

e – A net promoter score, answering the question "I would recommend Tesco as a place to shop"

f – Percentage of colleagues who agree or strongly agree with the statement "I would recommend Tesco as a great place to work"

g – Percentage of suppliers who responded positively when asked "Overall how satisfied are you with your experience of working with Tesco?"

Key Learning Point

Look at page 4 of the 2020 annual report that is headed "turnaround delivered." It gives comparative performance statistics for four stakeholder groups that show substantive improvement between 2014–2015 and 2019–2020.

BUT some of the measures differ from those defined in the big six.

The lesson here is to be wary of performance measures and check for consistency of definitions.

Dave Lewis, in his role as CEO, is granted much of the credit for the turnaround, and after outlining the next five-year strategic plan, he handed over the reins to Ken Murphy, formerly the chief commercial officer at Walgreens Boots Alliance, in late 2020. A new CFO is due to start in 2021, moving in from his current position as CFO of Tate and Lyle. Seemingly, Tesco has concluded that new blood at the most senior levels of management is good for business.

New senior management provides the opportunity to rethink both strategies and governance systems, and as it enters its second century of business, Tesco is moving closer to an ERM style of risk management. It is too early yet to judge if the three lines of defence will work well, and the competition for customers from the discounters remains unabated. Time will tell if "every little helps" really does work, but the current outlook certainly appears promising.

Conclusion

This case study illustrates how much can change within an organisation over the course of fifteen years and how risk management needs to be responsive to those changes. It also shows the way in which sometimes it takes a crisis to trigger transformation.

Pre-2014, with its strong emphasis on a collaborative culture and risk management focused on risk-based monitoring by internal audit, Tesco appears to have been lacking in many of the formal control systems that characterise mature risk management. This was risk management in a subtle, rather than a mature, form, and the emphasis on performance was not curtailed by internal controls. The price paid for this subtlety was very high, both financially and in terms of reputation, although on both counts Tesco PLC now seems well on the road to recovery.

Post-2014, strong new management clarified and reiterated its intolerance of compliance breaches and engaged in a campaign to reset the culture in favour of caring for the customer – going back to basics but this time with much tighter controls. Many things have changed very little, but there is now a clearer link between strategy, risk taking, and risk management. All are central to ERM.

Notes

1 He joined Tesco in 1979 after graduation as a marketing executive and was appointed to the board of directors in 1992. Leahy became chief executive just five years later in 1997.
2 The executive committee is a sub-division of the board, chaired by the chief executive and comprising all executive directors plus the company secretary.
3 The very different, simplified committee and governance structure post-2014, as described later in this case, illustrates well how changes in governance systems are commonly accompanied by a revised risk management system.
4 Figure 7.3 is my personal interpretation of the communication lines used within Tesco. It is intended to complement the governance model that is used internally by the group as is depicted in Figure 7.2.
5 The schemes work as follows: **Shares in Success**: Shares in the company are allocated to participants in the scheme up to Her Majesty's Revenue and Customs (HMRC)-approved limits (currently £3,000 per annum). The amount of profit allocated to the scheme is determined by the board, taking account of company performance. **Buy as You Earn**: An HMRC-approved share purchase scheme under which employees invest up to a limit of £110 on a four-weekly basis to buy shares at the market value in Tesco PLC. **Save as You Earn**: An HMRC-approved savings-related share option scheme under which employees save up to a limit of £250 on a four-weekly basis via a bank/building society with an option to buy shares in Tesco PLC at the end of a three-year or five-year period at a discount of up to 20% of the market value. There are no performance conditions attached to Save as You Earn options.
6 In 2012, for example, board members could earn bonuses of up to 200% of their salary, split 50:50 between shares, and cash in return for hitting a number of short-term performance targets, including profit levels for international and retail businesses, EPS, and sales growth. Long-term bonuses of an equivalent amount were also payable in share options.
7 For more information on OKR see *Objectives and Key Results. Driving Focus, Engagement and Alignment with OKRs* by Paul Niven and Ben Lamorte published by Wiley (2016).
8 Refer back to the sub-section on risk assessment, communication, and monitoring pre-2014 for evidence of this.
9 Community was added to the list in the 2020 annual report, although Tesco has been running community-based projects for several years.

References

Ahmed,K. (2015) "Tesco: Where it all wernt wrong". BBC.CO.UK. January. https://www.bbc.co.uk/news/business-30886632

Barrett, C., Agnew, H., & Felsted, A. (2014) "Q & A: What Went Wrong at Tesco." *Financial Times*, September 22, London.

CIMA (2005) *Official Terminology*. CIMA Publishing/Elsevier, Oxford.

Cinquini, L., Mitchell, F., Norreklit, H., & Tenucci, A. (2013) "Methodologies for Managing Performance Measurement." Chapter 21 in Mitchell, F., Norreklit, H., & Jakobsen, M. (eds.), *The Routledge Companion to Cost Management*. Routledge, London.

Croft, J. (2017) "Tesco Profit Overstatement Prompted 'tears and resignations'." *Financial Times*, October 3, London.

Croft, J., & Eley, J. (2019) "Tesco Fraud Trial Collapse Puts Deferred Prosecution Deals in the Dock. Store Chain Criticised for 'Throwing Executives Under the Bus' Over Accounting Scandal." *Financial Times*, January 23, London.

De Haas, M., & Kleingeld, A. (1999) "Multilevel Design of Performance Measurement Systems: Enhancing Strategic Dialogue Throughout the Organisation." *Management Accounting Research*, Vol. 10, pp. 233–261.

FCA (2018) "FCA Fines Tesco Bank £16.4m for Failures in 2016 Cyber Attack." *Press Release, FCA*, October 1, London.

Financial Reporting Council (2010) *UK Corporate Governance Code*. Downloadable from: www.frc.org.uk/documents/pagemanager/Corporate_Governance/UK%20Corp%20 Gov%20Code%20June%202010.pdf.

Financial Times (2014) "Picking Up the Pieces After Tesco's Stock Affair." *Editorial*. October 26, London.

The Grocer (2020) "The Winners of the Grocer Gold Awards 2020." *The Grocer*, November 13, London.

Helliar, C.V., Lomie, A.A., Power, D., & Sinclair, C.D. (2002) "Managerial Attitudes to Risk: A Comparison of Scottish Chartered Accountants and UK Managers." *Journal of International Accounting, Auditing and Taxation*, Vol. 11, pp. 156–190.

IIA (2013) *The Three Lines of Defense in Effective Risk Management and Control*. Institute of Internal Auditors, Lake Mary, FL.

Kaplan, R.S., & Norton, D.P. (1992) "The Balanced Scorecard – Measures That Drive Performance." *Harvard Business Review*, January/February.

Neville, S. (2014) "Inside Tesco's Bonus Fuelled Regime of Fear and Machismo." *Independent*, September 27, London.

Norreklit, H. (2000) "The Balance on the Balanced Scorecard – A Critical Analysis of Some of Its Assumptions." *Management Accounting Research*, Vol. 11, pp. 65–88.

OECD (2018) *Board Evaluation Overview of International Practices*. Organisation for Economic Co-operation and Development, Paris.

Ohmae, K. (1988) "Getting Back to Strategy." *Harvard Business Review*, Vol. 66, No. 6 (November/December), pp. 149–156.

Rankin, J. (2014) "New Tesco CEO Dave Lewis – Profile." *The Guardian*, July 21, London.

Selim, G., & McNamee, D. (1999) "The Risk Management and Internal Auditing Relationship: Developing and Validating a Model." *International Journal of Auditing*, Vol. 3, pp. 159–174.

Thomas, D. (2021) "Evaluations of UK Company Boards Face Tighter Scrutiny." *Financial Times*, January 20, London.

Thomas, N. (2014) "Tesco's £250m Accounting Black Hole First Flagged During Phil Clarke's Reign." *Sunday Telegraph*, September 28, London.

Vincent, M. (2017) "Terry Leahy's Retail Career in Two Acts." *Financial Times*, November 14, London.

Wilmott, H. (2014) "At Tesco Everyone Is at Fault and No One to Blame." *Financial Times*, October 7, London.

Useful Web Links

1. www.bbc.co.uk/news/business-29716885
   This is an article by the BBC's business editor Kamil Ahmed on the accounting scandal and what went wrong at Tesco to cause it to see its market value fall by 50% in one year in 2014.
2. www.allianz.co.uk/risk-management/trade-sectors/wholesale-and-retail.html
   A useful summary of the risk faced by retailers viewed from the perspective of an insurance provider. Note how the list of risks identified is incomplete relative to those identified by Tesco.

Discussion Questions

1. If you have ever worked as a shop assistant or member of staff in a big fast food outlet, try and recall what risks you were told to be aware of and how to manage them. To what extent do you think lower-grade staff in an organisation should be made aware of and responsible for risk management?
2. Tesco has added the idea of three lines of defence to its use of the steering wheel as a control tool. Are the two concepts complementary or contradictory?
3. Using information from their annual reports and other web sources, compare the style of risk management used in Asda and/or Morrisons with that deployed in Tesco. Critically assess their relative performance in this regard.

8 Risk Management in the Public Sector

Birmingham City Council
(2002–2020)

Aims

The aim of this chapter is to use a longitudinal study of risk management in Europe's largest local authority to illustrate that whilst the tools used to identify, prioritise, manage, and monitor risks are very similar to those adopted by the private sector, the challenges are both different and much greater. In both Akzo Nobel and Tesco, simplification of the business model was an important aid to the introduction of enterprise risk management (ERM). For local government, the option of simplification is largely unavailable, despite the huge diversity of the services provided. The big challenge for risk managers in this context is two-fold. Firstly, how to ensure common tools can be deployed in multiple different contexts across diverse services which are often competing for access to a limited pool of resources. Secondly, how to manage cross-cutting risks which impact on different services simultaneously.

In this chapter we will look in detail at:

- The historical background to the development of governance and risk management practice in local government from 2000 to 2020
- The broad profile of Birmingham City Council
- The evolution of risk management in Birmingham City Council from 2002 to 2020, including:

  - Principal risks
  - Roles and responsibilities for risk
  - Risk management tools
  - The problem of complex risks which cannot be offloaded

- Contrasting approaches to risk management 2002–2009 versus 2010–2020

Historical Background

Governance

Local government provides services, largely funded by the taxpayers, that are vital to many thousands of people. They are effectively huge publicly funded

DOI: 10.4324/9781315208336-8

businesses that have significant economic, social, and environmental impact, and so it is essential that they are underpinned by effective and robust risk management and governance processes. Decisions on how a council raises money and allocates its budget across different services are subject to statutory requirements that both limit the raising of money (e.g. capacity to borrow) and specify minimum levels of service provision. In theory, the elected council members have discretion to influence such decisions, but in practice, that discretion is very limited. Within these boundaries, the elected politicians (council members) define their own priorities in terms of objectives, and the council staff, led by a chief executive, are then required to implement the chosen policies.

In designing and implementing governance and control, local government can make full use of guidance such as ISO 31000 or Committee of Sponsoring Organizations' (COSO's) ERM framework, but specialised guidance and regulations applicable to the public sector also exist. Risk management sits within a local governance framework that was first developed jointly by Chartered Institute of Public Finance and Accountancy (CIPFA), Society of Local Authority Chief Executives (SOLACE) and the Local Government Association in 2001 (CIPFA, 2001). This was updated in 2007 and again in 2016 when it was re-issued along with revised guidance notes (CIPFA/Solace, 2016). The 2016 revisions incorporated legislative changes that now require local authorities to publish annual governance statements reporting on the effectiveness of their governance and internal control arrangements.

The governance statement pushes a council to focus on its effectiveness in achieving its objectives, including ensuring that services are delivered in a manner that ensures value for money. This means that in designing internal controls, risk managers need to acknowledge value for money as an organisational objective.

The new guidance needs to be seen in the context of the continuing austerity challenges faced by local authorities. Since 2009–2010 cuts to funding from central government have led to an average fall of 17% in councils' spending on local public services, whilst councils have simultaneously become increasingly dependent upon local taxation – such as council tax – as a source of income (IFS, 2019). The impact of the cuts has not, however, been equally distributed geographically. Consequently, the more deprived councils that are heavily dependent on grant income have been hit proportionally harder than those which were already more financially independent. The true scale of the impact of funding changes is made clear in a report from the National Audit Office, which calculated that local government spending power, funded from government grants and council tax income, fell in real terms by 28.6% between 2010–2011 and 2017–2018 (NAO, 2019).

This substantive drop in income has important implications for governance and risk management, with councils having to continue spending on priority services whilst simultaneously managing the new risks posed by alternative income sources such as partnership working or commercial income from trading and investment. The CIPFA 2016 governance guidance recognises the fact that the challenges can be locally specific, and so there is a strong emphasis on granting local authorities the autonomy to design their own local governance system within the boundaries of the suggested framework.

The 2016 CIPFA guidance defines governance as "the arrangements put in place to ensure that the intended outcomes for stakeholders are defined and achieved" (CIPFA/ Solace, 2016, p. 12) and emphasises that good governance involves working in the public interest to achieve sustainable economic, societal, and environmental outcomes. Six core principles of good governance are identified. These are adapted for local government use but are based upon the International Framework for Good Governance in the Public Sector (IFAC and CIPFA, 2014).

Two principles underpin the requirement to serve the public interest. These require a local authority to put in place arrangements that:

•   Ensure respect of the law, the maintenance of ethical values, and integrity
•   Incorporate widespread and open engagement with stakeholders

Further principles require a commitment to and effective arrangements for:

•   Sustainable economic, social, and environmental benefits to be used in defining outcomes
•   Specification of what is required to optimise the achievement of the intended outcomes
•   Developing the organisation's capacity, including leadership and staff capabilities
•   Managing risks and performance through robust internal control and strong public financial management
•   Ensuring robust and effective accountability through the adoption of good practices in transparency, reporting, and audits

In addition to defining the governance principles and associated guidance notes, the framework provides examples of best practice in governance reporting and transparency.

The CIPFA principles closely match those laid down in the UK Corporate Governance Code that regulates the private sector, under which the board of directors is responsible for establishing an internal control system and regularly monitoring its effectiveness. There are, however, two key differences between the public and private sector that make governance and risk management *significantly* more challenging in the former.

The first difference is that local councils have a statutory duty to provide certain services to the local community, including education, children's safeguarding and social care, adult social care, waste collection, planning and housing services, road maintenance, and library services. Unlike the private sector, therefore, a council cannot decide that one of these services exposes them to excessive risk and should therefore be stopped – they are legally obliged to provide such a service regardless of the associated risks and their level of funding.

The second difference is that local authorities are obliged to publish an annual governance statement that includes *the findings of* its annual review of the effectiveness of its governance framework and internal controls. The council's governance statement must be approved by a vote of all members and signed by the leader on behalf of the elected members and the chief executive. This contrasts with the private-sector regulations which simply require that the internal control system is reviewed; the findings do not have to be published.

Local authority governance is further complicated by the fact that decisions about service provision always include a political dimension, which means that staff may not be able to do what they consider ideal because the politicians – elected members – will not agree. For example, the person who oversees adult social care may feel that spending is best prioritised by focusing on putting people into a residential unit rather than care in the home, but the politicians may disagree. This can create tension between the staff and politicians, much the same as in central government between the permanent civil service staff and the politicians who are re-elected every five years.

In summary, the governance regulations faced by local government are more stringent that those faced by the private sector, particularly in light of the diverse range of services they are called upon to provide and the challenge of reduced funding combined with increased demand for services. It is perhaps not surprising therefore, that the NAO takes the view that compared with a decade earlier, "the risks from poor governance (are) greater in the current context as the stakes are higher, but the process of governance itself is more challenging and complex" (NAO, 2019).

Risk Management

Local authorities are required to maintain a sound system of internal control, including risk management, internal audit, and whistleblowing arrangements. The evolution of risk management systems within local government since 2000 is most easily understood as spanning two phases.

The first period, 2000–2009, was one in which there was seen to be a strong connection between risk management and a system of performance improvement called Best Value that was introduced in the 1999 Local Government Act. The act introduced a duty for all councils and other local government bodies to put in place arrangements to secure continuous improvement via a system known as Best Value. The act also gave the Audit Commission – an arm's-length government body – general powers to undertake Best Value reviews of individual services within councils. A subsequent Audit Commission paper (Audit Commission, 2001) emphasised the responsibility of both senior management and elected members in local government to manage key strategic risks and to develop formal risk management systems. The paper also highlighted how risk management might assist in the production and monitoring of the Best Value performance plans central to local authority performance improvement.

A broader form of performance inspection, Comprehensive Performance Assessment (CPA), was introduced in 2002. CPA took the form of an audit and inspection framework which reached a single judgement about the performance of a local body (Audit Commission, 2006, p. 2). The result was a CPA rating which classified a council as excellent, good, fair, weak, or poor. The rating system was revised for 2005–2008 with the introduction of a new methodology which used a five-point star scoring mechanism on a scale ranging from zero to four stars. The CPA rating was critically important to a council because it affected its access to funding – better councils got more money – as well as its broader reputation.

CPA directly increased the pressure on councils to introduce formal risk management systems by incorporating risk assessment and management procedures into the CPA judgement. The CPA assessment (Audit Commission, 2006) included a judgment on the extent to which risks and opportunities were incorporated into both strategic and operational decision making. Audit Commission inspectors also assessed the extent to which the internal control environment enabled a council to manage its significant business risks. In order to obtain the highest possible score under CPA, a council had to demonstrate that:

- Risk management practices and assurance frameworks were fully embedded in the council's business processes and overseen by an audit committee independent of the executive function.
- The framework followed terms of reference consistent with CIPFA's governance guidance.

In evaluating a council's performance in the area of risk management, the CPA inspectors looked closely at:

1. Basic structures for risk management, linking risks to strategic objectives, likelihood–impact analysis, and ownership of risks
2. The embedding of risk management into core processes, including policy making, planning, and performance management
3. Counter fraud and corruption arrangements, including both proactive and reactive work, and the encouragement of a counter fraud culture across the council
4. Systems of internal control and annual evaluation of internal control effectiveness, along with oversight by an Audit Committee

Given the importance of CPA performance to both funding and reputation, it is not surprising that it triggered significant efforts to introduce and improve risk management systems over the period 2000–2009. There were multiple sources for authorities to use in designing their risk management systems, including a core standard jointly drafted by the Association of Insurance and Risk Managers (AIRMIC), the Institute of Risk Management (IRM), and the

Association of Local Authority Risk Managers (ALARM) (AIRMIC/IRM/ ALARM, 2002). ALARM also published helpful guidance on issues such as the management of fraud, partnership risks, and the benchmarking of risk, as well as offering training programmes for both professional and academic risk management qualifications.

In 2009 CPA was replaced by Comprehensive Area Assessments (CAA), which sought to extend the inspection process to include local bodies not under council control (e.g. fire/police authorities). The intention was to assess local performance against economic and social outcomes that required councils to engage in partnerships with other organisations. CAA was intended as a step towards a regime that was more self-regulated and locally accountable, but it did not last long enough to be tested.

The year 2010 marked a step change in risk management in UK local government, with the newly elected Conservative government announcing the ending of CAA. The intention was to cut costs by eliminating inspections, but also reflected a political desire to emphasise locally independent decision making, underpinned by transparency and accountability. The newly appointed minister for decentralisation declared a desire to eliminate stifling bureaucracy and "make councils look to the public they serve, not to Whitehall" (GOV. UK, 2010). Two months later, plans to the close the Audit Commission were announced, though it did not finally shut its doors until mid-2015.

The Local Audit and Accountability Act 2014 formally abolished the Audit Commission and put in place new arrangements for the local audit of councils to be undertaken by private firms regulated by the Financial Reporting Council and professional accountancy bodies. Assessment of value for money was made an integral part of the audit process, and central government powers to evaluate value for money in local authorities were extended. Furthermore, the legislation placed a duty on a local auditor to consider the need to make a public interest report on any matter coming to their attention during the audit and relating to either the authority or a connected entity.

Additionally, the act introduced new regulations on councils to increase transparency of decision making. This built on earlier legislation from 2012 which had granted public access to attend meetings of the council's executive. The 2014 act introduced the right for the public to attend full council meetings and film, tweet, or blog at those meetings. The local community was also granted the right to a referendum vote on council tax increases if considered to be potentially excessive.

Post-2010, therefore, the role of central government in oversight of council affairs was dramatically reduced and replaced by oversight via transparency and accountability to the local community. Whilst public accountability and transparency is a laudable aim, for the purposes of this book, it is also useful to consider the resulting impact on risk management and service provision. New ways of communicating information in a way that the public can understand became central to transparency, and the increased level of media and public comment on decisions also required work to be done in response. These new demands on staff ran alongside the risk management pressures of retaining the required statutory service levels with a massively reduced budget, putting a strain on both staff and core services. In other words, the combination of greater accountability plus austerity ultimately increased the risks faced by local authorities.

In summary, the evolution of risk management within UK local government over the period 2000–2020 has developed within a context of autonomy of choice, but that autonomy is constrained by the current risk and governance standards and central government policies. Consequently, the story of risk management over this time can be split into two distinct phases:

Phase 1: 2002–2009
A period of development and formalisation of internal control and risk management systems and explicit recognition that effective risk management was central to successful achievement of objectives.
Phase 2: 2010–2020
A period of retrenchment for risk management in the context of reduced funding and greater public transparency. Attention has been increasingly focused on core services such as housing and education, possibly at the expense of non-essential ones (e.g. libraries or leisure facilities). Risk profiles have been raised by budget pressures and greater council involvement in commercial activities.

Before looking in depth at these phases, it is useful to look at the context via a brief profile of the city and the council.

Birmingham City Council Profile[1]

The City

Birmingham is England's second city, covering almost 300 square kilometres in the West Midlands conurbation, and the city is the hub of the region's economy. As the largest city in the conurbation, "the regional economy is driven by what happens in Birmingham and the Council's leadership role is critical to the prosperity and well-being of the region" (Audit Commission, 2007, p. 10).

The local authority area covers a population of approximately 1.2 million, although over 3 million live within the "travel to work" area. Despite significant levels of inward investment in recent years, the region has suffered from substantial job losses within its former core industries of car manufacturing and vehicle components. Consequently, the economy has refocused, and 80% of jobs in the city are now in the service sector. Nonetheless, Birmingham's unemployment level stood at 14.5% in mid-2020, almost 50% higher than a decade earlier, nearly double the national average of 7.8%, and the highest within the Core Cities group.[2] Low labour force participation rates are commonly linked to social deprivation, and average household incomes are below both the national and regional averages.

The population of Birmingham is characterised by its ethnic diversity, with 42% of the population made up of black, Asian and minority ethnic (BAME) groups (primarily South Asian). There is also great diversity in the level of prosperity across the city, with both affluent suburbs but also poor housing estates where levels of unemployment are high and health poor. Forty per cent of the city's population live in the most deprived decile areas in England. Overall, the levels of crime are lower than in most large cities, but health and skill levels in the population are significantly worse than the national average. For example, the life expectancy of men in Birmingham is 2.5 years less than the national average. Not surprisingly, therefore, in 2020 Birmingham was ranked as the seventh most deprived local authority in England.

The Council

Birmingham is England's largest local authority and one of the largest in Europe. The metropolitan authority employs approximately 26,500 people and for the 2020–2021 financial year, its budget is estimated at just under £3.2 billion. The council provides a wide range of services, both statutory and non-statutory. Statutory services, which they are required by law to provide, include adult social care, education, children's safeguarding and social care, waste collection, planning and housing, road maintenance, environmental health, and libraries. Local authorities can provide other services such as leisure, sport, and cultural facilities (e.g. art galleries) at their discretion. The sources of funding include central government, local taxes, rental income, and other forms of commercial activity.

The key statistics in Figure 8.1 give an overview of both the scale and range of services provided by the council.

- Funding of 238 schools and oversight of 186 academies and 19 free schools
- Provision of 29 libraries plus 7 co-managed with local community groups
- 60,185 houses provided and maintained by the council
- 4,700 hectares of parks maintained by the city council
- 412,130 tonnes of domestic waste collected
- 2 million phone calls and 65,000 emails received from citizens wanting to access council services
- Investment in and management of locally important subsidiary and joint venture companies (e.g. National Exhibition Centre; Birmingham Airport)
- 2,500 kilometres of road maintained
- 5,900 planning applications processed

Source: Birmingham City Council website

Figure 8.1 Key statistics (2019–2020)

It is clear that behind these statistics lies a complex and large-scale organisation facing a wide range of risks that need to be carefully monitored and managed. To begin to understand how this is achieved in practice, we need to consider the governance model through which the provision of services is managed.

The Governance Model

The model of governance used by the authority is a leader and cabinet system of publicly elected members. The cabinet is made up of nine senior full-time members (councillors) plus the leader of the council who acts as the chair, and together they are responsible for all the significant decisions within the council (excluding planning and licensing). The leader of the council is required by law to publish and maintain a forward plan of the work of the cabinet, covering all major decisions to be made over the coming four months, and a copy of this is posted on the council's website. Forthcoming meeting dates and the detail of both portfolio and ward-level decisions are made public.

Each cabinet member takes responsibility for a specific portfolio, such as health and social care or education, skills, and culture. Non-cabinet councillors monitor decision making and the workings of the council through their membership of a total of eight overview and scrutiny committees. Responsibility for chairing the main scrutiny committees is shared between the different political parties.

Whilst the cabinet oversees the budget and prioritises spending across the different services, in practice the service provision is the joint responsibility of both politicians and executive staff. Consequently, cabinet decisions are *implemented* by officers of the council, headed by the chief executive, supported by a management team made up of paid directors who head up the core central services and service directorates, as shown in Figure 8.2.

The council leadership team is the local authority equivalent of a private-sector board of directors and meets once a week for policy review and development.

Each directorate oversees several related services, and service directors carry overall responsibility for management of the operational staff. For example, in Birmingham the adult social care directorate provides support for adults with disabilities or requiring support due to old age. The directorates remit includes:

1. Provision of support for adults with mental health issues
2. Support for carers looking after elderly, disabled, or sick adults
3. Provision of elderly residential care homes and day centres
4. Adult education

Within the UK, the exact matching of services to directorates varies between different local authorities, but the overall governance structure remains very similar across the sector.

Chief Executive

Director of Finance and Governance	Assistant Chief Executive	Director of Digital and Customer Services	Managing Director City Operations	Director Inclusive Growth	Director of Education and Skills	Director of Adult Social Care	Director of Human Resources	Programme Director, Commonwealth Games 2022

Figure 8.2 Birmingham City Council leadership team

Source: Adapted from Birmingham, City Council Website 2021

Key Learning Point

The governance structure in local authorities requires interaction and good understanding between members and officers. The members make the policy decisions, and the staff implement them.

A good working relationship between the two groups is thus an essential prerequisite for effective service provision and risk and budget management.

Risk Management in Birmingham City Council (2002–2020)

Overall Strategy

The council formally adopted a framework for corporate governance in July 2002 that was based upon the CIPFA (2001) guidelines, and the associated risk management strategy has evolved over time but continues to reflect these underlying principles.

The introduction of formalised risk management control systems was triggered by several external factors:

1. The public-sector codes of governance, especially those issued by CIPFA and SOLACE
2. External audit
3. The introduction of the Best Value and CPA system and the inclusion of risk management arrangements within the key lines of enquiry used in CPA

The objectives of risk management as laid down pre-2010 were defined as:

1. Integrate risk management into the culture of the council.
2. Manage risk in accordance with the practice.
3. Anticipate and respond to changing social, political, environmental, legislative, and technological requirements.
4. Prevent injury damage and losses and reduce the cost of risk.
5. Raise awareness of the need for risk management by all those connected with the council's delivery of services.

Unsurprisingly, the city council's current risk management strategy document has retained the same objectives, simply prefacing the word practice with the adjective "good" to add ambition. Fundamental risk management strategies, definitions, and lines of responsibility have remained largely unchanged between 2002 and 2020, but the types of risks faced have evolved and the internal guidance provided has expanded and increased in detail.

Risk is defined as an event/series of events which may, partially or fully, prevent the council from achieving its planned objectives. Birmingham Audit (the internal audit function) carries day-to-day responsibility for implementing risk management policies and training, and the view is taken that

> risk management is very much looking at achieving your objectives and what's going to stop you . . . that's the way we sell it. It's part of helping them (Service Directors) to meet their targets and service plans and make it easier for them to see what's going to trip them up.
>
> (Head of Birmingham Audit)

At the same time, risk management is seen as making the most of opportunities to achieve objectives through a combination of risk transfer, risk control, and risk acceptance.

A 2017 document identifies the ways in which the objectives of the risk management strategy will be achieved:

1. Establishing clear roles, responsibilities, and reporting lines within the council for risk management, making it clear that everyone should take ownership for risk management
2. Incorporating risk management considerations into all levels of business planning
3. Providing opportunities for shared learning on risk management across the council and with partner organisations
4. Offering a framework for allocating resources to identified priority risk areas
5. Reinforcing the importance of effective risk management as part of the everyday work of employees by offering training
6. Monitoring of arrangements, at all levels, on an on-going basis by management

Source: Birmingham City Council Risk Management Strategy 2017

This list highlights the need for all staff to take responsibility for risk management within a well-defined framework that clarifies employees' roles and responsibilities. Embedding risk management across the council has always been a central aim, and this includes the politicians.

Principal Risks in Local Government

Unsurprisingly, the risk categories faced by local government are somewhat different from those in the private sector. In common with any organisation, Birmingham Council faces reputational, regulatory, technological, physical, and environmental risks. In their role as a provider of services to the community, funded from a mix of central and local sources, however, there are some additional risks that must be continuously monitored and managed:

1. **Political** – Politics can impact on the ability to make decisions (e.g. if there is no overall majority party), as well as the quality and style of leadership. Central government politics will affect funding and regulation in local authorities.
2. **Economic** – The type of services required locally will be influenced by levels of employment and poverty, and local property prices affect the capital receipts and growth of income from council tax.
3. **Social** – The demographic profile of the city, especially the age profile, can affect the demand for educational and adult social care services, as well as the requirement for different types of leisure/cultural services.
4. **Partnership risks** – In recent years, both regulation and the need to identify new ways of funding service provision have led councils into partnership with a range of public, private, and third-sector bodies, such as National Health Services (NHS) trusts, the police, universities, and social enterprises. All such partnerships introduce potential risks relating to service delivery, reputation, fraud, and performance management. Partnership working creates new governance challenges for council staff to ensure effective accountability and control.

In effect, the citizens of Birmingham are the consumers of the services, and so are equivalent to the customers in a private-sector arrangement. Current regulation, with its emphasis on transparency and accountability, makes councils directly answerable to this consumer base.

Roles and Responsibilities for Risk: Senior Management

It is the responsibility of the senior management team to identify new risks that may threaten the council and/or the city of Birmingham and ensure that the corporate risk register is up to date and complete. Many of the key corporate risks are cross-cutting in nature (i.e. impact on potentially multiple services within the council) and require close internal cooperation to be managed effectively.

At the executive level, the director of finance and corporate governance acts as the risk management "champion" amongst the officers (employees) of the council. The deputy leader carries responsibility for engaging and training elected members in risk management issues.

An annual governance review requires each directorate[3] (managed by an individual council director) and significant areas of service delivery/business units within each directorate to produce their own assurance statement highlighting significant governance issues and details of what action(s) are being taken to mitigate any risks. These assurance statements, provided by internal managers, together with evidence from internal audit, the external auditors, and other external assessment bodies, are used to reach the end-of-year opinion on governance effectiveness, signed by the leader of the council and chief executive, and published in the annual accounts. The following box shows an example of such an assurance statement.

Annual Assurance Statement

This statement shows that we have adequate arrangements which continue to be regarded as fit for purpose, comply with the council's local code of corporate governance, and demonstrates that we have met our legal and statutory obligations to our residents.

If the review reveals significant governance weaknesses, these must be identified, along with details of the tools being used to mitigate and correct them. Some examples of such governance failings and the associated statements are included later in this case study. Where a governance failure is considered highly significant by the external auditor, or they are concerned that an authority is not financially sustainable in the long term, the auditors can issue a Section 24 (Local Audit and Accountability Act, 2014) notice. In such cases, a council's external auditors append a written Section 24 "recommendation" to their annual audit letter that is also copied to the secretary of state. Such notices are very bad publicity for a council and require council members to respond within one month with a plan on how the issue will be satisfactorily addressed. Additionally, the secretary of state is empowered to order a Best Value Inspection of a Council to provide independent assurance that a council is complying with its Best Value duties. If such assurance cannot be given because the inspection suggests that the council lacks the relevant capacity, then commissioners are appointed to oversee the officers and the council as it progresses through a clearly directed improvement plan. The politically devastating practical effect of such an arrangement is that the council forfeits its autonomy over local decision making.[4]

On a day-to-day basis, internal controls require that all senior management (cabinet/committee) reports include a specific risk section that outlines:

1. The risks expected from a strategy/decision/action
2. The steps to be taken to mitigate these risks
3. An explanation of how the risks will be managed on an ongoing basis

All decisions of the executive are subject to scrutiny, and the scrutiny committees can "call in" a decision for detailed review to ensure that it matches council policy and is soundly based. In addition to a coordinating overview and scrutiny committee, other committees perform the same role within each directorate or major service area (e.g. education and children's social care overview and scrutiny committee/housing and neighbourhoods overview and scrutiny committee). Meetings of all of these committees are held in public and broadcast live on a webcast.

Within each directorate, the management team is responsible for undertaking risk assessments, and a nominated risk representative (formerly risk champion) is tasked with implementing and managing risk within the directorate, acting as the point of contact for provision of risk registers and liaison with internal audit. Additionally, each service director is required have in place a business continuity plan that will enable service provision to be maintained in the event of a major incident.

Roles and Responsibilities for Risk: Birmingham Audit

Day-to-day responsibility for the development and maintenance of the risk management processes rests with Birmingham Audit, which is the internal audit section of the council. Birmingham Audit emphasises, however, that

> good governance requires that risk management is embedded into the culture of the organisation, with members and managers at all levels recognizing that risk management is part of their job.

In other words, Birmingham Audit staff act as enablers of risk management by training and working with council staff to develop practical ways of managing risks.

Historically, the work of the internal audit function within local authorities has been focused on the provision of assurance on the core financial framework and systems and the detection, investigation, and prevention of fraud and corruption. Risk management, however, encompasses much more than financial controls, and this raises questions about the most appropriate location for risk management within councils. Birmingham has chosen to place responsibility within internal audit, but other councils take the view that risk management is essentially a performance management concern, and so the function lies there rather than with internal audit. Size is also a determining factor here, as some councils will not be sufficiently large to warrant a separate internal audit or risk management function.

In specifying the function that should hold supervisory responsibility for risk management, it is important to avoid any conflict of interest in the work of the function. If internal audit staff are testing control effectiveness, they should not simultaneously be involved in drafting those controls or advising on them. In practical terms, this means that separate teams of staff are required with different, clearly defined, areas of responsibility.

In Birmingham City Council the separation of duties is achieved by the internal audit section being split into those who conduct the internal audits per se and a separate risk team who provide the broader support for the risk management system and its application across the different services in the council. A relatively small proportion of the work of internal audit is now allocated to the audit of financial systems, and the remainder is devoted to risk management, corporate governance, and business/operational activities, although the latter does include an element of financial control review. The annual internal audit plans are prepared in accordance with the CIPFA Code of Practice for Internal Audit.

The creation of a specialist risk group is an explicit recognition of the size, complexity, and diversity of risks encountered within the city council, and the non-accounting nature of the work of this team is illustrated by the fact that they are training for the Institute of Internal Audit or Institute of Risk Management examinations rather than the management accounting–focused Chartered Institute of Management Accountants (CIMA) examinations. This also reflects growing evidence of the emergence of a new risk management "profession."

The risk team in internal audit are responsible for revising and updating the core risk management documents within the council. These include the policy and strategy statement, key responsibilities, risk management processes, and risk management toolkit, all of which are subject to both internal and external review. Working alongside staff from across the council's directorates, Birmingham Audit assist in the development of practical approaches to risk identification and monitoring and provide regular face-to-face training sessions together with an online learning module for all staff involved in the management of risk.

Corporate risk register reports are compiled by Birmingham Audit for submission to both the council management team and the Audit Committee. Reports from its internal audit teams provide detailed information on directorate-level risk management, and reporting to the Audit Committee, they inform the wider governance agenda.

Roles and Responsibilities for Risk: Audit Committee

Responsibility for independent assurance on the effectiveness of internal controls, risk management, and governance, as in private-sector organisations, rests with the Audit Committee, which receives regular reports from Birmingham Audit. Its independence serves to reassure the public of the objectivity of the council's reporting and accounts, and its authority provides backing for the work of Birmingham Audit. CIPFA guidelines (CIPFA, 2005, p. 13) define the role of the Audit Committee within a local authority as being to:

1. Consider the effectiveness of the authority's risk management arrangements, the control environment, and associated anti-fraud and anti-corruption arrangements.
2. Seek assurances that action is being taken on risk-related issues identified by auditors and inspectors.

3. Be satisfied that the authority's assurance statements, including the State-
    ment on Internal Control, properly reflect the risk environment and any
    actions required to improve it.
4. Approve (but not direct) internal audit's strategy, plan, and monitor perfor-
    mance. Review summary internal audit reports and the main issues arising,
    and seek assurance that action has been taken where necessary.
5. Receive the annual report of the head of internal audit. Consider the
    reports of external audit and inspection agencies.
6. Ensure that there are effective relationships between external and internal
    audit, inspection agencies, and other relevant bodies and that the value of
    the audit process is actively promoted.
7. Review the financial statements, external auditor's opinion, and reports to
    members and monitor management action in response to the issues raised
    by external audit.

Roles and Responsibilities for Risk: Council Staff and Members

Figure 8.3 shows the hierarchy for risk management that is used by staff within
Birmingham City Council. Elected members take political decisions that
reflect the council's chosen long- and short-term strategic objectives. Senior
management are responsible for the overall implementation of the political
decisions, but day-to-day operational management is done by the individual
directorates. Directorates are made up of divisions, which are further split into
specific services/business units and then projects.

The aim is to ensure that across all levels of the hierarchy, everyone com-
municates about risks – the existence, scale, likelihood, consequences, tools for
control, etc. – and those risks are regularly monitored and reviewed. Consequently, the left-hand side of Figure 8.3 is labelled "Communicate and Con-
sult," depicting the way in which risks are notified from the service divisions up
the hierarchy to senior management and the Audit Committee. For example,
within directorates, all individual risks are allocated to a risk owner, who carries responsibility for reducing the risk to a target level and reporting progress
to their directorate's risk representative for transmission up the hierarchy.

The right-hand side depicts the "Monitor and Review" processes, which are
continuous. Risk registers at both the corporate and divisional level are regularly updated and control tools revised when existing methods are ineffective.
In combination, the communication and monitoring processes form a control
loop, whereby a risk is identified and control tools selected; this information
is communicated up the hierarchy, and monitoring by internal audit helps to
ensure risks stay within the desired level.

Such a system requires that risk awareness and understanding permeate the
entire organisation, with all staff recognising risk management as part of their
job and something which helps in ensuring the achievement of the council's
overall objectives. Central to the development of such understanding are the
training sessions organised by Birmingham Audit.

A sample training exercise is illustrated in the following box.

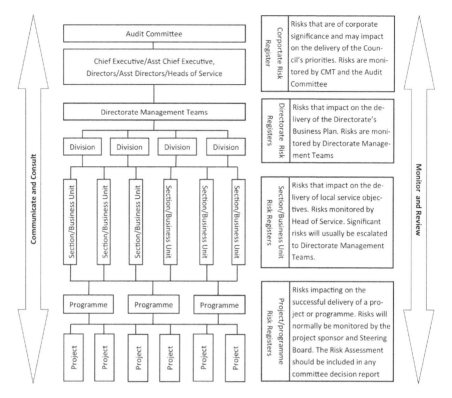

Figure 8.3 Risk management hierarchy

Source: Adapted from Birmingham City Council (2018)

Box 8.1 Training in Risk Identification and Control

Training in how to identify and monitor risks can start at a very basic level. For example, at a training session for new staff in Birmingham, members of the risk team within internal audit gave the trainees the task of getting a raw egg – unsupported – from one side of a large room to the other without breaking it. To help them in the process, teams were provided with access to any of the materials that they may wish to use from the department's stationery cupboard. Most of the teams were very concerned about the risk associated with the fragility of the egg, and so spent a lot of time building structures from cardboard, paper, string, and various other items to minimise the risk of breakage. The exercise ended with two members of the risk team throwing an unprotected egg from end to end of the room and simply being careful in the process of catching it. The lesson learnt was that it is easy to overestimate risk and also to spend a lot of money on protecting against it. The management of risk requires an ability to take a perspective on its importance, and hence how much to spend on managing it.

This particular training session took place within the offices of Birmingham Audit; training is also organised on site within the services themselves. Head of service and other line managers may request assistance from internal audit to help them identify and evaluate the risks that they may encounter based upon the service plan that they have drafted. The assistance does not take the form of telling them what risks may exist, but simply helping them to think about what might get in the way of the achievement of the plan's objectives. To some extent, risk management is about a particular mindset, and after staff have had some practice at going through the process of risk identification and assessment several times, many become adept at the process. At this point it can be argued that risk management is starting to become embedded within the culture and thinking of the organisation.

The Risk Management Framework

The risk management strategy and key lines of responsibility described earlier require the establishment of a very clear framework to provide the necessary tools to ensure that all levels of staff can fulfil their risk responsibilities. The framework used in Birmingham City Council is based on the three lines of defence model. Front-line service staff provide the first line of defence; the second line involves management oversight, complemented by some independent assessment and monitoring of controls (e.g. by Ofsted education inspectors); and the third line of defence is Birmingham Audit, whose work aims to provide assurance that the other defence lines and controls are operating effectively.

Within this framework, the risk management process is based upon the risk standard developed by the IRM (2002) and is broken down into five key stages:

1. **Identification** of risks/opportunities
2. **Analysis** of risks/opportunities
3. **Prioritisation** of risks/opportunities
4. **Management** of risks/opportunities
5. **Monitoring/review** of progress

The language used by Birmingham City Council varies little from that within the standard model of the IRM.

IDENTIFICATION OF RISKS/OPPORTUNITIES

Risks and opportunities are defined in terms of the aim of achieving the council's objectives in relation to service provision. A variety of methods can be used to help identify risks, including management experience, formal risk assessments, insurance data, and internal control reviews. Many different types of risk may be identified, and the causes are likely to be various and sometimes specific to individual services. Internal audit suggest a prompt list of risks that staff may wish to consider, including environmental, legal, political, financial, social, reputational, managerial, physical, and technological risks.

Every service area is required to identify risks and opportunities against the background of its service objectives, and all risks are then recorded on a risk register, which acts as a key reference point for the entire risk management system. An example of a risk register is included at the end of this section to illustrate how the whole framework ties together. The boxed example illustrates the breadth of risks that may be faced within an individual service area and formally recorded on the risk register. Note: The risks in this example are for illustrative purposes only.

Box 8.2   Example of Service-Level Risks

Waste Management Service
Risks may include:
- Failure to provide safe access for the public to household recycling centres
- Inadequate environmental controls at waste management sites
- Challenges in recruiting staff for work in refuse and recycling services
- Contractors failing to deliver services to the agreed specification
- Financial pressures leading to reduced repairs/maintenance

It is critical to note that the need for risk identification and management is not exclusive to the service level of the council. Directorates and the broader corporate level of the council will also face risks which may be either independent of or interact with the service-level risks. Such risks are defined as cross-cutting. Possibly the biggest challenge for risk managers in the public sector is the scale and range of cross-cutting risks that need to be managed, for example, in respect of child poverty. Poor households in a city may be unable to pay their council tax and be in receipt of multiple benefits, including housing benefits. The children are likely to be entitled to free school meals, which impacts the education service, and poor family health will cause increased pressure on local primary care services. In other words, multiple service areas covering housing, education, health, and local government income collection can all be impacted by a trend towards increased child poverty. Clearly, the management of risks that cut across multiple services needs to be controlled centrally and requires clear and timely cross-service communication.

Knowing the possible risks that may be faced is, however, insufficient for control purposes. More information is required to know where to prioritise the control effort and where risks are too small to really matter.

ANALYSIS OF RISKS/OPPORTUNITIES

After risks have been identified, they are grouped and ranked according to the likelihood of their occurrence and their expected impact. Likelihood/impact matrices are commonly used by risk managers. The exact design of the matrices will vary from organisation to organisation, but the underlying principle remains identical: the aim is to be able to classify risks in terms of the two dimensions. In Birmingham they use a 4 × 4 matrix with the classifications being high, significant, medium, and low. Tables 8.1 and 8.2 detail the definitions applicable to each of these classifications.

Initially, the risks being classified are the inherent risks (i.e. those which may occur assuming no management controls are in place to reduce their likelihood or impact).

An additional matrix of risks is drafted in terms of residual exposure levels, based on assurance – either from management or from internal audit – that the controls are demonstrably effective in reducing the risk. All residual risks are "owned" by a named member of staff, and the residual risks are regularly reported and compared to the target risk, which is defined as the long-term desired level of risk in the specific service area. The risk matrix for each service thus acts as both a feedback and feed-forward control for monitoring purposes.

RISK/OPPORTUNITY PRIORITISATION

Figure 8.4 shows the process used to prioritise risks or opportunities. Risks are marked on to the 4 × 4 matrix according to the classification of low to high likelihood and low to high impact, and the shaded zones of the matrix equate to a traffic light system: severe is a red light, material is amber, and tolerable is green.

Table 8.1 Likelihood

Classification	Definition
High	Almost certain in most circumstances. Higher than 80% probability.
Significant	Likely: 50% to 80% probability.
Medium	Possible: 20%–50% probability.
Low	Unlikely but could occur at any time. Less than 20% probability.

Table 8.2 Impact

Classification	Definition
High	Critical to achievement of objectives. Huge impact on cost/reputation and requiring a long-term recovery plan.
Significant	Major impact on costs and objectives. Serious impact on reputation or quality extending into the medium/long term.
Medium	Waste of time and resources but with moderate impact and potentially expensive medium-term effects.
Low	Minor loss/costs/inconvenience. Short- or medium-term impact only.

The definitions for these zones directly reflect the severity of impact upon service objectives if the risk crystallises, and the degree of severity is reflected in the subsequent level of control and frequency of monitoring. For example, in Figure 8.4 risk number two is classed as being of low severity and low likelihood. As a result, the level of control over this risk is likely to be low, because the impact will also be low. In contrast, risk number one is classed as being both high risk and high likelihood and hence severe. In terms of the definitions, this means that there is a strong likelihood of the risk occurring and jeopardising the achievement of council objectives. The only way to resolve this is to immediately introduce additional control systems.

All risks with a high impact and significant or above likelihood are classified as severe, and information about these risks and the related controls are automatically escalated up to the next level in the organisational hierarchy. In other words, if a service manager sees something as a severe risk, this fact will be made known to the service director, who then has a responsibility to ensure that controls and action plans are devised to reduce that residual risk to material rather than severe. Severe risks, which represent five of the sixteen elements of the matrix, are the subject of both weekly meetings and action plans within the relevant directorate. The action plans provide a record of the effectiveness of existing controls, who is responsible for managing the specific risk, and the nature and timing of the subsequent control actions taken.

Risks identified as having medium impact or below and with only a low likelihood of occurrence are classed as tolerable. Tolerable risks are regularly reviewed, and low-cost risk reduction strategies identified where possible, but they are not proactively managed, as they are acceptable within the existing management routines.

MANAGEMENT AND CONTROL OF RISKS

Six stages are involved in the process of the management of risk. These are as follows:

1. Establishing the risk appetite

Compliance With Regulations on Air Quality in Birmingham

Under the Environment Act 1995, the whole of Birmingham was classified as an Air Quality Management Area, requiring compliance with set limits on levels of certain air pollutants. A report in 2016 showed that levels of NO_2 needed to be reduced. Subsequently, the council's risk map dated March 2019 classified the risk of fines being imposed for poor air quality as being high and the impact medium. In other words, cost-effective control improvements needed to be identified to ensure regulatory compliance.

In response, the council introduced a Clean Air Zone in June 2021, aimed at discouraging polluting vehicles from entering the area. Daily charges of £8 per day for cars, taxis, and large good vehicles (LGVs) and £50 a day for coaches, buses, and heavy goods vehicles (HGVs) have been imposed on vehicles identified as not having clean enough engines.

This represents a low-cost response to controlling the risk.

2. Assessing whether to accept, control, modify, transfer, or eliminate the risk
3. Recording the reasons for the decision
4. Implementing the decision
5. Assigning individual ownership to each risk
6. Specifying the actions and timescale required to reduce risk to the target level

Risks are expressed and measured in terms of their impact upon the council's objectives, and they are managed in terms of the council's risk appetite. The risk appetite reflects the extent of risk which is deemed to be acceptable or tolerable. Tolerable is defined in terms of the traffic light system used in the matrix shown earlier. Once identified and prioritised, risks are therefore managed through acceptance, control, modification, or transfer. The aim is to bring the residual risk level down to a level classed as tolerable.

In choosing how to respond to a particular risk, staff must take into account the trade-off between the cost of controls and the costs incurred if objectives are not achieved. In crude terms, spending £100,000 on anti-fraud protection systems makes little economic sense if the maximum loss from fraud is estimated at £70,000. The cost of implementing and operating a control should not normally exceed the maximum potential benefit.

Once a decision has been made on how a risk will be controlled, individuals are assigned ownership of the risk and take responsibility for monitoring progress against controls to ensure that the risk remains within tolerable levels and does not threaten the achievement of objectives. Feedback from the monitoring is then used to review and possibly modify both the objectives and the control process itself.

Tools Used for Managing and Controlling Risks

Risk registers, allocation of risk ownership, and action plans all form important parts of the risk management process. Risk registers are reviewed at least quarterly to ensure that risks are deleted, added, or upgraded as appropriate. Where a risk is deleted, there is a requirement that the reasons for the deletion are fully recorded, together with an explanation of what has happened to the risk. The mechanisms adopted to review risks may be selected by service or directorate managers and may take the form of an agenda item at a management meeting, a special risk meeting, or a workshop organised through internal audit.

The review process will work through each risk on the current register to assess:

• If it is still valid
• If anything has changed, particularly the residual risk
• Whether to delegate/escalate the risk if required as a result of identified changes

Additionally, the review will identify any new risks that may have arisen and complete an assessment of the residual risk using the 4 × 4 matrix described earlier.

Council-wide consistency in relation to risk registers and action plans is achieved using standardised documentation. The same risk register template is used across all services, ensuring that when risks are aggregated across the whole council, internal audit knows that equivalent approaches have been adopted in all directorates.

The risk register template is reproduced in Table 8.3.

The action plan that forms the lower section of the template ensures that it is clear what actions are necessary to reduce risk, who carries responsibility for these, and if progress is being made. This documentary record forces staff to face up to the need to monitor risks in order to keep them under control and to see risk identification and measurement as a perpetual cycle rather than an irregular event. By being forced to record the decisions taken and the basis for them and to ensure that controls are regularly reviewed for effectiveness, people become answerable for their actions and begin to understand the link between risk and performance.

Consistency is also monitored by the internal audit process itself, with staff knowledgeable about which directorates or service areas are more or less focused on risk management issues and good or bad at maintaining up-to-date risk information. Internal audit also carries responsibility for checking whether the risk controls are working effectively, thus fulfilling the role as shown on the

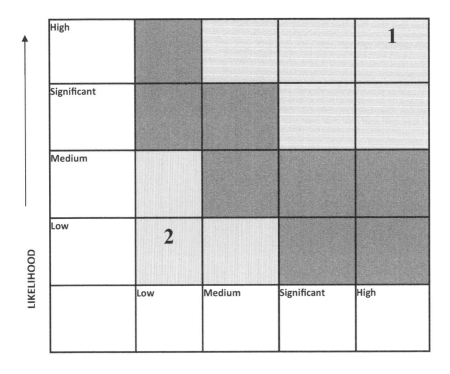

KEY:

	SEVERE	Immediate control improvement to be made to enable business goals to be met and service delivery maintained/improved
	MATERIAL	Close monitoring to be carried out and cost effective control improvements sought to ensure service delivery is maintained
	TOLERABLE	Regular review, low cost control improvements sought if possible

Figure 8.4 Prioritisation matrix/risk heat map

Table 8.3 Risk Register Template

Risk No.:		**Risk Title:**	

Risk Description:

Risk Owner:	**Risk Lead:**	**Risk Type/Category:**

Inherent/Gross Risk			Residual/ Current Risk			Target Risk		
Likelihood	Impact	Prioritisation	Likelihood	Impact	Prioritisation	Likelihood	Impact	Prioritisation

Current Controls Mitigating Inherent Risk:	**Sources of Assurance on Effectiveness of Identified Controls:**

No.:	Actions to Reduce Risk to Target	Owner	Target Date	Progress	RAG
1					
2					
3					
4					
5					

Updated by:	**Date:**

right-hand side of Figure 8.3. Birmingham Audit uses a risk-based approach for internal audit, which prioritises those directorates and service areas which may carry significant "corporate-level" risks as well as operational risks.

Information Support Systems for Risk Management

Information and communications technology (ICT) is fundamentally important to the maintenance of the risk management control system in Birmingham because the technology is integral to the risk control process. When the risk management system was first being developed, documentation and risk guidance were posted on the intranet, but it was felt that its usefulness for risk management purposes was limited. As a result, the risk team chose to purchase Magique, a dedicated piece of commercial risk management software. The team was also responsible for the system's installation.

The role of Magique is four-fold:

1. **Training** – Online training packages help to get the risk message across to staff at all levels within the council, whilst simultaneously easing the pressure on staff resources within internal audit.
2. **Real-time update of risk registers** – Real-time updating ensures that up-to-date council-wide risk registers are continuously available to both internal audit and senior council staff. The software does not, however, automatically update the internal audit plan in response to changes in the service-level risk registers. Instead, these have to be completed manually by internal audit staff.
3. **Maintenance of an events log** – The events log is used for both audit planning and the redesign of risk controls to reduce the likelihood of future events.
4. **Management of cross-directorate risk information** – By granting real-time access to information across all services, the software facilitates the management of cross-directorate risk information. For example, the council's CPA score is aggregated from across a broad range of council activities, and senior management therefore need to be aware of the risk of the score changing because of shifts in risk data across all of the relevant directorates. Magique enables analysis of cross-directorate information because it can present slices of risk profiles both vertically and horizontally across the organisation.

Magique therefore enables internal audit to pull together all of the information needed to draft the annual assurance statement on risk management and internal control. In the absence of such technology, the database would have to be maintained manually, and the preparation of the assurance statement would clearly be more time consuming.

Birmingham directly recognises the role played by Magique in supporting the risk management infrastructure by recording it as a permanent item on the corporate risk register. There is no expectation that it will ever be removed.

The interdependencies between service delivery, ICT, and risk management can be usefully illustrated by reference to the problem of fraud control within the benefits section of Birmingham City Council. One of the benefits that is available to people living in the city is a reduction in the amount of council tax payable for one-person households. Sharing information across directorates and other public agencies can help to reduce the high risk of fraudulent claims for this benefit. ICT can facilitate this information sharing by enabling cross-referencing of the information provided by individuals to different sections of the council (e.g. housing benefit and the electoral register). One benefit of the investment in ICT is thus that it frees up fraud control staff time.

Linking Risk and Performance Management

Risk and organisational objectives are intrinsically linked, and the challenge in practice is to make the link work and demonstrate this by *proven* improvements in performance.

For Birmingham City Council, the challenge of demonstrating how risk management works to help achieve objectives is made even more difficult by the fact that it is a public-sector body and a political organisation. Council objectives are determined by elected members, with their own political agenda, although the day-to-day management is largely done by paid officers.

As a service provider to a huge and diverse community, the council's corporate plan is very wide ranging in scope. The 2018–2022 plan seeks to create a green, clean entrepreneurial city that fulfils the aspirations of younger citizens and the service needs of the older citizens and maximises the benefits of the 2022 Commonwealth Games for its residents.

Such objectives are admirable but need to be "translated" into specific objectives which can be applied to all the directorates and services across the council, cascaded down to operational staff, and provided with the required corporate support. The performance planning framework has evolved over time and aims to ensure that objectives and performance targets for the city, councils, directorate, and local constituencies are linked together to form a coherent whole.

Successful performance management requires all members of staff to understand the council's objectives and their individual role in helping to achieve them. Local government, in contrast to much of the private sector, has traditionally been very good at linking corporate-level objectives down the organisational hierarchy to individual performance targets. In Birmingham this is done using a balanced scorecard type of approach, further details of which can be found in Woods (2009).

At the heart of the performance management system is a series of linked plans that establish objectives and targets at each hierarchical level, which are regularly monitored and reported. At the council level, overview and scrutiny committees have internal responsibility for scrutinising and reviewing the performance of the council as a whole. The council's plan for 2018–2022 defines six core outcomes and eighty-two associated performance indicators, and Table 8.4 details the six core objectives and illustrative performance measures used for evaluation purposes.

Results in terms of meeting or not achieving targets within an acceptable tolerance level are reported to the cabinet and compared to the previous time frame. Performance against the plan is highly visible to the wider public via the publication of both quarterly updates and an annual performance report, highlighting what has or has not been achieved, ongoing challenges, and the current focus. The council is sensitive to the fact that service performance can drive funding opportunities, and so monitoring and success are critical.

At the directorate level, performance plans for service delivery specify both the desired service quality and outcomes. Summary performance reports for services are published quarterly on the website, based upon sixty-nine performance measures, with performance classified under one of four categories:

1. Blue – target exceeded
2. Green – target met
3. Amber – below target within tolerable limits
4. Red – target missed

Benchmarking of service performance against that of other UK local authorities is also used to both encourage improvement and increase accountability.

Table 8.4 Target Council Outcomes and Performance Measures

Target Outcome	Illustrative Performance Measures
Entrepreneurial city to learn, work, and invest in	• Number of jobs created • Number of small/medium-size enterprises starts and closures
An aspirational city to grow up in	• Key stage 2 educational attainment • Percentage of children overweight or obese at year 6
A fulfilling city to age well in	• The proportion of people who use services who reported that they had as much social contact as they would like • The percentage of people who receive adult social care in their own home
Great, clean, and green city to live in	• Reduced collected household waste – kg per household • How safe do you feel outside in your local area after dark (citizen perception measure)?
Maximum benefit from the Commonwealth Games	• Volume of games contracts awarded to Birmingham/West Midlands companies • Percentage rise in young people and adults engaged in physical activity
A city that takes a leading role in tackling climate change	• To be agreed

For example, the Adult Social Care Outcomes Framework (ASCOF) measures how well care and support services achieve the outcomes that matter most to people, based upon surveys of both carers and service users. Birmingham's adult social care service is huge (its budget was £264 million in 2018–2019) and reports its ranking across 150 local authorities for each of the twenty-eight performance measures used by ASCOF. This ranking system helps to highlight where improvements are required, as the council's position varies from the very best to the close to worst and all points in between, depending on the chosen performance measure. This is clearly illustrated in Table 8.5.

The control loop between planning, delivery, and monitoring of performance is illustrated in Figure 8.5. This is not taken from the council's own documentation, but is a generic example of how a council's plans and scorecards for performance can be cascaded downwards from the very general vision quoted earlier into individual performance plans for every member of staff.

If the performance plans also include risk plans which specify where the responsibility for risk lies, then risk becomes part of the mechanism by which performance is evaluated. The risk and performance functions then run in tandem, and it can truly be said that risk management is embedded into the organisation. This is the ultimate aim, but it is very difficult to achieve because of the complexity and interdependence of some of the council's objectives.

Complex Objectives Generate Complex Risks

One of the key ways in which risk management in the public sector differs from that in the private sector is in the challenges created by complex risks.

Table 8.5 ASCOF Illustrative Performance Rankings: Birmingham City Council (2018–2019)

Performance Measure	Ranking (out of 150)
The proportion of people who use services who receive self-directed support	1
Long-term support needs of older adults (aged 65 and over) met by admission to residential and nursing care homes per 100,000 population	37
The proportion of adults in contact with secondary mental health services living independently, with or without support	99
The proportion of people who use services who find it easy to find information about support	122
The proportion of carers who report that they have been included or consulted in discussion about the person they care for	146

Source: Local Account 2018–19 Birmingham City Council Adult Social Care:

www.birmingham.gov.uk/downloads/download/40/local_performance_account_reports

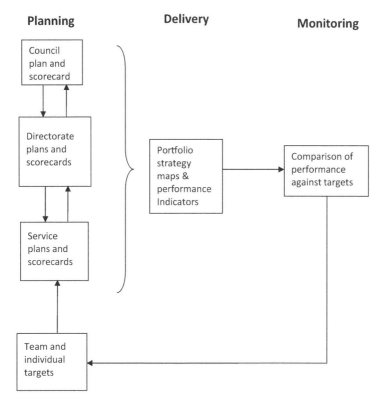

Figure 8.5 The performance management control loop

Complex objectives such as those relating to children's social care require the involvement of multiple services and organisations if they are to be achieved, resulting in what are commonly termed cross-cutting risks (i.e. those which cross service/organisational boundaries). They commonly involve a large and diverse set of stakeholders, and because the service delivery requires multi-party involvement, cross-cutting risks are more difficult to monitor and control.

Multi-party working creates a potential for conflicting priorities, lack of co-ordination, and issues of differing organisational cultures (NIA, 2008). Recognising the challenges faced in this regard, in July 2014 the leader of Birmingham City Council requested an independent review into the governance and organisational capabilities of the council, which included recommendations on ways to improve its efficiency and effectiveness. A key area of concern was children's social care, which had been classified by the government inspectors at Ofsted as providing inadequate care and requiring intervention through "special measures" since 2009. The challenge of providing this complex service in an environment subject to increased budget austerity is widespread. In 2017 an investigation revealed that children's services in a record thirty-one authorities – one in five (!) – were under some form of government intervention due to the combined pressures of rising demand and shrinking budgets.

The 2014 Ofsted report into children's social care in Birmingham concluded that the service was inadequate and showed widespread and serious failures that left children and young people at risk of harm. The same year, the independent review into Birmingham Council, commonly referred to as the Kerslake Report (Kerslake, 2014), was similarly hard hitting, suggesting that deep-rooted cultural change was required and that the council did not have "credible plans" to meet the significant budgetary challenges it was facing.

The risk of failing to effectively respond to the Kerslake Report was still on the council's risk map in March 2019 and classed as of medium likelihood but significant impact, and so requiring close monitoring and cost-effective control improvements. Focusing solely on the challenges of managing children's social care, it is useful to analyse the cross-cutting issues that arise and their implications for risk management.

The problems faced by Birmingham children's social care service from 2009 ff included:

- Lack of consistent management. Six different senior managers were in the post from 2008 to 2016.
- Long-term staff shortages, leading to high workloads, high staff turnover, and budget pressures from high usage of agency workers.
- Rising demand. The service covers an area with some of the highest rates of poverty and deprivation in the UK.
- Lack of support from partner agencies such as the police/schools/health services, especially in relation to information sharing.
- Budget cuts. Total council income from grants and sale of services fell from £4049 million in 2011–2012 to £3324 million in 2019–2020, a drop of almost 18%.

All of these factors create risks and an environment in which identifying priorities that could be funded and getting staff buy-in was severely challenging.

In December 2018 the service was deemed by Ofsted to no longer be inadequate – the first time in ten years – but still requiring improvement to be good. The key change that led to the reduced risks and performance improvement was the decision to transfer the service out of the council to an independent council-owned voluntary trust.[5] The 2018 inspection report from Ofsted noted significant improvements in staff morale, highly visible management providing clear and effective oversight, and a revised performance management system that facilitated the prioritisation of risks. Where improvement was still needed, however, was in relation to partnership working. In serious case reviews, including children's deaths, it was felt that there was still a lack of fully effective information sharing between the council, schools, police, nurseries, and health services. All of these parties will have their own performance management systems, and culture, and if no single party has the right to bring them into alignment, then there is a risk that serious cases get missed as they fall into an information gap created by weak interaction across the agencies.

Key Learning Point

Partnership working brings huge challenges and increased risks. The public sector's approach to managing cross-cutting risks may have useful lessons for the private sector, such as setting up a separate entity to control services and risks which straddle traditional organisational boundaries.

Changing Risk Priorities: 2000–2010 versus 2010–2020

Risk management is inextricably linked to corporate objectives, and so it is inevitable that changes in objectives will result in revisions to which risks are given priority. This evolution of risk thinking has already been clearly illustrated earlier in this book in Chapter 4. Technological risks and the threat of climate change represent responses to evolving market conditions. The growth of internet-based sales and accompanying customer databases have created new technological risks; similarly, growing public awareness and concern over climate change have pushed the issue onto the corporate agenda, as companies seek to keep their stakeholder base happy by demonstrating how they control such risks.

In the case of Birmingham City Council, political matters have played a central role in determining what objectives matter most, and hence which risks require prioritising. As we saw earlier in this chapter, the period 2000–2010 was one in which there was a strong emphasis on external assessment of the council's performance. The period 2000–2009 was the era of Best Value reviews and then CPA undertaken by Audit Commission inspectors. A council's CPA rating affected its access to funding, and so service ratings became the key performance indicators. This was also the decade in which risk management systems were first being developed, and so they grew alongside the CPA regime, with risks commonly defined in terms of CPA scores.

The successor to CPA, comprehensive area assessment, was more wide ranging and challenging, but very short lived, and the change of government in 2010 led to a shift in risk management thinking. More emphasis was placed on value for money and the authority's arrangements for securing economy, efficiency, and effectiveness in its use of resources. The audit reports included in the annual statement of accounts now detail what the auditors perceive to be any key risks that may threaten such arrangements. For example, the 2019–2020 audit report by Grant Thornton states:

> We identified five significant risks in respect of the Authority's arrangements for securing economy, efficiency and effectiveness in its use of resources in respect of:
>
> - the Authority's resilience and financial sustainability
> - waste service continuity and industrial relations
> - contractual arrangements relating to the highways PFI Scheme
> - the financial impact of the Commonwealth Games and
> - contract monitoring and management.
>
> Source: Birmingham City Council Statement of Accounts 2019–20, p. 230

These comments clearly demonstrate that maintaining financial capacity is still very important and also that contracting out of services is also problematic, as many councils have little experience of the necessary negotiating skills required in such an environment. The need for such contracting reflects the huge challenge of maintaining service provision when total income is falling. The Kerslake report highlighted the need for the council to develop plans to manage the expected financial challenges and operate a balanced budget. This was first achieved in 2015–2016 but only through cutting down or eliminating non-essential service provision (e.g. public libraries) and using contractors to cut fixed costs. Such an approach reflects central government political thinking and can lead to conflict if local councillors feel that certain services should be retained.

Simultaneous with the shifting emphasis towards financial stability were the new legal requirements for transparency. Fulfilment of the resulting, more detailed reporting needs led to some change of focus within Birmingham Audit. Compliance with financial and accountability requirements moved up the agenda, and broader performance issues were possibly (perhaps inevitably) sacrificed in the process. There has been a long learning curve, but in 2021 in a review of the council's financial management capability, CIPFA ranked the city council as a three-star authority on a ranking of one to five stars – up from the one-star rating awarded in 2019 and delivered a year ahead of schedule. CIPFA's report concluded that "Birmingham City Council should be considered an exemplar in the transformation of financial management capability given the extent of improvement achieved over the last two years" (quoted in Report to Cabinet, 2021).

The shift towards firmer financial foundations provides the council with an opportunity to rethink its priorities and revise its key risk register. Most importantly, the long-term perspective allows us to see that risk management is far from static. It evolves and responds to changing external conditions, be they political in the case of Birmingham City Council, or market related in the case of private-sector organisations.

Conclusion

Birmingham City Council is a huge and complex organisation with wide-ranging social, economic, and political objectives. Establishing the objectives and then establishing the necessary control systems to achieve them is a massive operation. Risk management is a fundamental element of the broader management control system and is strongly linked to performance management because risk is defined in terms of the ability to achieve objectives. What is seen as constituting good performance, however, has changed over time.

The risk team within internal audit have created a very formal, well-documented, and structured framework for risk management, and its effectiveness as a control tool is reported upon annually. In the end that effectiveness is driven not by the system itself but by the people who implement it – the council members and staff. Risk management is only as good as the people who deploy it, and the local government sector in the UK has gone through something of a performance management revolution since 1999, which has been accompanied by a step change in the quality of risk management. The complexity and cross-cutting nature of many of the risks faced by local government present massive challenges, the management of which also provides useful lessons for the private sector.

Notes

1 The material used in the case study is drawn from several different sources. Phase 1 (2000–2010) material is primarily based upon internal documentation from the city council and interview transcripts. Extended interviews, attendance at management meetings and training sessions, and a guided walk through the software used to manage risks were all used to collect further evidence on both the risk management structure and how it is used in practice. Interviewees included the head of internal audit, other members of staff in Birmingham Audit, and the council's chief executive. Phase 2 (2010–2020) material uses information from the public domain – mainly the council's own website, but also central government, media, and academic sources.
2 The Core Cities Group is composed of the eleven main cities of the UK (excluding London) – namely Belfast, Birmingham, Bristol, Cardiff, Glasgow, Leeds, Liverpool, Manchester, Newcastle, Nottingham, and Sheffield. They form the economic and urban cores of wider surrounding territories, the city regions, and are home to 25% of the UK population.
3 In Birmingham there are eight directorates, each managed by an appointed director of the council – Adult Social Care and Health, Education and Skills, Inclusive Growth, Finance and Governance, Neighbourhoods, Digital and Customer Services, Partnerships, Insight and Prevention, and Human Resources.
4 Liverpool City Council received such an inspection in late 2020, and commissioners were appointed in March 2021 for an initial three-year term. Further details of the case and the identified governance failings are readily available online by searching for "Liverpool City Council Best Value Inspection."

5 A growing number of councils are choosing to engage in this form of outsourcing, which is promoted by central government as freeing the system from local bureaucracy, allowing staff to focus totally on service provision.

References

AIRMIC/IRM/ALARM (2002) *A Risk Management Standard*. Airmic, London.

Audit Commission (2001) *Worth the Risk: Improving Risk Management in Local Government*. Audit Commission, London.

Audit Commission (2006) *Briefing on the Audit Commission's Comprehensive Performance Assessment Frameworks*. Audit Commission, London.

Audit Commission (2007) *Corporate Assessment, Birmingham City Council*. February, Audit Commission, London.

Birmingham City Council (2018) *Risk Management Framework*. Birmingham City Council, Birmingham.

CIPFA (2001) *Corporate Governance in Local Government: A Keystone for Community Governance Framework*. CIPFA, London.

CIPFA (2005) *Audit Committees: Practical Guidance for Local Authorities*. CIPFA, London.

CIPFA/ Solace (2016) *Delivering Good Governance in Local Government*. Framework, London.

GOV.UK (2010) "Pickles Strips Away Pointless Town Hall Red Tape Targets. Ministry of Housing Communities and Local Government." *Press Release*, June 25, London.

IFAC and CIPFA (2014) *International Framework: Good Governance in the Public Sector*. IFAC, London.

IFS (2019) *English Local Government Funding: Trends and Challenges in 2019 and Beyond*. Harris, T., Hodge, L., & Phillips, D. (eds.). Institute for Fiscal Studies, London.

Kerslake, B. (2014) *The Way Forward: An Independent Review of the Governance and Organisational Capabilities of Birmingham City Council*. Sir Bob Kerslake. Department for Communities and Local Government, London.

NAO (2019) *Local Authority Governance*. National Audit Office, Ministry of Housing, Communities & Local Government, London.

NIA (2008) *Ensuring Delivery of the Cross- Cutting Themes in the Programme for Government*. Northern Ireland Assembly. Research and Library Services Briefing Note 89/10.

Report to Cabinet (2021) *Outcome of CIPFA's Assessment of the Council's Financial Management Capability*. Birmingham City Council, Birmingham.

Woods, M. (2009) "A Contingency Theory Perspective on the Risk Management Control System Within Birmingham City Council." *Management Accounting Research*, Vol. 20, No. 1, pp. 69–81.

Useful Web Links

1. A useful PDF document provided to managers within the council with the aim of helping them to learn how to identify and manage risks. It includes a helpful appendix illustrating the wide range of cross-cutting risks they may encounter. www.birmingham.gov.uk/downloads/file/711/ risk_management_toolkit

2. An example of risk reporting within the council. This is a report from the assistant director of audit and risk management to the Audit Committee concerning the council's management of the key risks in the corporate

risk register. (From the electronic version of the book, follow the detailed hyperlink, or you can find the document by searching online for "Birmingham City Council Audit Committee report on corporate risk register.")
  https://birmingham.cmis.uk.com/Birmingham/

Discussion Questions

1. What are the key differences, if any, between risk management in the private sector versus the public sector?
2. Draw a diagram, with indicative performance measures, to show how an objective to provide residential care for all elderly people in need can be translated down to personal objectives for a member of staff in a care home.
3. Discuss the extent to which firm financial foundations are an essential prerequisite of good risk management.

9 Best Practice Risk Management

Key Lessons

Introduction

In combination, the three detailed case studies of Tesco, Akzo Nobel, and Birmingham City Council provide us with substantive detailed information about widely variable risk management experiences across very different sectors. Learning from others – both their successes and their mistakes – is perfect for a practical subject such as risk management, and so the aim of this chapter is to summarise the lessons that can be learned from the case studies. For the purposes of this chapter, most of the discussion will use the generic term risk management as opposed to the more specific enterprise risk management, simply because it is more widely applicable.

The lessons discussed in this chapter originate from the case studies but are expanded to incorporate academic and broader practitioner comment on the issue(s), so that the pedagogical benefits are maximised. For the reader, the challenge is to then assess the extent to which they can be applied to risk management in their own organisation.

Lesson One: Risk Management Systems Are Both Time and Organisation Specific

Chapter 2 described the two main theoretical frameworks used globally in the design of risk management systems – Committee of Sponsoring Organizations' (COSO's) Enterprise Risk Management (COSO, 2017) and ISO 31000 (2018). The chapter concluded that risk management systems in all organisations display common features that are derived from one or another of these standards, but that their detail and complexity will vary. The case studies confirmed this mix of similarity combined with variability, with the variability being explained by both the point in time being analysed and specific organisational traits.

Time

Risk management is not static – regulations and guidance have evolved hugely over the last twenty years – and simultaneously, the risk management needs of

DOI: 10.4324/9781315208336-9

an organisation change as its strategies and markets develop over time. Consequently, it is important to be cautious about what can be learned from a point-in-time snapshot of risk management in a specific organisation. The picture is likely to be incomplete, and it is for this reason that the case studies straddled long time frames, which revealed the findings discussed next.

The Impact of New Strategies and Objectives on the Risk Management System

Risk management is linked to corporate objectives and strategy, which change over time. For example, in the case of Tesco, the first phase of the case is a period of rapid expansion of the business, both internationally and into new sectors such as non-food and online retail. The risk management system was therefore very performance focused, particularly in terms of financial results, but that focus engendered a culture which ultimately lost sight of certain risks and failed. Retrenchment was required to re-establish codes of behaviour that were supportive of risk management and a revised strategy of refocusing on the core grocery business.

In Akzo Nobel, the purchase of ICI in 2008 and refocusing of the business on paints and coatings served to facilitate a shift towards centralised processes such as procurement. Centralisation of corporate services ensures greater consistency of decision making and reduced risks, so the focus of risk management was revised in the direction of establishing standardised procedures.

The Impact of External Events on Risk Management Systems

Whilst many risks (e.g. regulatory, reputational, or market risks) are long standing in nature, new risks also emerge over time as a result of external events. What mattered in 2010 is not necessarily what matters now for any given organisation.

For example, Birmingham City Council began the millennium with a risk management system directly connected to performance management and risk levels defined in terms of the expected ability to reach target performance scores, which were externally audited by the government. A change of government in 2010 led to a complete revision of how government oversight of local authority management and finances was managed. As a result, risk management in Birmingham refocused its efforts on meeting the new objectives of transparency and operating a balanced budget (i.e. risks were redefined).

In Tesco, one external event that ultimately forced risk management changes was the emergence of the discount supermarket chains Aldi and Lidl. Initially not seen as much of a threat, the discounters ultimately stole significant shares of the UK grocery market and pushed Tesco into finally recognising that price was an important component of customer needs. Aldi "price matches" now form part of the strategy, and risk management tools are in place to monitor relative prices more closely.

More broadly, in Chapter 4 we saw that cyber risk has become increasingly significant, despite hardly being mentioned ten years ago, so much so that this new edition of the book includes a new chapter on technology risk. Similarly, the COVID-19 pandemic, in combination with Brexit, will have resulted in many UK-based organisations being forced to revise certain strategies in terms of their target markets, sources of supply, and employment arrangements. All of these will have implications for risk management. For example, Brexit may have led to a loss of sales in mainland Europe, and so strategies need to be developed to replace these sales, but this creates new risks, as every market is different. COVID-19 has increased the proportion of staff working from home, with an associated increase in technology risks from insecure Wi-Fi connections and misuse of employers' laptops, etc.

The Impact of New Management on Risk Management Systems

The arrival of a new chief executive officer (CEO), Dave Lewis, at Tesco in 2014 illustrates this idea well. His appointment was particularly significant, as he was the first "outsider" (from Unilever) to be given the post. As Chapter 6 reveals, his appointment was followed by extensive management re-organisation and the appointment of other non-Tesco-trained directors to the board. The new management slimmed down the performance indicators to "the Big Six," which brought closer alignment between risk and performance management. Operational risk appears to have disappeared from the key performance indicators (KPIs), and staff involvement in setting targets and performance monitoring has increased, replacing the previous emphasis on top-level financial performance measures.

The case of children's social care in Birmingham City Council also demonstrates the importance of senior management change as a tool for rethinking risk management. Between 2009 and 2014 this service was classed by Ofsted as being "in special measures" and providing inadequate care for its users. The case study showed that the causes of the problem were multiple and compounded by increasing pressure on the council's finances combined with growing demand for the service. Operating such a complex service within the constraints of local government bureaucracy and financial controls was extremely challenging. The service had also been plagued by a lack of consistent management, with six different senior managers in the post over an eight-year period.

The service was taken out of local authority control, placed under an independent trust, and new managers put in place. The new management style was much more visible – they introduced a new performance management system that also facilitated a clear prioritisation of risks and provided clear and efficient oversight. Staff morale was significantly boosted, and the service removed by Ofsted from its inadequate status in 2018.

Organisational Traits

The three case studies covered different economic sectors, both public and private, and whilst their risk management systems all incorporated tools for risk identification, analysis, prioritisation, management, and monitoring, the way in which these were done varied across the organisations. There are multiple reasons for such variations, discussed next.

Sector

Each specific sector has its own challenges and organisational format that will impact upon risk management. For example, Tesco is described as a pyramid-style structure, with relatively few senior managers but a very large number of operational staff working in stores/warehouses, etc. This generates a different risk management approach to a flatter organisational structure. Additionally, as a retailer, its greatest risk is loss of custom, and so risk management systems will be focused on building and maintaining customer loyalty. This idea is reflected in the revised performance management measures introduced post-2014 and the revival of the core Tesco Values (a culture of risk management) in line with those measures.

Akzo Nobel, as an international manufacturing company in the chemical sector, needs to be very conscious of operational and health and safety risks, and their risk management approach is focused on ensuring organisation-wide consistency built around a code of conduct applicable to all staff. The working environment means that operational staff are probably already risk aware, but central to Akzo's thinking is the idea that "unidentified risks are a threat; identified risks are a managerial issue." In other words, speak out if you spot a new risk, and we can then look at how it might be managed.

Birmingham City Council operates within the confines of regulatory oversight by national government and the financing provided by central government, other grants, and sale of its services. Most importantly, it cannot opt out of offering certain services simply because they are too complex or too expensive. Statutory obligations require that services such as social care, planning control, and housing must be provided. Furthermore, many of the risks faced by the council straddle multiple services, and this makes them especially complex to manage. This means that, unlike the private sector, local government cannot easily simplify its "business model" to reduce its risks. The decision by Akzo Nobel to simplify down to a paints and coatings company does not have a public-sector equivalent. The scenario is made even more complex by the need for effective working between elected members and council staff, as well as multiple local partners such as the police, health service, and schools.

In summary, whilst the principles of risk management are identical for both the public and private sectors, the challenge in practice for the public sector is significantly more substantial.

Geographic Location

The location of an organisation's headquarters will determine the regulatory framework, which in turn will determine its governance and risk management system. It is this factor that largely explains the mix of COSO- versus ISO 31000-based systems described in the case studies.

For example, Akzo Nobel operates in line with Dutch law and so has a two-tier board system, with risk management responsibility resting with the supervisory board. As the company had a US stock market listing at the time, it was required to comply with the 2002 Sarbanes-Oxley Act (SOX), and so when Akzo Nobel began to formally develop its risk management system in 2004, it was structured in a way that ensured compliance with the COSO framework endorsed by SOX. The result was that enterprise risk management became the language of risk management in Akzo Nobel, and this persists today even though the company's shares are no longer traded on NASDAQ, but simply in the Over The Counter market.

In contrast, Tesco complies with UK law and has a single board of directors responsible for setting the group's risk appetite and establishing and maintaining appropriate risk management control systems. The group must comply with the UK's Combined Code, which contrasts with US regulation in its requirement that the roles of the chairman and CEO are separated. Perhaps the most significant difference between UK and US regulation is that COSO only holds the board responsible for evaluating and reporting on the effectiveness of internal control over financial reporting. In contrast, the viability statement (see Chapter 3) now required under the Combined Code embraces all types of risk, not just financial, and means directors now attest to the viability of their company's ability to operate. The risk management system adopted by Tesco reflects this regulatory framework, although it has evolved over time. Pre-2014, the focus was on seeking to integrate performance management and risk management via the use of the steering wheel and adoption of the core tools described in ISO 31000. Post-2014, a diluted version of the steering wheel remains, but is now combined with the three lines of defence model, which more clearly defines risk management responsibilities across different levels of the organisation. In the United States, the three lines of defence did not form part of the COSO debate until after 2015, and so Tesco's systems are clearly UK driven, although in its management of community and sustainability issues, it is broadening its definition of organisational boundaries in a manner synonymous with enterprise risk management (ERM).

In summary, the choice of ERM and the COSO approach versus ISO 31000 is commonly driven by the geographic location of an organisation and whether it has a US stock market listing. A US listing, requiring compliance with SOX, has traditionally resulted in firms adopting a COSO-based system. COSO is therefore more commonly found in US-based companies or huge multinationals. At the same time, the broader-based approach to risk, extending well beyond financial controls, that characterises ISO 31000 means that it is applicable to any type of organisation, including those in the public sector, which serves to broaden its appeal.

One further organisational trait which is a core determinant of risk management style and systems is culture, but this is an issue that warrants more detailed discussion.

Lesson Two: Organisational Culture Is Critical to Risk Management Effectiveness

Despite its importance, there is little consensus on the precise meaning of the term organisational culture (Watkins, 2013). Culture is often described as incorporating issues such as how things are done, the way in which individuals interact, and the values and rituals that "glue" the individuals in an organisation together. In many respects, it acts as a social control system that encourages people to think and act in particular ways. Risk culture is a subdivision of organisational culture, which specifically relates to the level and form of risk awareness amongst staff. Ashby et al. (2012, p. 7) define risk culture as "the habits and routines which are relevant to risk taking and its mitigation." In all the case studies, it is clear that great efforts were made to establish risk awareness amongst staff and to use training to encourage people at all levels to take responsibility for risk management. The importance of developing a strong risk culture cannot be overemphasised, and there is useful guidance on the topic in the Institute of Risk Management's (2012) publication (see the references), which highlights the link between the broader organisational culture, the internal risk culture, and the resulting behaviour and attitudes of individual staff to risk-related matters.

The challenge of introducing risk management into an organisation where there is no recognised risk culture is huge, as confirmed by this comment from the Institute of International Finance (IIF, 2008) in relation to financial institutions: "the development of a 'risk culture' throughout the firm is perhaps the most fundamental tool for effective risk management" (IIF, 2008). The IIF comment was made in relation to financial institutions in the wake of the global financial crisis, but it is common for all types of organisations to look closely at culture and seek to revive risk awareness in response to a risk management failure.

In Akzo Nobel, several regulatory breaches by its executives and punitive heavy fines damaged both its finances and reputation and served as an important trigger to the organisation's decision to develop an ERM system. Indeed, the first four years of the ERM journey focused on nurturing an ethical culture to revive the corporate reputation. The result was a code of conduct that defined staff responsibilities and was complemented by other tools to define risk boundaries: a set of business principles, corporate directives, and authority schedules together with a statement on sustainability.

Similarly, in Tesco, it was the investigation by the Serious Fraud Office (SFO) into the misreporting of profits in 2014 that triggered a wake-up call to rethink the group's risk culture via a group-wide programme emphasising the importance of culture, integrity, and ethics. The 2015 relaunch of the code of conduct was accompanied by a group-wide training programme that addressed key risk areas and laid down behavioural guidelines.

The lesson from both cases and from the financial crisis is that a weak risk culture can lead to governance and risk management failure. This suggests that it is important to monitor risk culture in an organisation, but as it is both invisible and difficult to document, how can it be tracked? Information drawn from the case studies provides us with a few useful tools to monitor the level of risk awareness and engagement amongst staff.

What Is the Profile of Risk Staff/Risk Management in the Organisation?

This question is concerned not just with the status of the risk management function and its staff but also the extent to which risk managers interact with and work alongside operational staff. Think about the following contrasting examples:

- In a major UK bank, the risk management department – separate from internal audit – has traditionally been located on a single floor of the bank's HQ building, only accessible to departmental staff. Operational staff were located elsewhere in the building, grouped according to their area of work.
- In Akzo Nobel, each business unit and major function has its own risk and compliance control committee (RCC), and within each business area, a management team member is appointed as the "compliance focal point" or "risk champion."
- In Birmingham City Council, within each directorate the management team is responsible for undertaking risk assessments, with assistance from Birmingham Audit as required, and a nominated risk representative is tasked with implementing and managing risk within the directorate.
- Within Akzo Nobel, details of the top ten risks and the relevant responses are reported up from the project level, through business units and the executive committee, right up to the supervisory board. The identification of risks is done by operational staff aided and advised by risk management employees, but both work together on the task.

The lesson here is that risk staff should not be siloed. Applying the three lines of defence model, operational staff are best placed to help identify risks based on their day-to-day experience, but designing the required controls is the specialised role of the risk managers, and the two parties need to work together to maximise the effectiveness of the third line of defence (i.e. the control system itself).

The level of seniority given to staff in the risk function can also be an indicator of profile. Is there a chief risk officer on the board of directors? At business unit level, is there a representative of risk and internal control on the board?

To what extent is the head of risk in an organisation asked to comment on key strategic decisions such as a takeover or merger?

The evidence on these issues from the case studies is mixed. In Tesco, the internal audit staff (pre-2014) were always involved in store location decisions – and presumably still are – because location is a core driver of retail success. Nonetheless, the accepted view in Tesco was that the specific term risk management was not helpful to operational staff and that expressing problems in terms of failure to meet objectives was preferable. The result was perhaps that internal audit and risk management staff held a low profile overall. This may, in part, account for why they found it difficult to get their voice heard regarding the accounting scandal – the focus was not on the risks, but on performance. Post-2014, the situation has changed, with risk (particularly compliance) training getting a higher profile now, but a continued emphasis on performance.

The profile of risk management staff and the overall profile of risk in the organisation are clearly interlinked. The picture from Akzo Nobel is one of an organisation that believes that simple, direct messaging to staff about risk is helpful. A clear illustration of this is the inclusion of safety as one of the three core principles in the code of conduct (see Table 6.3). Ultimately, their view is that a corporate culture that emphasises risk awareness *and* accountability amongst all employees is critical to the success of ERM, and so the risk profile is high.

Evidence on the outcomes of whistleblowing services can also serve as an indicator of risk profile. A well-used service that clearly results in disciplinary action, where appropriate, is suggestive of an organisational culture that nurtures risk awareness. In Akzo Nobel, in Chapter 6 we learned that between 2009 and 2019, both the number of confirmed code violations reported via the Speak Up! line and the subsequent employment terminations fell dramatically. In contrast, in Tesco, the fact that finance and other staff resigned over the issue of misreporting of profits *before* the senior accountant finally had his voice heard in the legacy paper is very significant and suggests that staff lacked confidence in the whistleblowing service or their capacity to be heard by their managers.

Perhaps one explanation for the observed differences across the cases is the extent to which the culture encourages openness versus fear in respect of the reporting of risk matters.

Is There a Culture of Openness or of Fear in Respect of Risk Issues?

Front-line staff form the first line of defence against risk, but if they are afraid of reprisals when they report problems, then a culture of fear is engendered. This seems to be what happened within the finance department and specifically the commercial income section in Tesco. The danger is that fear nurtures wilful blindness amongst staff, through which they ignore information that they really need to be aware of, and in so doing they engender a broader institutional silence about breaches of risk boundaries. The consequences of such blindness will vary across sectors but can range from financial or reputational to physical damage.

One useful historic example of wilful blindness is the case of the B.P. Texas City Refinery Fire of 1995, which killed 15 people and injured 180 more. The US Chemical and Safety Hazard Board report into the accident was highly critical of the risk management arrangements for the site, noting that the organisation:

> lacked a reporting and learning culture. Personnel were not encouraged to report safety problems and some feared retaliation for doing so. The lessons from incidents and near misses, therefore, were generally not captured or acted upon. Important relevant safety lessons from a British government investigation of incidents at BP's Grangemouth, Scotland, refinery were also not incorporated at Texas City.
>
> (US Chemical and Safety Hazard Board, 2007, p. 26)

In this instance staff feared retribution for reporting problems, but another reason for silence is a sense of futility – that complaints will go unheard and not acted upon, and as such are a "waste of effort." Whatever the cause, it is helpful to recall the link between risk culture and the broader organisational culture. Ultimately, people want to "do a good job," and this is often translated into conforming with the organisational norms and culture, and if silence is the norm, then it can be difficult to change.

In Akzo Nobel, behavioural norms were established via the code of conduct, which includes safety risk, and a recognition that a culture of appropriate behaviour cannot be imposed from above – it is everyone's responsibility. This approach is mirrored in the Tesco Values, although these are focused more on treating fellow employees and staff correctly and seeking to help where possible, rather than risk management.

One useful example of how openness to the admission of risks can be encouraged is that of the UK's Civil Aviation Authority (CAA), which has transitioned from a "blame" to what is termed a "just" culture. The change occurred in response to an EU regulation introduced in recognition of a failure within the civil aviation industry to learn from previous accidents and dangerous occurrences – very similar to the criticism made of BP regarding the Texas City explosion. The CAA defines a just culture as "a culture in which front-line operators or other persons are not punished for actions, omissions or decisions taken by them that are commensurate with their experience and training, but in which gross negligence, wilful violations and destructive acts are not tolerated" (CAA, 2014).

The core features of a just culture are:

- Confidence to report without fear of blame
- Confidence that confidentiality will be maintained
- No punishment for unintentional errors

- Gross negligence, violations, or dangerous actions are not tolerated
- All data collected is analysed and used for organisational learning

The underlying principle is that openness that encourages risk reporting also serves to provide useful information on how to avoid future risks. This is a lesson that it is useful for all organisations to learn.

The differences in risk culture across the case studies are subtle but worthy of note because they suggest that codes of behaviour and whistleblowing systems can help to engage staff, but they need to be complemented by formal, standardised control systems such as defined risk boundaries for specific tasks and continuous recording, monitoring and re-evaluation of risks. In other words, establishing a strong risk culture is just the start of the journey towards enterprise risk management, as discussed next.

Lesson Three: Be Patient! Building a Mature and Effective Risk Management System Takes a Long Time

The academic literature abounds with efforts, mostly US based, to define and assess the level of maturity of enterprise risk management systems across different organisations in order to test whether mature systems increase market value (see for example Eckles et al., 2014; Hoyt and Liebenberg (2015) or Farrell and Gallagher, 2015). For the risk practitioner, the question of maturity is subsumed by the practical problem of how to develop and improve an existing system.

One of the benefits of case studies that cover such long time frames is that they allow the reader to better understand the whole evolutionary process of risk management, and a common pattern of development is demonstrated in all the cases. The case evidence suggests a four-stage process that takes at least ten years overall but continues to evolve for much longer.

The four stages are discussed in the following sections.

Formulate a Code of Conduct/Ethical Framework and Establish Core Risk Boundaries

Both Tesco and Akzo Nobel did exactly this in response to their respective governance failures, and since 2002 Birmingham City Council has sought to integrate risk management across all levels of staff by incorporating risk issues into personal performance plans. Akzo describes the Code of Conduct as "one of the critical foundations of good corporate governance" (Akzo Annual Report, 2005, p. 69).

Develop a Risk-Aware Culture

Central to reinforcing the importance of codes of behaviour and conduct is risk management training as a tool for increasing risk awareness amongst staff.

In Birmingham, all employees are invited to participate in training sessions run by internal audit, and similar sessions addressing risk awareness are run by the deputy leader for all elected members of the council.

Within Akzo Nobel, all training was similarly managed in house and cascaded from the top down, so that managers became involved in training their own staff. Nonetheless, the case study shows that just the process of constructing a code of conduct and ethical boundaries took almost four years, and it was a further five years before the directors committed to providing risk training for all staff worldwide. Today, linked codes, and accompanying requirements for compliance, apply not just to employees but also to contractors and business partners.

Training and a code of conduct, however, only have value if compliance is closely monitored, and it was in this regard that Tesco demonstrated weaknesses pre-2014. Additionally, some whistle blowers expressed a lack of confidence in the telephone service's early effectiveness in protecting confidentiality and enforcing change, and so compliance failures were probably underreported. The revised code of conduct, launched in 2015, included new sections on key areas of risk and was accompanied by mandatory training for all staff. It will still take some time to evaluate the effectiveness of this revised approach.

The experience in Birmingham relating to compliance was interesting, as which risks were monitored more closely evolved over time to reflect changing priorities. Initially, the focus was on auditing performance targets to match external demands and financing opportunities. Post-2010, once austerity began to bite, audit staff refocused attention on financial and accountability requirements to minimise the risk of compliance breaches. Unsurprisingly, performance in other respects consequently suffered – hence the problems with children's social care.

In Akzo Nobel, compliance at the individual level remains high on the agenda, as demonstrated by the decision to use the term "integrity and compliance function" to monitor and control compliance with the code of conduct. Integrity and compliance staff are concerned with issues of compliance in areas such as competition law, anti-bribery and anti-corruption, export control and sanctions, data privacy, and human rights. In other words, their role is that of a risk management function.

Develop Standardised Control Tools to Create Organisational Coherence in Risk Management

A code of conduct provides a foundation upon which a risk management system can be built. Training and compliance monitoring help provide reinforcement, but for greater solidity, all the components of the risk management system, from training through to risk reporting and monitoring, need to be consistent across the organisation. This is made easier if there is underlying organisational strategic coherence. In the Akzo Nobel case study, the core strategy was to consolidate the group's interests in the paints and coatings sector and sell off non-core businesses, and the implementation of this strategy coincided with moves to centralise internal processes such as procurement. The centralisation helped to promote consistency in decision making in relation to risk. It was still nine years after the appointment of the group's first risk manager, however, that a Business Directives portal was launched to provide staff with a one-stop source of information on all directives, manuals, rules, etc.

The evidence from Tesco suggests that it is heading in a similar direction. The diversity of its businesses by 2010–2012 created a complexity that made risk management more difficult, as needs and priorities were not consistent. Rationalising and refocusing on the UK grocery market has created a coherent base on which to build a more solid risk architecture.

Look Outwards and Redefine Enterprise Boundaries in Terms of Risk Management

What is meant by the term enterprise, and what are its boundaries? Does the term relate only to its staff and physical boundaries, or does it include any and all of the stakeholder groups that may be impacted by its activities? This question requires an answer before we can define the exact meaning of the term enterprise risk management, and the broader the definition of the boundaries, the more challenging that ERM becomes.

There are two interconnected strands to the redefining of boundaries. The first strand relates to who and what is deemed to be part of the enterprise in terms of the boundaries of compliance with codes of conduct and core principles. The second involves rethinking the meaning of enterprise risk in relation to who and what is impacted by the actions of the organisation.

The first strand has very clear implications for who is required to comply with risk management controls and is tricky to implement, except perhaps for a very large organisation which has strong influence. Within Akzo Nobel the term "enterprise" now includes the core organisation plus all associated joint ventures and suppliers, distributors, and agents. All employees, vendors, and contractors are required to comply with the code of conduct. A parallel code for business partners, such as suppliers, requires them to comply with both the law and Akzo's three core principles of safety, integrity, and sustainability, or their own equivalent set of principles.

In Tesco, the situation in terms of compliance requirements outside the main group is perhaps less formalised. The code of business conduct and human rights policy applies to all staff across the Tesco group and details Tesco's obligations to customers, colleagues, and communities in its own operations and its supply chain. In addition, Tesco works with its suppliers to ensure compliance with the Ethical Trade Initiative (ETI) base code and undertakes due diligence to help them meet internal standards on human rights. The whistle-blower Protector Line is also accessible by suppliers and their staff if they wish to raise confidential concerns. Within the company's product division, a group responsible sourcing director leads the human rights strategy of the business, reporting to the board's corporate responsibility committee, which meets three times a year.

The contrasting approaches of Tesco versus Akzo Nobel mirror their respective organisational mindsets in relation to risk. In the former, risk is managed less formally via the performance management system, whereas in Akzo Nobel, standardised procedures, directives, and rules have created a more formal system. The differences probably reflect the sectors in which they operate as much as organisational culture.

In defining the boundaries of sources of risk and who and what is impacted by organisational activities, there is much greater similarity between Tesco and Akzo Nobel. The same year that the ERM programme was launched (2004), Akzo Nobel became a signatory of the UN Global Compact and a member of the World Business Council for Sustainable Development. Sustainability has been high on the corporate agenda ever since, as detailed in Chapter 6. There is a clear recognition of the need to try and minimise the environmental impact of both manufacturing processes and the products themselves, and the group has been publishing corporate social responsibility information since 2005. More recent annual reports include detailed sustainability statements that make interesting reading.

The diverse, but very clear, sustainability performance targets that are set (e.g. kg of CO_2 emissions per ton of production) mean that the range of risks faced by the group has been extended. This presents a substantial challenge and requires a high level of sophistication in the risk management system. There needs to be confidence that core risks are already well managed before more ambitious ones can be added to the list!

Extended organisational boundaries in Tesco have traditionally been expressed in terms of the "community," which has long been identified as a stakeholder. The term is wide ranging and incorporates direct support for local communities such as food banks, as well as responsible product sourcing and caring for the environment. For example, in their annual reports Tesco detail their work with suppliers to reduce plastic packaging levels and food waste and their donations of surplus food from stores through a Community Food Connection. In 2020 Tesco launched a new performance measure – the sustainable basket metric – intended to assess progress in halving the environmental impact of the average UK shopping basket against seven key sustainability measures. That said, community and sustainability do not feature in the Big Six performance measures, and so the wider concept of enterprise is not perhaps as well embedded as it appears to be in Akzo. Certainly, its management appears to be again less formalised.

The four phases of development of enterprise-wide risk management illustrate how long it can take in practice to develop an effective and mature system. What is more, if there are any major failures of governance or risk management en route, then it may be necessary to retrench and start all over again by refocusing on cultural dimensions. Despite the rhetoric about ERM being widespread, the cruel reality is that few organisations can truly claim to have a strong, effective, and mature system.

Lesson Four: Risk Management and Performance Management Don't Always Agree

ISO 3100 (2018) defines risk management as the set of co-ordinated activities used to direct and control an organisation in respect of risk, with risk seen as "the effect of uncertainty on objectives." Palermo (2017, p. 139) defines performance management as "concerned with defining, controlling and managing the achievement of expected outcomes as well as the means used to achieve these results." Both are therefore concerned with the achievement of objectives, but risk management is specifically focused on managing the uncertainties that may threaten success. This suggests that whilst they are complementary control tools, there is also scope for tension at the interface between risk and performance management systems. Importantly, if the two are in conflict, which one dominates? The case studies offer interesting insights into this issue.

In all three case studies, the ultimate aim was to integrate risk management across all levels of the organisation. When integration is working, individual operational staff are linked back to corporate performance objectives via performance scorecards, such as those used in the Tesco steering wheel, or the personal performance plans deployed in both Akzo Nobel and Birmingham City Council. Scorecards can be developed for each level of the organisation, cascading down from the corporate level, through divisional and business units, to the individual line managers and their staff. At each level the scorecards are underpinned by plans showing the link between strategic objectives and targeted outcomes and may be complemented by strategy diagrams or maps which set out the plans and actions that will deliver the performance measured by the scorecards, as well as the relevant performance targets.

Using scorecards which cascade down through the corporate hierarchy ensures ownership of targets and links them to the strategic plan. Recording the allocation of targets to individual managers in the performance database also provides an audit pathway for each performance indicator. The principle of cascading down responsibility for performance can also be applied to risk management.

Under ERM, the underlying aim is to ensure that at all levels of an organisation staff:

- Are aware of the risks that may affect performance in the areas over which they have responsibility
- Take responsibility for management of those risks
- Conduct performance and risk monitoring in parallel to ensure achievement of corporate objectives

The strategic maps that define how performance targets will be achieved can be complemented by risk maps that identify the key threats to successful delivery at each level of the organisation. In Birmingham, for example, the case shows that this was done by the creation of directorate-level risk maps. In Akzo Nobel, the top ten risks at project, business unit, and divisional levels are reported up the hierarchy.

At the same time, responsibility for management of those risks can be specified by identifying "owners" of risks and including details of such ownership in the performance management system. In Akzo Nobel, mechanisms such as the use of non-financial letters of representation and the code of conduct help to ensure managerial and personal accountability and are fundamental to the ERM system. In Birmingham, there are examples of both political (councillors) and staff ownership of risks. In Tesco, individual members of the executive committee are accountable for specific principal risk, and for other managers, personal performance plans will include a risk management component. In other words, risk management and performance management can become fully integrated systems, as illustrated in Figure 9.1.

Figure 9.1 shows that at all levels of the organisation, from corporate down to the individual, objectives *can* be linked to both performance targets and risk maps. If the system works properly, then if a manager is hitting the performance targets, and he or she must simultaneously be managing the risks. If the performance targets are not linked across to risk maps, then there is a danger that performance will be achieved by taking on risks that exceed the organisational risk appetite. The key to effective integration lies with monitoring to compare risk and performance and ensure consistency of approach. The case studies reveal three useful examples of when this was not done.

In Tesco, the largely informal risk management style that characterised the period 2000–2014 was overwhelmed in practice by a domineering performance management system and a leadership style that placed heavy emphasis on particular aspects of performance. As already discussed, the relatively low profile of the risk and internal audit staff did not help the situation, and so financial performance overrode the need to avoid the risk of overstatement of profits.

In Akzo Nobel, the regulatory breaches that led to the decision to introduce ERM arose out of a performance-focused system that sought sales, almost irrespective of the risks taken to achieve them, perhaps simply because there was little or no oversight of risk, except those relating to health and safety or financial management.

In Birmingham, the work of staff in Birmingham Audit shifted focus post-2010. It might have been assumed that having sought to integrate risk and performance for eight years by that point that the two systems were well aligned. For children's services, however, this was not the case. There was a clear conflict between the need to meet statutory service targets such as speed of response to incidents and staff workload levels versus the demand to meet financial targets and a balanced budget. This meant that certain objectives had to be prioritised,

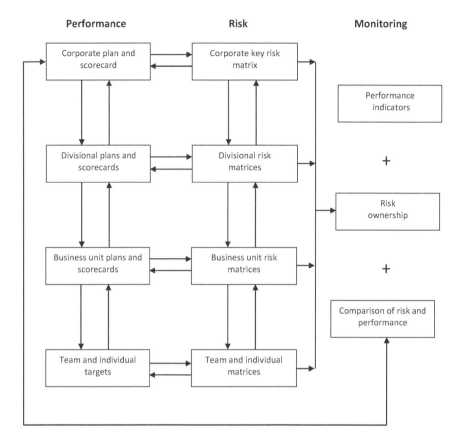

Figure 9.1 Integrating risk and performance management

and it would appear that the impact of this on risk was not sufficiently well evaluated or monitored.

The examples show that if there is either no effort to link specific performance targets with the associated risks or that certain performance targets get prioritised and risk assessments are not adjusted in response, there is a misalignment that can result in the crystallisation of risks. Continuous monitoring and matching up of performance targets – at all levels – to the associated risks is essential to the full integration of performance and risk management.

Summary

The case studies provide some useful lessons for risk managers, both in terms of what mistakes to avoid and what systems to aim for. Put simply, they also show that both formal and relatively informal systems can work, but both have their limitations. Instead, it seems that multiple styles of control are required in order to build an effective risk management system. In research that is widely cited in the academic world, Robert Simons (1995) suggested four different ways in which control systems could function. His work was not specifically about risk management, though it does get mentioned. The four types of control systems are:

- Belief systems – that communicate the core values of an organisation and encourage them to commit to organisational objectives
- Diagnostic systems – used to monitor the efficient achievement of key goals
- Interactive systems – designed to enable top-level managers to focus on strategic uncertainties via interaction with their staff
- Boundary systems – used to establish the ground rules and prevent inappropriate decision making

Simons (1999, p. 92) commented that "the levers, simply stated, are mechanisms managers can adjust to control risk as a company pursues its strategy," and it is helpful to look at this more carefully. Lesson Three from the cases was the need to be patient and view the development of an ERM system as a series of stages. The stages identified from the case studies closely mirror the levers of control. Stage 1 involves establishing a cultural base that sets clear boundaries on behaviour. This equates to setting up a boundary control system. Stage 2 was developing risk awareness, shown to be critical in Lesson Two, which amounts to a belief system of control through which staff can connect to corporate objectives. Stage 3 is the development of standardised documentation for risk management and controls to embrace the whole organisation. Interactive control systems do exactly this by encouraging managers and staff to work together to identify and manage risks that threaten organisational objectives. Simon's diagnostic systems work across all three of these stages by using monitoring to ensure that objectives are being met. Collectively, the four levers of control set in motion powerful forces that reinforce one another.

In reviewing the link between performance management and risk management systems, it was noted that things break down when there is not continuous monitoring of performance targets against the assessed risks. This suggests that Simon's diagnostic control system is the glue that binds everything together. All four control systems have a part to play, but diagnostics are critical.

Hopefully, this provides plenty of food for thought for both present and future risk managers. I hope you have enjoyed this book and found it useful.

References

Ashby, S., Palermo, T., & Power, M. (2012) *Risk Culture in Financial Organisations: An Interim Report*. London School of Economics, London.

Civil Aviation Authority (CAA) (2014) *Just Culture*. Sean Parker, Safety Reporting Programme Lead, London.

Eckles, D.L., Hoyt, R.E., & Miller, S.M. (2014) "The Impact of Enterprise Risk Management on the Marginal Cost of Reducing Risk: Evidence from the Insurance Industry." *Journal of Banking & Finance*, Vol. 33, pp. 247–261.

Farrell, M., & Gallagher, R. (2015) "The Valuation Implications of Enterprise Risk Management Maturity." *The Journal of Risk and Insurance*, Vol. 82, No. 3, pp. 625–657.

Hoyt, R.E., & Liebenberg, A.P. (2015) "Evidence of the Value of Enterprise Risk Management." *Journal of Applied Corporate Finance*, Vol. 27, No. 1, pp. 41–47.

IIF (2008) *Financial Services Industry Response to the Market Turmoil of 2007–2008*. Institute of International Finance, Washington, DC.

IRM (Institute of Risk Management) (2012) *Risk Culture*. Resources for Practitioners, London.

ISO 31000 (2018) *Risk Management – Guidelines*. International Organization for Standardization (ISO), Geneva.

Palermo, T. (2017) "Risk and Performance Management. Two Sides of the Same Coin?" Chapter 10 in Woods, M., & Linsley, P. (eds.), *The Routledge Companion to Accounting & Risk*. Routledge, London.

Simons, R. (1995) "Control in an Age of Empowerment." *Harvard Business Review*, March–April, pp. 80–88.

Simons, R. (1999) "How Risky Is Your Company." *Harvard Business Review*, Vol. 71, pp. 85–94.

US Chemical and Safety Hazard Board (2007) Investigation Report No. 2005–04-I-TX Refinery Explosion and Fire. Washington, DC.

Watkins, M. (2013) "What Is Organizational Culture? And Why Should We Care?" *Harvard Business Review*, May.

10 A Risk Management Perspective on COVID-19

Aim

The aim of this chapter is to review the impact of the COVID-19 pandemic from a risk management perspective. The specific focus is on the lessons that can be learned from the experience of living through the pandemic and how organisations can prepare and respond to such substantive and potentially catastrophic risks in the future. The chapter is subdivided into sections which address:

- The social and economic impact of COVID-19
- The preparedness of UK government and organisations
- Planning for highly uncertain critical future events
- Conclusion – lessons for risk management

Social and Economic Impact

The COVID-19 virus reputedly originated in Wuhan in China, in the Huanan Seafood Wholesale market in late 2019. According to the *South China Post*, the first case was identified on 17 November 2019, and as the number of cases increased, almost two thirds were traced back to the wholesale market. This led scientists to conclude that the virus started in animals – possibly bats or pangolins – and then crossed into humans. The first reports of the new virus reached the World Health Organization (WHO) on 31 December 2019. Early cases were confined to Southeast Asia, but by late February the number globally had reached almost 81,000. Zero restrictions on global travel enabled the virus to spread rapidly, and by the time the WHO declared it a global pandemic on 11 March 2020, more than 121,000 people across Southeast Asia, the Middle East, Europe, and the United Stated had been infected and at least 4,373 had died. Infections rising from zero to 121,000 in just three months seemed scary enough, but much worse was to come.

By April 2021 the total cases of COVID-19 recorded worldwide had reached 146.4 million and the total death level 3.1 million. This is much less than the

DOI: 10.4324/9781315208336-10

1918 Spanish flu outbreak, which killed around 50 million people, but the impact is still huge, and whilst the number of deaths relative to cases appears relatively low, this highly infectious disease caused havoc through the economic and social devastation it generated. Examples of such impacts are shown in the following box.

Box 10.1 Economic and Social Impact of COVID-19

- Canada – Recorded a budget deficit for the year ending March 2021 of C$354.2 billion, 16% of its gross domestic product (GDP).
- In the United States the $1.9 trillion American Rescue Plan amounts to 15% of GDP.
- In the UK, government borrowing for the year ending March 2021 reached £303.1 billion, up by £246.1 billion on the previous year. Total borrowing was at its highest level in peacetime and more than at any time since WW2.
- By late April 2021 the UK had recorded:

  - 4.4 million cases of COVID-19
  - 127,450 deaths from the disease
  - 3.42 million fewer elective surgery treatments*
  - A 240-fold increase in patients waiting over one year for treatment in the National Health Service (NHS)*
  - 28% of households suffered a drop in income**

Sources:
*Pressure points in the NHS, BMA 15 April 2021.
** How has COVID-19 affected the finances of UK households? Bank of England, August 2020.

Such statistics hide a much more complex picture in which the impact of the pandemic is very uneven across economic sectors, geographic regions, and individual organisations and households. For example, the major supermarkets, especially those offering online deliveries, thrived in lockdown, as people spent more time at home, and eating out became impossible. In contrast, the hospitality sector – food and accommodation service industries – has been very seriously damaged by COVID. In the UK, the Office for National Statistics (ONS) reported that as of early March 2021, 55% of such businesses had temporarily ceased trading during the pandemic, 56% of eligible jobs in the industry had been furloughed, and 19% had little confidence that their business would survive the next three months, despite planned reductions in lockdown restrictions. London's hospitality businesses were particularly badly hit because of their dependence upon international tourism, which ground to a halt. Hotel occupancy rates in London fell, for example, from 90% to just 20% between July 2019 and July 2020. Hotels have been especially badly hit, but simultaneously some restaurants have shifted to "cook at home" services which have allowed them to continue trading and hopefully survive until indoor dining is once again possible. The organisational consequences of the virus are proving incredibly mixed, which raises the question of how well prepared the world was for such an event.

Government and Organisational Preparedness

In risk management terms, pandemic infectious diseases represent a risk to organisational and societal continuity. Transport and logistics systems have been closed down or restricted, creating supply chain problems, which have been further exacerbated by employee illness, and new cyber risks have emerged as the number working from home has risen dramatically. Whilst a global pandemic might seem a very low probability event, and such uncertainty makes planning difficult, there is growing evidence that organisations that had business continuity plans in place have fared better than those engulfed by the surprise.

A pandemic can be classified as a macro-level risk, as it is outside the control of a single organisation but could nonetheless have dramatic consequences. A useful reference point for both ongoing and newly emerging macro risks are country-level risk registers, such as the UK's National Risk Register (NRR). First published in 2008 and in the public domain, the NRR is updated every two years and represents "a classified assessment of risks that could happen in the UK over the next five years" (NRR, 2017, p. 5). Risks are categorised under a number of headings, including natural hazards, diseases, major accidents and malicious attacks, and the register is used to assist both central and local government planning for a major emergency.

An infectious disease pandemic has been on the register since 2008, but with a stronger emphasis on pandemic flu rather than newly emerging infectious diseases. The 2017 NRR, the most recent prior to the emergence of COVID-19, noted that "the emergence of new infectious diseases is unpredictable but evidence indicates it may become more frequent . . . the likelihood of this risk has increased since 2015" (NRR, 2017, p. 7).

The register's 5 × 5 impact:likelihood matrix rated a flu pandemic as having an impact level of 5 and a likelihood of occurrence (within five years) of 4. In contrast, emerging infectious disease had an impact of just 3 and the same likelihood of 4. Consequently, the forecasts of a flu pandemic were between 20,000 and 750,000 fatalities in the UK and high levels of absence from work, compared with a new infectious disease causing just several thousand to fall ill, with up to 100 fatalities. In hindsight, the latter forecast was far too low and may in part explain the resulting lack of preparedness in terms of protective equipment and ventilators. A future public enquiry may provide some answers to such questions, but speculation is not appropriate in this context.

It is reasonable to assume that major organisations, and possibly some smaller ones, use the NRR as an indicator of the potential major risks that might strike and use them in developing their internal risk plans. Table 10.1 shows the way in which a pandemic disease might affect specific sectors and was (if at all) identified as a principal risk in the 2019 annual reports of ten FTSE

Table 10.1 Did FTSE 100 Companies Include a Pandemic as a Principal Risk in 2019?

Sector/Company	Potential Impact on the Sector	Pandemic Disease Risk Identified in Principal Risks/ Uncertainties	Categorisation of Pandemic Risk
Oil and Gas			
Royal Dutch Shell	Collapse in demand leading to a fall in prices and lost revenue (e.g. airline fuel sales)	Yes	"Catch-all" category covering social instability, terrorism, acts of war, and pandemic diseases
BP		Unclear	Could be placed under financial liquidity due to impact on oil prices and investment capacity
Financial Services			
Barclays PLC	Increased level of loan defaults and	No	
NatWest PLC	overall credit risk	No	
Pharmaceuticals			
Glaxo Smith Kline	Positive if one of the manufacturers	Yes	Supplier continuity
Astra Zeneca	of effective treatments; negative if not, or other healthcare treatments drop as a response to COVID	Yes	Supply chain, business continuity, and resilience
Hospitality			
Intercontinental Hotels Group	Lost income caused by business closures	Yes	Macro external factors, including war, infectious diseases, and terrorism
Whitbread PLC		Yes	Pandemic or terrorism, though the emphasis appears to be on the latter
Food Retailing			
Sainsbury PLC	Increased sales from people staying at home	Yes	Business continuity and operational resilience
Tesco PLC		No	

Sources: Annual Reports 2019. Section on principal risks and uncertainties.

100 companies. The selection of companies is not intended to be representative but paints a useful picture of current practice.

Three out of ten organisations did not identify pandemic disease as a principal risk. Both of the financial services companies fail to mention such a risk in their report, even though the economic impact on business and personal customers could be huge. Businesses being unable to repay debts or forced to close, combined with increased personal debt levels and a growth in mortgage arrears, could have a massive impact on both a bank's balance sheet and its profits. It is difficult to explain why the financial services sector failed to report this risk, but one possible reason may be simply historical.

Traditionally, the primary risks faced by banks have been viewed as financial in nature and categorised under the headings of market, credit, and liquidity. Operational risk in banking is defined by the Basel Committee on Banking Supervision as the risk of loss resulting from inadequate or failed internal processes, people, and systems or from external events, and so a pandemic would fall into this category. The committee first laid down principles for the management of operational risk in 2003, which have subsequently been revised several times in the light of the 2008 financial crisis and other events. Nonetheless, risk management thinking within banking remains focused around the primary financial risks. In 2020, reflecting lessons learned from COVID-19, the Basel Committee made further proposals to place greater emphasis on organisational resilience to major events via tighter management of operational risk. The 2021 reports of the banks may therefore reveal a new principal risk – a check would prove interesting.

The third company not to include a pandemic risk was Tesco. On the one hand, this could be explained by the board taking the view that the perceived benefits – extra revenue, etc. – outweighed the additional cost of new sanitation controls and staff absences. We can never know, but it is interesting that one of their major competitors, Sainsbury's, declared a pandemic to be important as a threat to business continuity and resilience. Historically, many businesses have opted to see macro risks as too uncertain and remote and have seen business interruption as an issue that is commonly short-term and often localised. COVID-19 has proved the dangers of such an approach.

Table 10.1 also reveals other evidence of "common" practice within a sector, this time in terms of the categorisation of pandemic risk. In pharmaceuticals, supply continuity is the key concern, as it was for Sainsbury's, whilst in hospitality, the pandemic falls into a macro risk group that includes terrorism. Shell also uses a catch-all category for a pandemic, but this approach is open to criticism. What can the reader of an annual report make of knowing that terrorism and a pandemic are both recognised as principal risks? The reader themselves could predict that – what they want to know is more specific: How exactly will Whitbread or Shell be affected and what plans are in place to manage those risks? In summary, the evidence from this small sample of risk reporting practice in the FTSE 100 shows that there is much room for improvement. Businesses need to plan for long-term resilience and acknowledge that business continuity means more than just a few months of downtime from a fire or major incident. There is potential for a long-term crisis that must be managed, and the starting point for such management is a major risk plan.

Planning for Highly Uncertain Critical Events

Insurance

Huge uncertainty about an event's likelihood and/or consequences inevitably makes planning difficult. One possible way of managing the risk is to offload the uncertainty by taking out insurance against business interruption, but although the UK government declared it a notifiable disease and forced businesses to close from 16 March 2020, many policy holders have found their claims under COVID-19 rejected.

The scope of coverage provided by policies and their specific wording vary widely, resulting in confusion over what could and could not be claimed. Some policies allow claims for loss of income or profit subject to the policy's definitions of these terms. Increases in the cost of working (e.g. due to the need for social distancing or provision of laptops for home working) may also be covered, but it is quite common for claims to be subject to limits restricting the amount that can be claimed and/or the time frame within which a claim must be made. One problem faced by many smaller businesses was the refusal of their claim under COVID-19 because of debate around specific policy wordings, including the need to prove the presence of infection in a restricted area around the business premises.

Not surprisingly, the insurance industry strongly defended its position, with the Association of British Insurers (ABI) declaring "standard business insurance policies are designed and priced to cover standard risks and are therefore unlikely to provide cover for the effects of global pandemics like Covid-19" (BBC News, 2020). In response to multiple complaints to the financial ombudsman's service that insurers were adopting a narrow interpretation of whether insurance claims were payable, however, the UK regulator (the Financial Conduct Authority [FCA]) took a test case to the High Court in 2020. The aim was to provide clarification of liability for both the insured and the insurers, and the 2021 Supreme Court judgement on a set of specific policy wording is legally binding on the eight insurance companies that agreed to be parties to the case.[1]

There are still ongoing disputes about the calculation of policy pay-outs, most notably on how to account for government support received by firms to compensate for business closures. Nonetheless, a key outcome of the case has been the production by the FCA of an online guidance calculator which can be used by policy holders. The calculator uses data published by Imperial College London on infection rates at the lower tier local authority level to estimate the presence of COVID-19 in a locality, in support of a claim.

It remains the case, however, that the vast majority of businesses are uninsured for global pandemics, and the Office for Budget Responsibility has called for the government to act as the "insurer of last resort" in cases such as coronavirus where businesses are damaged by an uninsurable "act of God" (FT Adviser, 2020). The Treasury Committee is reviewing alternative insurance options, including a re-insurance model that pools public and private liabilities for future pandemics. This approach is favoured by the industry, but the discussions are continuing.

Detailed Planning

In developing a plan to respond to a major external risk such as a pandemic, an organisation needs to address three core questions in terms of risks:

1. Which risks will arise?
2. Which risks matter most in terms of impact (e.g. lost revenue, employee risks, supply chain)?
3. Which risks have the highest probability?

In other words, what is required is an impact:likelihood matrix framed around the broader macro risk. This means that multiple assessments of impact and likelihood might be required for disease threats versus terrorism or natural disaster.

For example, in the case of a food retailer, many different types of risk arising from a pandemic can be identified, including:

*   Disrupted supplies due to transport issues and problems with suppliers
*   Increased costs from providing security services to manage social distancing and hand sanitising by customers
*   Risk of customers attempting to stockpile goods
*   High levels of employee sickness or absence
*   Scope and cost of a shift to online selling

The risks identified need to be prioritised and management effort then focused on controlling the most important risks. At the same time, there is a need to re-evaluate counter party risks such as IT provision or dependence on a limited number of key suppliers, because such risks can perhaps be managed in advance.

Simply ask the question "how much stress can we cope with?" This may then also lead to a more fundamental review of organisational risk appetite at the board level.

Factors that should be included in all major risk plans include:

1. **Technology**
    a. Will it work if the business is shut down?
    b. Is the internet bandwidth adequate for home working?

    c.   Do staff have laptops, and how secure are the access systems?

    d.   Do we have established protocols for home working?

2. Staffing

    a.   Do we have key staff back-up?

    b.   What fall in staff attendance will cause severe disruption?

    c.   Do we have an emergency communication plan in place?

3. Key Contracts (for Buying and Selling)

    a.   Do they include "force majeure clauses"?

    b.   Do they include a specific pandemic/terrorism/war clause?

    c.   Are we happy with the associated terms and implied risks that result?

4. Financial Strength

    a.   What is the cash flow forecast if we shut down?

    b.   How long can we last before we lose the liquidity to operate?

    c.   Do we have readily saleable assets?

    d.   How can we cut costs quickly?

    e.   Are systems in place to record extraordinary expenses to support claims to government insurance providers?

    f.   Have we any business interruption insurance, and do we understand the limitations of the coverage?

5. Risk Forecasts

    a.   What is the time frame of our risk forecasts?

    b.   At what point in the year are risks greatest?

    c.   Do the forecasts incorporate repeated shutdowns, possibly weeks apart as in COVID-19?

This list of what should be included in a plan is purely indicative and can be refined to fit specific organisational needs. In addition, the plan's contents, drafted by line managers, should be reviewed and evaluated by both the risk management and internal audit functions to ensure that they are comprehensive and aligned with the existing control system. Armed with such information, any organisation should be able to declare itself prepared for a major risk.

Conclusion

The COVID-19 pandemic has proved extremely challenging for both individuals and organisations, not only because its effects have been so widespread and painful but also because it hit so unexpectedly and rapidly. As discussed earlier, at the government level, a global pandemic within five years was considered likely, but its severity was massively underestimated. It is helpful to look at what lessons can be learned from the crisis – what was done right and what could have been better managed – and use that knowledge to prepare for any future global disruption. We therefore conclude this chapter with six lessons for risk managers.

Lesson 1

Global hyper-connectivity creates a potential for disruption to supply chains at a global level. Increased global connections have been driven by a search for greater economic efficiency, but the World Trade Organization is now encouraging companies to be aware of a risk versus economic efficiency trade-off. The UK's Economic Intelligence Unit is encouraging a shift towards regional supply chains to increase corporate resilience to macro risks.

Lesson 2

Disruption may not be short-lived. Many countries are experiencing a third wave of COVID-19 infections, and some expect a fourth. Resilience implies a capacity to cope with repeated disruptions.

Lesson 3

Beware of computer-based forecasting models based on assumptions of normality. Many forecasting models assume that prices fluctuate around a norm, and wild market movements ultimately revert back to the mean. The financial crisis proved this not to be true in the banks' use of value at risk models, and in the recent pandemic hedge funds have faced huge problems because when the S&P 500 sank into bear territory, it was assumed the jump back would be rapid. It was not, and millions of dollars were lost as a result. The rules of normality may not apply outside financial circles either. For example, although take-away food became a new norm instead of eating out at a restaurant, it may not remain so.

Lesson 4

Have back-ups in place for senior management teams. The UK-based hi-fi, home cinema, and TV company Richer Sounds reported problems in 2020 after their newly appointed finance director was forced to take long-term sick leave (FT, 2021). At the senior management level knowledge needs to be shared and understudies prepared to take over as and when necessary.

Lesson 5

Embrace flexible working and marketing methods. The traditional model of office-based working has been thrown into disarray by the pandemic, and individual members of staff may vary in the working style they prefer. To get the best from staff, companies should be prepared to be flexible and offer face-to-face, office-based, and home working options to their staff.

Similarly, in terms of marketing, those who have fared better in the pandemic have been those who have been flexible and adapted to new demands (e.g. home delivery, click and collect services, cook at home versus restaurant-based eating).

Lesson 6

Be aware that new ways of operating can create new, unexpected risks. For example, there was a huge growth in scamming and cybercrime levels in 2020, and attacks were not confined to small businesses. The car firm Honda had to suspend global production for a full day after some employees lost access to their work laptops following a ransomware attack. If you have hundreds of thousands of staff using laptops on their unsecured home Wi-Fi networks, such attacks are highly likely and need to be planned for.

These are all useful lessons which support the case for strong risk management. As Richard Branson argues:

> It is only by being bold that you get anywhere. If you are a risk-taker, then the art is to protect the downside.

Risk managers are a vital part of the protection armoury.

Note

1 The insurers are Arch Insurance (UK) Ltd., Argenta Syndicate Management Ltd., Ecclesiastical Insurance Office PLC, MS Amlin Underwriting Ltd., Hiscox Insurance Ltd., QBE UK Ltd., Royal and Sun Alliance PLC, and Zurich Insurance PLC.

References

Akzo Nobel Annual Report (2005). https://www.akzonobel.com/content/dam/akzonobel-corporate/global/en/investor-relations-images/result-center/archive-annual-reports/2009-2000/Akzonobel-annual-report-2005.pdf

BBC News (2020) "ABI Comment on Coronavirus and Commercial Insurance." *BBC News*, "Government Clarifies Coronavirus Insurance Stance." March 4.

Committee of Sponsoring Organisations of the Treadway Commission (COSO) (2017) *Enterprise Risk Management Integrating with Strategy and Performance*. Committee of Sponsoring Organizations of the Treadway Commission, NJ.

Financial Times (2020) "Leaders' Lessons. The Value of Mistakes." February 25, 2021.

FT Adviser (2020) "OBR Says Govt Should Cover Insurance Claims Related to Virus." *Amy Austin*, March 17, 2020.

National Risk Register of Civil Emergencies (2017) Cabinet Office, London.

Useful Web Links

1. The latest version of the UK's National Risk Register can be found at www.gov.uk/government/publications/national-risk-register-2020

2.   Institute of Risk Management. Risk Predictions 2021. Resilience, Risk & Recovery. IRM. London. Available from: https://issuu.com/irmglobal/docs/risk_predictions_2021_final_compressed

Discussion Questions

1.   Has your organisation undertaken a review of its preparedness for COVID-19? If you don't know, then can you ask risk management or internal audit staff this question? If you do know, can you identify what lessons have been learned from the exercise that can be used in future planning?
2.   Critically discuss the pros and cons of flexible working (i.e. combining office-based and home-based working) from a risk management perspective.
3.   Download the latest national risk register for your country of residence, and rank the key risks identified in terms of their potential impact on your own workplace or place of study. Discuss the extent to which the organisation has clear plans in place for such events.

Index

Note: Page numbers in *italics* indicate a figure and page numbers in **bold** indicate a table on the corresponding page.